*f***P**

MANAGING
A NONPROFIT
ORGANIZATION

Updated Twenty-First-Century Edition

THOMAS WOLF

Illustrated by Barbara Carter

FREE PRESS

New York   London   Toronto   Sydney   New Delhi

NOTE TO READERS

FREE PRESS
A Division of Simon & Schuster, Inc.
1230 Avenue of the Americas
New York, NY 10020

First Free Press trade paperback edition July 2012

FREE PRESS and colophon are trademarks of Simon & Schuster, Inc.

For information about special discounts for bulk purchases,
please contact Simon & Schuster Special Sales at 1-866-506-1949
or business@simonandschuster.com.

The Simon & Schuster Speakers Bureau can bring authors
to your live event. For more information or to book an event
contact the Simon & Schuster Speakers Bureau at 1-866-248-3049
or visit our website at www.simonspeakers.com.

Design by Esther Paradelo

Manufactured in the United States of America

10 9 8 7 6

Library of Congress Cataloging-in-Publication Data
Managing a nonprofit organization : updated twenty-first-century
edition / Thomas Wolf ; illustrated by Barbara Carter. p. cm.
Rev. ed. of : Managing a nonprofit organization
in the twenty-first century. c1999.
1. Nonprofit organizations—Management. 2. Nonprofit organizations—Finance.
I. Wolf, Thomas, Managing a nonprofit organization in the twenty-first century. II. Title.
HD62.6.W649 2012
658'.048—dc23   2012001416
ISBN 978-1-4516-0846-5
ISBN 978-1-4391-3489-4 (ebook)

In memory of my parents
Irene and Walter Wolf
who committed time, money, and children
to nonprofit organizations

And to my grandchildren
Asa, Sasha, Lyla, Isaiah, and Elias
who I hope will continue the tradition

CONTENTS

PREFACE

PREFACE

This book represents a fifth version of a manuscript originally developed for a course at Harvard University in the early 1980s. I wrote the first version because no textbook existed that covered the material in a fashion that I thought my students required. Most of them had some experience working in nonprofit organizations, but they were hungry for simple, practical advice. The class material was oriented toward the challenges of staff, board, and other volunteers of smaller nonprofit organizations who were completely unschooled or had learned what they knew on the job.

When a publisher asked me to collect the class material into a book in 1983 and the book was subsequently published under the title *The Nonprofit Organization*, I was surprised to discover that experienced professionals in larger organizations were buying and using it. Bulk orders were being placed by organizations that were distributing it to trustees and staff. Foundations were purchasing the book and giving it to their grantees. And the book was being used in a growing number of university courses. Thus, a second edition was prepared called *Managing a Nonprofit Organization*, which dealt with a wider variety of situations and challenges. As the millennium was approaching, I updated the material again in light of what appeared to be emerging issues for the twenty-first century, and I expanded the title to *Managing a Nonprofit Organization in the Twenty-First Century*.

No one could have predicted the scope of the changes that would be brought on by the march of innovation on the one hand and by the cataclysmic events of the early twenty-first century on the other. In the aftermath of the terrorist attacks of September 11, 2001, a fundamental reassessment of the role, governance, and management of nonprofits began and was expanded due to the high-profile failure of several global for-profit companies and the financial meltdown that followed toward the end of the decade.

But there were other fundamental changes that this book documents related to technology, accountability, and sustainability:

- One of the greatest unanticipated changes was *the impact of technology on nonprofits*. In the 1999 edition, there was no mention of websites or email, and social media was largely unknown to practitioners within nonprofits. To talk about any aspect of nonprofit management today—especially marketing and fund raising—without mentioning these advances would be unthinkable. Subsequent to the first edition, I have always thought it made little sense to include a separate chapter on technology inasmuch as it changes so rapidly that such chapters quickly become dated. Rather, what I have continued to do is incorporate into existing chapters reference to technological tools and approaches that have become basic to effective management.
- In the wake of the scandals that engulfed the corporate community in the first decade of the twenty-first century, *accountability* and *the need for transparency* soon became watchwords not only in the for-profit sector but also among nonprofits. The impact on governance and management has been significant. Especially in the chapter on governance, you'll note a new emphasis on these topics.
- Finally, the economic challenges (including the near financial collapse of the United States economy) that characterized the end of the first decade of the twenty-first century came at the same time there was tremendous expansion in the nonprofit sector. Inevitably, there has been a *renewed emphasis on the question of sustainability*. In some cases, this has meant organizations have learned to get leaner and stronger; in others, it has led to strategic alliances, partnerships, and mergers; in still others, organizations have gone out of business.

I have worked with nonprofit organizations for over fifty years, and the people I have come in contact with have enriched my life immeasurably. My first job was as a part-time director of a small music festival. I have also worked as executive director of a grant-giving foundation, served as a trustee of several other nonprofits, and, more recently, provided consulting services to thousands of nonprofit organizations with budgets ranging from less than $5,000 to over $100 million. I am continually amazed by how much of what we value as a society is made possible by nonprofit organizations and the people who work in them. It is for these people that this book was originally conceived, and it is their needs that I continue to have uppermost in mind.

In reacting to previous editions of this book, readers told me that they found the examples and anecdotes particularly helpful. Reading case histories made the surrounding prose come alive and make sense. In many cases, I was asked if I had used actual organizations. In some cases, I was asked for addresses. Needless to say, protecting the anonymity of organizations was critical to my using them as examples. In some cases, I adjusted the facts or chronology so that organizations and individuals would not be readily identifiable. Many of the examples are actually composites of more than one organization. In almost every case, the events reported have occurred, but their occurrence may have been in a different organization at a different time.

I am grateful to several people who collaborated with me on this book. Barbara Carter offered her wonderful illustrations, which bring the book's concepts to life with refreshing and humorous visual imagery. Jane Culbert tackled the financial chapters again and made sure other chapters seemed relevant and up to date. Carole Brand provided many valuable suggestions for chapters 3 and 4. Without Naomi Grabel's help, I could never have done such a comprehensive job updating the marketing chapter. I appreciate the advice of John J. Sanford on the section concerning trustee liability and Eric Rayman on other legal matters. Finally, this new edition would not have been possible without Dominick Anfuso, Maura O'Brien, and Sydney Tanigawa at Free Press, a division of Simon & Schuster, Inc.

To all these individuals and to my wife, Dennie, and my children, Lea and Lex, I owe a great debt of thanks.

Thomas Wolf
Cambridge
2012

ONE

Understanding Nonprofit Organizations

The Spencer family lives in a small city in the western United States. Sam Spencer runs a plumbing supply business; Jane, his wife, teaches at a school for the learning disabled. On a typical day, their lives—like the lives of most Americans—are touched repeatedly by the world of nonprofit organizations.

- At 7:30 A.M., Jane takes Sammy Jr., aged three, to a day-care center housed at the Baptist church to which the family belongs. She then goes directly to her school, which serves learning-disabled high school students. The day-care center, the church, and the school are all nonprofit organizations.
- At about the same time that Jane leaves, Sam is loading his truck with plumbing supplies for the regional hospital, which is located in their city. The hospital, which employs more than a thousand people, is also a nonprofit organization, one that makes a significant contribution to the local economy.
- Before leaving home, Sam reminds son John, aged nine, that he should pack his bathing suit and towel because there is swim practice after school at the local YMCA. The YMCA is the city's principal recreational organization and is organized as a nonprofit.
- On this particular day, Jane is on release time from the classroom, taking an in-service workshop on language arts instruction at the local college. The college is the largest nonprofit organization in the city.
- While Jane is on release time, half of her students are on a field trip to the science museum, and the other half are attending an open rehearsal at the local symphony. Both of these organizations are nonprofits.
- Meanwhile, Sam has completed his delivery of plumbing supplies and drives over to the job training center where he teaches

the essentials of plumbing two mornings a week. Although supported almost exclusively with government funding, the center is a nongovernment, private nonprofit organization.

- When school is over, Jane meets with a group of teachers who are working on a special grant proposal that they will submit to a local foundation. They are seeking funds to support a computer-based language arts program in their classrooms. The foundation, whose income is derived mainly from a large endowment and is exempt from taxation, is a nonprofit organization.

- After leaving school, Jane drives over to a local nursing home to visit her father. The nursing home is a nonprofit organization.

- Sam leaves work early to go to a public hearing. A local builder, one of Sam's customers, has proposed a new development in what was formerly marshland. An environmental group, organized as a nonprofit organization, is opposing the development and is presenting its testimony at the public hearing.

- When Jane arrives home, there is a letter from daughter Amy, who is spending the fall of her junior year in South America as part of an exchange program. The exchange was organized by a national nonprofit organization with a local chapter in the city where the Spencers live.

- Finally, after dinner, the Spencers receive a call from the public radio station. It is pledge week, and the caller asks whether the Spencers will renew their membership in this nonprofit organization. Jane leaves soon after for a planning meeting for the local Girl Scouts' cookie drive. The Girl Scouts is a prominent national nonprofit organization.

There are over 1.5 million nonprofit organizations in the United States, a number that has increased by over 30 percent in the past decade.[1] This includes public charities active in health care, religion, culture, education, human services, and the environment. It also includes advocacy organizations, labor unions, business and professional associations, and social and recreational clubs. The public charities, identified with the special 501(c)(3) designation by the United States Internal Revenue Service (IRS), alone number over a million organizations. This subsector grew by 64 percent over the decade from 1999 to 2009.

Many of these nonprofit organizations have relatively small operating budgets. Indeed, fully 45 percent of the sector in 2008 had budgets of under $100,000. Move up to the $500,000 level, and almost three quarters of the organizations had budgets less than that. Fewer than 5 percent have budgets of over $10 million, though they account for 85 percent of all expenditures.[2]

With so many small organizations, what is their financial impact? Actually it is quite dramatic. In total, the sector's spending was approximately 11 to 12 percent of the nation's gross domestic product in 2007.[3] Based on 2008 statistics, nonprofits employ over 15 million people, or 13 percent of all private-sector workers.[4] But beyond this, their contribution to the nation's quality of life is incalculable. American households contributed nearly $2,000 per year of their personal money[5] to nonprofits plus substantially more in contributed hours. In fact, at the end of the first decade of the twenty-first century, over 63 million Americans (27 percent of the population) volunteered their time to nonprofit organizations with an estimated value of over $278 billion.[6]

Despite the tremendous size and impact of the nonprofit sector, it is not well understood by most people. The purpose of this chapter is to describe what nonprofit organizations are, what distinctive features they possess, and what special challenges they pose for the people who manage and govern them.

WHAT IS A NONPROFIT ORGANIZATION?

Suppose you asked someone, "What is an elephant?" and the person answered, "An elephant is a nonhorse." You would probably find the answer unsatisfactory. Yet, the term *nonprofit organization* describes something that is *not* something else—it suggests a business enterprise not organized to make a profit. But it tells us very little about the essential characteristics of this type of entity.

It is not easy to describe nonprofit organizations, and this is partly what makes managing them such a difficult task fraught with challenges and problems. Unlike management issues in the profit sector, which tend to be clear and related to specific economic measures, issues in the nonprofit environment are more nebulous because they relate to the somewhat abstract concept of *public service*. In a profit-making company, a manager generally knows whether he or she is doing a good job, but it is often less clear in a nonprofit organization in which the primary purpose is not to make money but to serve the public.

Some say that the essential defining characteristic of nonprofit organizations is the fact that they are established to provide a service to the public, and to some extent this is true. But this idea of a public service mission can be misleading. For one thing, there are a number of nonprofit organizations that are not organized to serve the public (for example, country clubs and labor unions). For another, the idea that nonprofit organizations are simply organized to solve some societal problem or deliver some much-needed public service flies in the face of the exclusivity often associated with their respective constituencies. This is perhaps most clear when nonprofit organizations are compared to public (or government) organizations and agencies working in the same area of activity. Although the nonprofit organizations often have a stated public service mission, they do not necessarily have a requirement of equity (that is, a mandate to serve everyone) the way public agencies usually do. As a result, the nonprofit organization's actual constituency may be far more limited than that of a public agency working in the same field.

Others claim that the essential defining characteristic of nonprofit organizations is that their mission is not to make money. Again, this is partly true. But many nonprofit organizations are quite entrepreneurial (again, this distinguishes them from most public or governmental agencies working in the same field). Many nonprofits engage in all sorts of money-making ventures that bear a close resemblance to profit-making entities, and this has been cause for some concern among those working in commercial endeavors whose businesses must compete with nonprofits for customers.

In fact, a nonprofit organization is neither in the for-profit sector nor in the public sector but sits somewhere between the two. This position allows the nonprofit great flexibility in its operation but also requires great skill in its management. On the one hand, managers must learn the same management techniques and analytical strategies that apply in profit-making companies. However, while these techniques are relevant in the nonprofit world, their application is dissimilar. Although both profit-making and nonprofit organizations engage in planning, budgeting, accounting, and marketing; although both have to contend with issues of governance, personnel, and information management; and although both have to raise money from time to time, these activities are carried out in markedly different ways. Similarly, while it may be useful to know about the workings of a public agency and the development of public policy, it is not sufficient preparation for the nonprofit manager or trustee. Governance, organizational accountability, financial reporting, and long-range planning are very different in nonprofit organizations whose special defining characteristics are laid down in state and federal law.

Toward a Definition

In this book, the term *nonprofit organization* refers to those legally constituted, nongovernmental entities incorporated under state law as charitable or not-for-profit corporations that have been set up to serve some public purpose and are tax-exempt according to the IRS. All must have the following five characteristics:

- They must have a public service mission.
- They must be organized as a not-for-profit or charitable corporation.
- Their governance structures must preclude self-interest and private financial gain.
- They must be exempt from paying federal tax.
- They must possess the special legal status that stipulates gifts made to them are tax deductible.

Consequently, nonprofit organizations *as described in this book* do *not* include three other categories of organizations:

- Entities that have been set up to make a profit but are failing to do so
- Organizations that are governed informally by a collection of people who, although they have banded together to serve some public good, have been granted no special corporate status by federal and state authorities
- Organizations that are recognized as nonprofit by the IRS but do not have a public purpose (for example, trade associations, labor unions, country clubs, and fraternal organizations)

Because these various classes of organizations do not have *all* the characteristics previously listed, their missions, governance structures, or method of management may be significantly different from what is described in this book.

This chapter considers four major challenges that face nonprofit organizations as a consequence of these special characteristics. The challenges are:

- Articulating a clear public service mission
- Engaging in risk/survival analysis
- Identifying and involving the constituency
- Testing for "Organized Abandonment"

By looking closely at each of these, we will continue to refine our understanding of the special nature of nonprofit organizations.

CONSEQUENCES OF A PUBLIC SERVICE MISSION

An essential difference between for-profit and nonprofit organizations centers on the concept of mission. The ultimate mission of the profit-making entity is to earn money for its owners. Ownership can come in many forms, of course, from outright ownership of the organization by a single individual to shared ownership (by partners or shareholders or some other group). The concept of *ownership* is completely absent from nonprofit organizations, and consequently the nonprofit's mission has a totally different thrust. There can be no owners in a nonprofit organization, because such an entity is intended to serve a broad public purpose and the law is clear in specifying that ownership (with concomitant private gain) is incompatible with public purpose. This is not to say that nonprofit organizations cannot make money. Nonprofit organizations can and do make money—in the same way profit-making entities do—but the money that is taken in must be directed toward the public purpose for which the organization was set up, held in reserve, or turned over to another organization with a public purpose.

It is much more difficult to identify and articulate the mission of a nonprofit organization and consequently to develop criteria by which success can be measured. In a profit-making organization, because the mission is clear, success criteria are also clear. The mission centers on profitability; thus the criteria for success (and for decision making) include the bottom line, return on investment, sales, profit margins, market share, and other easily calculated measures. In a nonprofit organization, where the mission centers on public service, it is not only more difficult to define purposes, but it can be a bewildering task to try to find the proper yardstick by which to measure success. If the purpose of a school is to produce well-educated citizens, if a peace group is established to oppose the use of military force, if a recreation center is to offer constructive activities to urban teenagers, what criteria should each use to measure success? There will always be quantitative measures at hand—College Board scores for the school, statistics on attendance at political rallies for the peace group, and numbers of participating teenagers in the case of the recreation center—but these measures are only indirect indexes of success.

Because the missions of nonprofit organizations center on the concept of public service, one might look to the public sector for models that demonstrate how mission statements are articulated and tested. Unfortunately, there is a problem with this approach. In the public sector, as we have already seen, there is an implied or stated mandate of equity in every mission statement. That is, public agencies are obligated to serve anyone who is eligible for assistance. For that reason, quantitative measures of success are often possible on the basis of the numbers of people served, their geographic distribution, their racial and socioeconomic diversity, and the cost-effectiveness of service delivery. For nonprofit organizations, these criteria may be relevant, but more often than not they are only indirect measures of success. Consider a nonprofit university-affiliated teaching hospital. Unlike the public hospital down the street, it cannot directly measure its success by counting the numbers of patients served and the cost-effectiveness of medical treatment. The nonprofit hospital's mission of promoting excellence in medical practice through exemplary training is less concrete, and success criteria are more difficult to establish.

Thus we come to the first major challenge for a nonprofit organization—that of articulating a clear public service mission. The challenge is not only to come up with a statement that defines what the organization is and what it has been set up to do, but to state these things in such a way that the organization can evaluate its success in carrying out this mission over time.

Developing a Mission Statement

The challenge of developing a good mission statement includes creating a text that is sufficiently broad to encompass the many possible activities that the organization may wish to engage in. This is crucial inasmuch as the law obligates the trustees of the organization to limit their activities to those covered by the mission statement as articulated in the organizing charter. However, in addition to a broad statement of purpose, a mission statement is only valuable if it gives some specific guidance on the direction the organization should take in regard to programs, services, and activities.

In designing a mission statement, whatever is decided on is not cast in stone. Although the filing of the statement of purpose with the organization's incorporation papers is an important step, this document can be updated and changed through a clearly articulated legal procedure, and in many cases, working mission statements are modified regularly without going through the legal process. Mission statements should be reviewed and revised periodically because such a process is itself valuable in helping to clarify the assumptions and desires of those most involved in the organization. How is a mission statement created? Let's look at a case history.

THE UTOPIAVILLE ARTS COUNCIL

The city of Utopiaville wanted to create a local arts council that would oversee the cultural activities in the community. City officials appointed a committee to look into the question of how best to proceed, and the group held public meetings to determine what kinds of activities would be most appropriate for the organization. The group wanted something simple and easy to remember and initially developed the following statement:

> *The purpose of the Utopiaville Arts Council is to develop, foster, and promote the arts as central to the lives of the citizens of the city of Utopiaville.*

While this statement certainly met the standard of being broad, the city council members were not satisfied. They felt the statement was too broad and did not provide enough of a sense of direction and intent. The planning group devised several more complex statements but could not find one that had the resonance of the first.

Finally, they went back to their notes from the public meetings and the lists of responsibilities and activities that people said should be part of the local arts council's mandate. They returned to the original mission statement but provided clarifying language as follows:

The purpose of the Utopiaville Arts Council is to develop, foster, and promote the arts as central to the lives of the citizens of the city of Utopiaville. Toward this end, it will undertake the following activities:

- Initiate programs in art, music, dance, and theater to benefit the citizens of Utopiaville
- Advise the city council on all matters concerning the arts, including pending legislation
- Work closely with the Utopiaville School District, with colleges and universities, and with other educational institutions in the city on the development of appropriate arts education programs
- Allocate public and private funds to organizations, agencies, or individuals who provide arts programs or products of high quality that are beneficial to the community
- Seek and apply for state, federal, and private funds available in support of the arts
- Review and make recommendations on all works of art to be acquired by the city, either by purchase or gift, and make recommendations concerning their proposed locations
- Develop a website that contains directories of local arts groups, artists, and performing and visual arts spaces; assemble calendars and schedules of arts events; and other material as appropriate to promote the arts in Utopiaville
- Conduct ongoing planning, researching the arts needs of the city, including new arts facilities, and developing, updat-

ing, and evaluating progress against periodic written plans
for the growth of the arts in Utopiaville
- Develop an awareness in the business community, in local
government, and in the general public of the value of the
arts in Utopiaville
- Promote and encourage the cultural diversity of the city and
assist in preserving the cultural heritage of the area
- Engage in any other activities that will enhance the arts and
cultural life of Utopiaville

This new mission statement was far stronger than the first.
Not only did it include the original compelling opening words
(which are all that most people committed to memory), but it
also included a more detailed framework from which the organization could develop a coherent program. And, of equal importance, it provided a structure against which some meaningful
evaluation of the organization's effectiveness could be carried
out in the years to come.

PUBLIC SERVICE AND RISK VERSUS SURVIVAL

James Sully is the president of the board of a summer camp in Northern California. The camp was founded in 1949 primarily to serve the
needs of at-risk youth, and it runs a special program for inner-city
teenagers on its pristine acreage in the mountains. The camp's program
has been based on a curriculum of outdoor survival skills, and teenagers
of all ethnic and racial backgrounds have been encouraged to work in
groups to foster increased understanding, trust, and affection for one
another.

Despite the popularity of the camp, costs have been rising and
funding has been diminishing for its core inner-city youth program.
At a meeting of the board, Sully put the problem plainly: "For several
years we've had a serious financial problem, and until that's solved,
we won't be continuing the program for the disadvantaged. We will
be taking only full tuition-paying campers. Balancing the books has
become our top priority."

James Sully's survival-and-safety-first attitude suggests that he may have forgotten the camp's original mission or has relegated it to a second-level priority. He seems to be telling us that running a non-profit organization is just like running a business and that financial problems have to be tended to first. In some ways he may be right. After all, no organization, for-profit or nonprofit, can lose money forever and survive. But perhaps it is not quite that simple. There may be many ways to meet a financial crisis, some more consistent with the organization's mission than others. As one board member said in response to Sully's statements, "Given the present crisis, it is clear that changes will have to be made; it's the nature of the changes that has people concerned."

Here is a classic manifestation of one of the great dilemmas for non-profit organizations. Which is more important: to ensure the continuity and survival of the organization or to stay true to the organization's mission even if this involves certain financial and institutional risks? Consider the following cases:

- A legal aid group, in the face of continuing cuts in government funding, must decide whether it will begin to charge clients a modest fee in order to generate much-needed earned income (the mission statement talks about providing free legal aid).
- A church must decide whether to take a stand on women in the priesthood. Regardless of the position it takes, it risks alienating a large number of church members. Yet the minister believes that the mission of the church is to provide guidance on moral issues.
- An all-male school, responding to decreasing enrollments, has been advised by a marketing consultant to go coed. Yet the faculty and many alumni feel that the original mission to offer a quality education to young men is still valid.
- A symphony orchestra, organized to improve the quality of the musical life of its city, must decide whether to increase the number of pop concerts and decrease its regular subscription concerts of classical music. The programming change would assist the organization in meeting its payroll but, some say, would compromise the mission of the organization.
- A women's health organization, founded as a collective, must decide whether it will reorganize around more conventional

management lines in order to increase efficiency and professionalism. Several of the organization's founders believe that collective management is central to the organization's mission.

Each of these examples suggests a choice between risks and compromises. The original missions of the various organizations suggest
one direction; prudence and good management sense suggest another.
Staying true to the original missions may be risky and expensive, yet
focusing only on the relative security of organizational survival may
lead to a compromise in principles. The tug between these two competing tendencies is constant in the nonprofit environment, and it
becomes extreme when organizations are under pressure, when funds
are scarce, and when there is lack of agreement about basic purposes.

Once again, the contrast with the public and profit sectors is
striking. In the public sector, risk is measured in political terms and
agencies generally have a clear idea of how far they can and should
go. The authorization to operate comes from elected officials who set
limits on what is permissible. To extend those limits requires political
persuasion, advocacy, and, in extreme cases, a change brought about by
voters who put new people in office. In the profit sector, businesses are
constantly faced with choices involving varying degrees of risk. But
the risks are almost always measured in terms of the ultimate return
or payoff. If the effect of a risky decision today is greater profitability
tomorrow, then the decision may have merit.

The situation for the nonprofit organization is different because
the standards of value are not stated primarily in political or financial
terms. Who can decide how much it is worth to take a moral stand,
perform more classical music, preserve a collective decision-making
structure, or continue to provide free legal aid especially if risk in
each case will not lead to greater profitability? In fact, in most cases,
the risks described will place greater financial burdens on the organization. Thus there is no single, simple criterion on which to base a
decision. It is a judgment call. On one side are the people who say the
organization cannot afford to put itself in jeopardy; on the other side
are the people who claim that a nonprofit organization that does not
stay true to its ideals should not continue to operate.

For all practical purposes, there is rarely a correct place to draw
the line between organizational security and a public service mission.

A nonprofit organization that is responsibly governed and managed finds itself debating the question continually, issue by issue, decision by decision. This is the second major challenge for a nonprofit organization—risk/survival analysis, or the search for the proper balance between organizational extension and risk taking on the one hand and organizational security on the other. Meeting the challenge involves the willingness of the governing group to:

- Engage in an ongoing planning process
- Analyze future options from both a practical and an idealistic point of view
- Debate the pros and cons of each proposed action in terms of the organization's stated mission and its long-term security

Consider the following example of an organization that successfully met this challenge.

LEGAL EDUCATION SOCIETY

The Legal Education Society has been in existence for several decades. Its mission is to provide legal assistance in a variety of ways—legal advice to individuals who cannot afford it, legal assistance to nonprofit organizations, and scholarly contributions to advance the public's understanding of the law. The multiracial board of directors of the Legal Education Society is composed of lawyers, judges, and private citizens representing different socioeconomic groups. At present, the organization is adequately funded, has a modest endowment, and has a permanent staff of twelve people.

In 2003, the Legal Education Society hired a woman who was widely recognized as one of the brightest young lawyers in the country to be the society's executive director. She had been on the *Law Review* at a prestigious law school, had contributed significantly to the law literature, and had spent two years clerking for a Supreme Court justice. Her appointment was hailed as a turning point in the history of the Legal Education Society. However, it was a turning point in a way that no one had expected.

During the first four years of her tenure as executive director, the young woman pleased everyone. She added programs, secured increased funding, wrote important articles, attracted new staff (including minorities and women), and appeared to be the dynamo that everyone thought she would be when they hired her. After four years, her interest began to shift. With her growing prominence in the field, organizations throughout the country wanted to hire her as a consultant to advise them on setting up legal education programs. At first, she accepted these assignments only on weekends and vacations, having received permission to do so from the board of directors. But as the demand for her consulting services grew, as her own interest in these projects increased, and as the scope of the projects demanded greater time commitments, she asked the board whether she might set up a small consulting program through the Legal Education Society, bringing the consulting contracts through the organization. The advantage, she explained, would be that the Legal Education Society could earn income and expand its influence nationally in the field of legal education.

At first, the arrangement worked well. Two large contracts during the first year netted the organization $82,000 in additional income. The Legal Education Society was cited as a leader in its field. The executive director, with the assistance of several key staff people, continued to be happy with the challenge and growth of the consulting work, but the Legal Education Society's primary constituency back home was becoming restless. The focus of the organization was changing. Individual staff members appeared to be less interested in their constituents' problems as they became more focused on the problems facing people halfway across the country. The board of directors was receiving conflicting signals. The national press and funding agencies throughout the country were praising the work of the Legal Education Society; the local constituency (individuals and organizations seeking services) was complaining about inadequate response and attention.

On the fifth anniversary of the executive director's tenure, she proposed a major restructuring of the Legal Education Society in which the consulting business would become—within five years—the major activity of the organization. Her plan, brilliant in its conception, saw the organization doubling its budget and staff during that period and becoming far less reliant on grants. Legal assistance would still be provided, but it would be offered through a number of subcontracts, and the Legal Education Society would simply act as broker. One of her justifications for the plan was especially compelling. At the time, federal and state governments seemed to be placing less priority on the funding of legal aid programs, and the private sector did not indicate enthusiasm about making up the difference. Realistically, there was less money available and greater competition for that money. By way of contrast, she explained, the consulting business offered a very promising financial future.

There was no doubt in the minds of those serving on the board of directors that the executive director could pull off the plan. Her ability had been proven time and time again. There was also no debate on the question of the funding outlook. Simply stated, the funding picture for basic legal services looked bleak. However, the board of directors was concerned about what impact the change would have on the organization's central and original mission. Although a consulting business would ensure organizational survival and continued growth, it would also mean a major shift away from basic legal services for the poor and for nonprofit organizations. That need existed, now more than ever, and several community members of the board of directors argued passionately that the organization must return to its original purpose.

The question was debated for two months. Surveys were conducted among both constituents and national authorities. At first, the majority of trustees seemed to favor the executive director's plan. But another group stated unequivocally that it was the legal obligation of the board of directors to safeguard the organization's mission, and they threatened to seek the support of the state attorney general to compel the board to reject the plan. In the end, the board of directors, in a close vote, turned down the executive director's request and called for a new plan that would return the organization to its original mode of operation. A year later, the Legal Education Society had a new executive director, a smaller (and mostly new) staff, a smaller budget, many new board members, and a clear sense of its place in the community. In the interim, the previous executive director had started a consulting firm and staffed it with many of her former employees. One of her first clients turned out to be the Legal Education Society, which even now continues to draw on her experience and expertise.

Did the board of directors make the right decision? Some people would say yes; others would disagree. It is unlikely that the state attorney general would have intervened in the case— although in theory he would have had legal standing to do so had some of the trustees convinced him that the organization's mission was being compromised. Regardless of the merits of the case, the fact that such a legal action was threatened indicated the troubling aspects of the executive director's plan in the minds of some trustees. In the end, there was no right decision because "right" depended on each person's point of view. In spite of this, there was a correct and responsible course of action, which was the decision to debate the executive director's plan in an open and informed manner. The trustees considered the question of mission on the one hand and organizational security on the other. They weighed their options and came down in favor of a recommitment to the original mission. Those who disagreed (the executive director, some of the staff, and some of the board members) left the organization, and although they were disappointed with the decision, all believed in the integrity of the decision-making process. The organization had successfully met the challenge of risk/survival analysis.

HOW LARGE AND DIVERSE A PUBLIC?

The mission of every nonprofit organization centers on serving the public. But what precisely does that mean? The public, in the broadest sense, is everyone; yet few nonprofit organizations see themselves as offering their services to everyone. Unlike public agencies, they do not operate under any such implied or stated obligation. Therefore, every nonprofit organization must decide how broadly to define its constituency and how large or diverse a public to serve.

This decision is not simply a theoretical one. It is practical. The decision has ramifications for programs and activities, fund raising, budget planning, and staff size and structure. It touches on questions of constituency representation on the board. It is a question that cannot be finessed through a mission statement that refers in a general sort of way to "serving the public." The organization must demonstrate the scope of its service and interests through its governance, its staffing, its programs, and its activities.

The contrast with profit-sector organizations sharpens our understanding of this special characteristic of nonprofits. In the profit sector, an organization's public is determined by its need to sell products and services. Therefore, its public consists of those who have either a direct or indirect effect on profitability: its customers and clients, its employees, and those significant others who can either promote or hamper the organization's ability to carry out its activities. Significant others, in the case of an oil company, might include a senator considering environmental restrictions on drilling; for a major bank, it might include a group of journalists who regularly cover economic and financial issues.

Each of these constituency groups—customers and clients, employees, and significant others—is important to a profit-making entity to the extent that it can influence the business enterprise, and the primary strategy for dealing with each group is determined from a business perspective. For example, a profit-making company may survey the attitudes and predilections of its customers and clients, adjust its products and services accordingly, and then adopt marketing strategies to promote an image of service. It might offer its employees a generous benefits package or a bonus to promote good management/employee relations. In some cases, it might decide to make certain kinds of investments to promote a positive public image among those whose opinions can affect the conduct of business and, ultimately, profitability. The business may make contributions to political candidates to try to influence legislation, or it may make charitable contributions to promote an image of a caring organization. When these decisions are explained to the organization's owners or investors, they can be justified on the basis that they promote the business's own interests. In all cases, service to and involvement of various constituency groups is seen as a strategy, and in no case is involvement of the constituency in the decision-making process seen as essential.

In the nonprofit world, the situation is completely reversed. Service to the public is not seen as a strategy; it is an end in itself. While a nonprofit organization can engage in many of the same activities that were described for the profit-making business—surveying its constituency to adjust products and services, promoting harmony among employees, and even, occasionally, making contributions to other charities—it does so out of a conviction that these activities further the organization's service mission. In order to be effective, the organization cannot keep its public at arm's length. Broad involvement of its public at all levels of operation is absolutely necessary to achieve effective nonprofit administration.

Yet, the nonprofit organization does not have the same kind of public mandate that the government (or public) agency does. The public agency, because it is tax based, theoretically must offer its services to anyone. In many cases, "anyone" is restricted to people or organizations meeting certain eligibility requirements. But there are two significant points here. First, eligibility is always defined precisely, usually in quantitative terms (for example, people over sixty-five, people who earn less than $10,000 per year, organizations with budgets of less than $100,000 per year, or nonprofit 501(c)(3) organizations). Second, once eligibility criteria are set, anyone who meets those criteria is eligible to be served. Not so with the nonprofit organization. Such an organization has the luxury of picking and choosing who it wishes to serve. But this very flexibility is also a challenge. Defining the constituency too narrowly or failing to include representatives of that constituency in the operation of a nonprofit organization may have negative consequences.

This is the third major challenge for a nonprofit organization, the challenge of constituency identification and involvement. A nonprofit organization must identify clearly those it intends to serve, and once it does so, it must work toward an organizational structure—through board, staff, and activities—that reinforces its commitment to that group. The various decisions that follow the identification of an organization's constituents establish its specific image in the community, provide a clue to potential funders concerning its public commitment, and either attract or repel the people the organization wishes to serve.

Why is this issue so important? Consider the following situations:

- An art museum fails to secure a grant from its state arts agency because its programs "serve only an elitist and affluent audience." It is encouraged to find ways to reach out to a broader public.
- A health clinic based in an urban neighborhood claims to be serving its community, composed of 80 percent black residents. Yet, despite efforts to attract blacks to the clinic, nearly all of the clinic's patients are white. Significantly, so are its entire board and staff.
- The board of directors of a community recreation center is mystified by the low attendance at a newly planned series of events. The problem stems from the fact that the events were planned by a consultant who failed to seek community input.
- The IRS challenges the tax-exempt status of a nonprofit literary marketing service on the grounds that membership is open only to a select few who derive clear financial benefits from the association.

Each of these organizations finds itself in a dilemma. In each case, the concept of public involvement has been defined too narrowly:

- In the case of the art museum, the director of the funding agency that dispenses public tax dollars says her grants committee is unwilling to "see the taxes of poor people going to pay for the pleasures of the rich." She claims that her agency might feel very differently if the museum offered subsidized admissions for senior citizens, attempted to make the facility accessible to the disabled, provided informal programs in community locations, or offered an educational program for local schoolchildren.
- In the case of the health center, the organization's mission statement refers to service to its community, but the organization's all-white board and staff (all of whom live elsewhere) transmit

a different message to the black people who are local to the neighborhood. It is an example of actions speaking louder than words.

- In the case of the recreation center, the organization appears to have alienated its primary community constituency by placing too much confidence in the abilities of a consultant. Perhaps if community representatives had been involved in the planning process from the start, there would have been a greater sense of ownership once the programs were established.
- Finally, the literary organization offers a chilling preview of what can happen when an organization defines its membership and services too narrowly. The consequences of ambiguity about the nonprofit intent of the organization are possible loss of funding and ultimately of tax-exempt status.

For a nonprofit organization, then, defining its service to the public involves the following components:

- A well-defined understanding of an organization's constituency
- Involvement of this constituency at all levels of the organization, but particularly at the trustee level
- Programs and activities that demonstrate a strong commitment to the constituency

THE TEST FOR ORGANIZED ABANDONMENT

One of the most important steps for a nonprofit organization, as we have seen, is to determine its mission. Doing it well requires a lot of thought and discussion. But there is another aspect of mission that is even more challenging—deciding at what point it is no longer appropriate, or determining where there are other organizations that can fulfill the mission more effectively. This test for organized abandonment is so difficult to apply that many nonprofit organizations simply struggle along year after year without ever facing up to the fact that their existence is of very little consequence to anyone outside of the organization itself.

Consider the organization whose mission centers on the eradication of a particular disease. What should happen to that organization when a cure for the disease is discovered, medicine made available, and the disease eliminated? At first glance, it would seem obvious that the organization should disband. But should it? It has over the years built up a loyal constituency. Might that constituency be encouraged to join the fight to eliminate another disease?

Or consider the organization that has been allowed to atrophy over the years and now finds itself surrounded by a number of younger, more vital organizations that appear to be carrying out its mission more effectively. This would appear to be a clear case where the organization should disband. But again, one should not jump quickly to conclusions. By whose standards is the organization judged moribund, and by what criteria is it determined that others are carrying out its mission more effectively?

The concept of organized abandonment is central to our understanding of nonprofit organizations and illustrates one of the principal difficulties in responsible governance and management. *Organized abandonment* refers to the planned phasing out of an organization's operation. The word *organized* is used to characterize a kind of disbanding that is the result of careful deliberation rather than of unwelcome and unexpected financial reversals, management upheaval, or other external or internal crises. One of the major problems in the nonprofit world is that the test for organized abandonment is difficult to apply because the criteria by which judgments are made are relative and subjective.

Once again, the contrast with the profit and public sectors is clear. In the profit sector, when an organization loses money for any length of time and the future does not promise a turnaround, it is usually a signal that something must change. Investors move in to cut their losses, and the organization may be sold, disbanded, or reorganized. There are two essential differences in the nonprofit sector. The first is that it is not nearly as obvious when things should change because there is not a single, objective criterion by which to measure success or failure. Second, there is no predictable outside pressure to reorganize or disband. There is no voting group moving quickly to protect its investments, and the governing group and staff can continue operating for years without a real sense of purpose or standard of excellence.

In the public sector, there is also a clear difference in knowing when to cease operations. For a government agency, publicly elected individuals hold the purse strings and review the agency's achievements and plans. The agency must perform to the elected individuals' satisfaction or its funding, and sometimes its continued existence, is threatened. Periodically, the agency may be further subjected to some form of "sunset review" that requires a formal justification of its continued existence before it is authorized to continue operating. No such external pressures are brought to bear on private nonprofit organizations.

We have arrived, then, at the final critical challenge for a nonprofit organization—the challenge of testing for organized abandonment. This challenge requires that the organization:

- Has defined its mission clearly
- Has established success criteria by which it can evaluate the relevance and effectiveness of its mission
- Has set up a formal system by which it can determine whether the mission is still relevant and whether it is carrying out the mission effectively

The following case may provide insight into how this can be accomplished.

THE REGIONAL HEALTH NETWORK

In the late twentieth century, a federal agency, in partnership with three state agencies from northern New England and with the help of several area corporations, put together a funding package to promote exemplary health education programs in rural Maine, New Hampshire, and Vermont. A new private nonprofit organization—the Regional Health Network—was established in New Hampshire. Its mission was twofold: first, to improve the quality and quantity of health education in the three northern New England states through workshops, seminars, classes, and community events, and second, to upgrade the expertise of schools and community groups in establishing permanent ongoing programs at the local level.

For ten years, the Regional Health Network thrived. Its budget increased, its staff grew to ten people, it was given a home within a large university, and its program was cited as a national model. Then things began to change. The funding of the Regional Health Network became more precarious because the federal agency changed its funding priorities and state agencies followed suit. The funding crisis was the result of a policy shift for which the Network was not to blame and over which it had no control. The Network's federal and state funders had decided to establish regional health education organizations, but the definition of the New England region was six states. The Network, because it served only three states, was not considered an appropriate recipient of funding. Hence, through a technicality in federal and state policy, continued funding for the Network appeared to be uncertain.

Money was not the Regional Health Network's only problem. From its inception, the Network's constituency had been composed largely of volunteers with little experience in health education. Initially, teachers, parents, and other volunteers continually praised the technical assistance provided by the Regional Health Network staff, stating that "we never could have done these programs without you." But ten years later, the Network's constituency was becoming far more sophisticated. Many of the local programs were staffed by professionals, and these people were demanding either that the Network provide better and more extensive services or simply turn the scarce federal and state money directly over to them.

It is fortunate that the Regional Health Network had defined its mission clearly, set up evaluation criteria, and was willing to engage in the test for organized abandonment. By doing so, it was able to provide improved services to its constituents, preserve all of its important programs, find satisfying new jobs for its staff members, and ultimately, to disband.

The organization went through the following steps to determine whether organized abandonment was appropriate. An evaluation was done to determine how well the organization had fulfilled or was fulfilling its mission. Through the evaluation, it was discovered that the ten years of developmental work in rural northern New England had spawned a large number of ongoing, self-sufficient programs in both the schools and community organizations—a discovery that pleased the board but indicated that the need for developmental work had diminished. The evaluation also revealed that while the need for health education, technical assistance, and resources was still great, the Network's constituents were looking to larger and better-funded organizations to provide these resources and the Network was becoming less important to them.

Subsequent to the evaluation, the board and staff of the Network talked to funders in both the public and private sectors to analyze the financial prospects for the future. While most of the funders said they would be willing to help the organization by making small gifts toward its programmatic activities, no funder was willing to underwrite basic administrative costs. The federal and state agencies that had originally provided the administrative underwriting were in the process of designating another organization (which serviced six states) to be the official regional organization, and federal policy required that only one organization per region could receive basic administrative underwriting. Thus, the Network's financial future did not look good.

The board and the staff of the Regional Health Network met for several months to consider the situation. Could the organization change its mission in order to secure basic administrative funding? Should the organization charge for its services? Should the staff be cut to one or two people so that the organization could continue to run a token program, hoping for a better future? Each of these alternatives and many others were considered. But each was rejected. The original mission of the organization had been right for its time. Much of what the organization had set out to do had been accomplished. Now there were other organizations that were carrying out the balance of the mission with greater effectiveness and financial viability.

The board voted to disband but set up a nine-month timetable to make sure that every significant program of the Network was placed in another organization, that each member of the staff had another place to go, and that a history of the organization and its accomplishments would be written to become a part of the public record. Several of the programs were absorbed by the new six-state regional organization, based in Massachusetts, and to ensure continuity through the first year of transition, that organization hired the Network's executive director as a full-time consultant/coordinator for program implementation in the three northern New England states. Fifteen years after it had been established, the Network closed its doors for good. It did so after a champagne reception to celebrate its accomplishments and the future of its programs.

The history of the Regional Health Network is a success story in nonprofit administration. Its success is represented not only by what it accomplished during its twenty-plus years of existence but also what it accomplished in disbanding at the right time and in the right way. There are many nonprofit organizations that would benefit from a close analysis of the history of the Network, particularly the events of the final two years. This history demonstrates how one nonprofit organization met the challenge of accountability to its mission.

The purpose of this chapter has been to describe some of the more important characteristics of nonprofit organizations and the consequent challenges that face those who govern and manage them.

Nonprofit organizations are private-sector organizations with public purposes. This combination gives them great flexibility in their operations. However, flexibility is a double-edged sword. It offers opportunities yet poses certain dangers. Most particularly, it can cause ambiguity and uncertainty in the areas of mission, constituency, and activities. A nonprofit organization must address these dangers by:

1. Articulating its mission clearly
2. Engaging in ongoing analysis of the risks versus the benefits of each proposed action
3. Identifying its constituency and involving representatives of that constituency in all phases of its operation

4. Testing for organized abandonment in order to ensure that the organization remains needed and wanted

These challenges, when properly met, provide a basic framework for responsible governance and management in nonprofit organizations.

CHECKLIST QUESTIONS FOR CHAPTER 1

1. Has the mission statement of your organization been reviewed within the last five years?
2. Does the mission statement contain both a broad statement of purpose and a more detailed framework from which your organization can develop a coherent set of activities?
3. Has a planning process been developed that balances the need for organizational and program development with long-term financial security?
4. Who are your organization's constituents? Are they well represented in the organization? Are they well served by the organization's activities?
5. Has there been a formal test for organized abandonment in your organization within the last decade?
6. What criteria have been developed to evaluate the continued relevance and appropriateness of your organization's mission and activities?

TWO

The Board

Mary Clarke founded the Compton Community Center eleven years ago. Had she known then what she knows now, she would have done things differently. Who could have imagined back then, when the center was just an idea in her head, that the idea would become a reality, that within ten years the community center would be serving more than fifteen thousand people every year, that it would own a building (a former schoolhouse that was purchased from the town for $1), and that it would have a paid staff of twenty-two people and a budget in excess of $1.5 million? Had she known all these things were possible, she might have taken the advice of people who told her to go more slowly and carefully. But, at the time, she felt she had to move quickly and decisively. She had to garner support from anyone who would help. She had to show confidence even when she was not sure she was doing the right thing. Her philosophy was that enthusiasm is contagious and it is enthusiasm that builds community organizations.

Mary Clarke's biggest regret is that she did not exercise greater care in assembling a board of trustees. Her mistake is completely understandable given the circumstances. The community center had operated for two years as a project of the local YMCA and had not needed to incorporate. It was a convenient relationship. The YMCA provided space, took care of all the necessary bookkeeping, and lent its tax-exempt status to the center so that Mary could go out and fund raise. Eventually, she knew, she would have to worry about separate corporate status, but many people advised her to wait until the program was well established. However, something unexpected happened that required a change in her timetable. When Compton's school board decided to close one of the local elementary schools, several influential people in town felt that it should become the new home for the Compton Community Center. The idea was the fulfillment of Mary

Clarke's dream, and she was not about to claim that the organization was not ready for such a step.

After that, things moved quickly. There was a special town referendum in which the voters agreed that the school should be sold to the Compton Community Center for $1. Lawyers for the town met with lawyers representing the YMCA and Mary Clarke's committee. All agreed that under these new circumstances Mary Clarke's project had gone beyond the point at which the YMCA could assume a fiscal agent status and that separate incorporation for the Compton Community Center would be a necessity. It was further agreed that Mary needed an official nonprofit corporation to which the property could be deeded.

It was at this point that Mary Clarke made her first serious mistake. In her haste to get the corporation together, she asked a group of her friends to serve as the trustees. "It is just to satisfy the lawyers," she said, "and to put some names on the incorporation papers. I promise that you won't really have to do anything." These were words that she soon came to regret. She regretted them when the Compton Community Center needed to begin serious fund raising, when she needed to mobilize support in the community for a zoning change, and when she came to realize that one person could not single-handedly assume responsibility for an organization as large and complex as the Compton Community Center. Like many nonprofit organizations, Mary's was incorporated in haste, and a governing group was thrown together that knew nothing about the considerable responsibilities of trusteeship. This was to haunt Mary Clarke for the next five years.

Perhaps all of this would have been clearer if Mary Clarke herself had understood the specific role that the law has carved out for trustees[1] in connection with the governance of a legally constituted nonprofit organization. Chapter 1 indicated that nonprofit organizations are granted several very lucrative concessions and immunities by the federal and state governments, especially after they have received permission to operate as tax-exempt corporations. Once the organizations are declared tax-exempt, several governmental authorities at the federal, state, and, in some cases, the local level give up their right to tax. Furthermore, the IRS generally agrees to allow individuals and institutional donors to claim tax deductions when they make gifts to these organizations. This is no less than a generous public subsidy. In making this concession, the government is assuming that the organizations are somehow serving the public and not operating for anyone's private financial gain.

By giving up the power to tax and granting the status of tax deductibility on gifts, government taxing authorities are making tremendous concessions and in many cases bestowing a great deal of indirect financial assistance on nonprofit organizations. For example, in a particular organization that is receiving $500,000 in individual contributions each year, we can assume that at least $100,000 of that is indirectly provided by the government through taxes not paid to the U.S. Treasury. For the nonprofit field as a whole, forgone taxes from individuals total in the billions of dollars. For this reason, there needs to be some protection built into the system so that the government can feel that the public purposes of nonprofit organizations are in fact being carried out. It requires that a group of people act as guardians of the public trust—individuals who have the public's interest at heart. These people are trustees. It is their task to act as stewards, accountable to the state governments that granted the organizations their respective charters, accountable to the federal government that granted tax-exempt status, and ultimately accountable to the public itself.

In order to ensure that trustees of nonprofit organizations have the public's interest at heart, the individuals should not serve in order to derive financial benefits from trusteeship, as would be the case in a profit-making organization. They may not personally own stock in the nonprofit organization or have an owner's equity in any of an organization's assets as would be the case in a for-profit corporation. For the most part, they are expected to serve without compensation (except reasonable reimbursement for out-of-pocket expenses).[2] Indeed, instead of serving as trustees for the financial benefits that might accrue to them, they are expected to carry out their duties as volunteers for the public good, and to exercise, on behalf of the public, a legal and fiduciary responsibility. They must make sure that the organizations they serve are carrying out their missions as articulated in their articles of incorporation and that their financial activities are both legal and proper, given federal and state requirements.

In this context, trusteeship is a serious business carrying extensive legal obligations. It is not simply an honor. Nor is it simply attendance at luncheons and tea parties, as trustees who have been sued have learned to their dismay. It is an activity that requires knowledge, commitment, and time. In selecting trustees, Mary Clarke should have found people who understood this; she should have searched out people with proper legal and financial skills. Most important, she should have looked for people who understood something about the responsibilities and duties of trusteeship.

THE RESPONSIBILITIES AND DUTIES OF TRUSTEES

There are six principal areas of responsibility for trustees. Trustees should:

- Determine the organization's mission and set policies for its operation, ensuring that the provisions of the organization's charter and the law are being followed
- Set the organization's overall program from year to year and engage in longer-range planning to establish its general course for the future
- Establish fiscal policy and boundaries, with budgets and financial controls
- Provide adequate resources for the activities of the organization through direct financial contributions and a commitment to fund raising
- Select, evaluate, and, if necessary, terminate the appointment of the chief executive
- Develop and maintain a communication link to the community, promoting the work of the organization

Important as it is to understand what the duties of trustees include, it is equally important to understand what they do not include. Trustees should not:

- Engage in the day-to-day operation of the organization
- Hire staff other than the chief executive
- Make detailed programmatic decisions without consulting staff

Let us look in more detail at the six responsibility areas of trustees.

POLICY MAKING

By law, the board of trustees is responsible for setting policy for a nonprofit organization. This begins with drafting (and amending when necessary) two documents that set out various rules, regulations, and procedures. These are the *articles of incorporation* (sometimes called the *articles of organization)* and the *bylaws.* In addition, the trustees may wish to develop other documents such as a personnel manual that establishes all policies in regard to staff and a trustee manual to further clarify roles, responsibilities, duties, and general board policies. In many nonprofit organizations, additional policies are drafted in the areas of conflict of interest, whistle-blowers, use of organizational funds by board and staff (for such things as travel and entertainment), and other matters pertaining to the particular activities of the organization.

Developing policies for the smooth operation of a nonprofit organization has two advantages. From a very practical point of view, a set of rules, regulations, and operating procedures ensures that there is a standard against which to measure employee and trustee actions and that the standards provide grounds for dismissal when individuals do not conform to them. More broadly, fully documented policies partially protect the trustees from liability for things that may go wrong, as will be described later in this chapter. Lawsuits are far less likely when the trustees have taken the trouble to develop, debate, revise, and adopt policies that demonstrate their involvement in the affairs of the organization.

The first document that the trustees must concern themselves with is the organization's *charter* referred to in some states as the *articles of incorporation* and in others as the *articles of organization.* The articles are initially submitted at the time the organization petitions the state for corporate status, and they are reviewed in the state office that maintains corporate records (e.g., Department of Corporations or the Secretary of State's office). That portion of the articles that sets out the basic operating framework of the organization is almost always drafted with the assistance of an attorney to ensure conformity with the laws governing nonprofit corporations, although the portion containing the corporate purpose should be drafted with the input of the trustees.

Once the articles of incorporation are approved, the original copy remains in the state office and serves as official documentation of the corporation's structure, purpose, fiscal year, and so on. Because so much of the organization's character and reason for being are contained in the articles of organization, the trustees should review it at least once every three years. Changes should be stated as amendments, approved by the trustees, and subsequently filed with the state. It is important to remind the trustees that part of their legal obligation is to make sure that the corporation is carrying out its activities and fulfilling its mission as specified in the charter. Thus the trustees should be supplied with a copy of the charter at the time they join the organization.

The board of trustees is also responsible for drafting a second document, called the *bylaws*, which serves as the organization's operating constitution. Bylaws go beyond the general material contained in the charter and discuss more detailed and specific procedures affecting the trustees themselves. For example, the bylaws set out the number, tenure, and election procedure for trustees and discuss how and when meetings are called, how officers (president, treasurer, clerk, and so on) are elected and what their powers are, how votes are taken, how board vacancies are filled, and a host of other small details essential to the smooth operation of the organization.

Bylaws, like articles of organization, must be reviewed periodically and updated. Furthermore, it is the responsibility of the trustees to see that the provisions are followed in order to avoid legal complications. Consider the following case.

PETERSON PARK ZOO

The executive director of the Peterson Park Zoo, a nonprofit organization with a budget of $10 million, had been warned several times by the president of the board that the trustees were unhappy with his performance. After six months, the president of the board held a special meeting of the executive committee, and a vote was taken to terminate the appointment of the executive director with two months' notice. The executive director was informed of the decision and, unbeknownst to the trustees, secured the services of a lawyer. Meanwhile, a search committee was formed, and a new executive director was hired.

When the time came for the first executive director to leave, he stated that he had not been legally removed from his job and was therefore still the executive director. He pointed out that according to the bylaws, the executive committee was not empowered to terminate him because he was an officer of the corporation and that such an action required a majority vote of the entire board at a full board meeting. Furthermore, according to his contract, three months' notice was required between the official vote to terminate and actual termination of services.

The Peterson Park Zoo now had two executive directors, each threatening a lawsuit, and the trustees were in a quandary. Three weeks elapsed before the full board could meet to discuss the problem and take a vote on the first executive director's termination. During that time, the executive director mobilized considerable support from disgruntled trustees who were angry at the incompetence of the executive committee. During the board meeting, the lawyer for the executive director successfully convinced a majority of trustees to provide two years of severance pay for his client, an expense that the Peterson Park Zoo could ill afford and that could have been avoided had the board given proper attention to the bylaws.

Subsequently, a group of trustees who had not been part of the executive committee and had not been consulted in the original decision to fire the executive director threatened to bring suit against members of the executive committee (as was their legal right under state law). In order to avoid the potential financial consequences of legal action, the executive committee members voluntarily resigned from the board in exchange for having the suit dropped.

In addition to the articles of organization and the bylaws, some organizations develop two rule books, one primarily for staff and the other for the board. The staff rule book is called a *personnel manual* and is discussed in detail in chapter 4. It provides information about hiring and firing, vacation and sick days, leaves, performance and salary reviews, working hours and conditions, and benefits. The board rule book, or *trustee manual,* is discussed later in this chapter. It provides a more detailed account of the roles and responsibilities of trustees.

Either included in both the personnel and trustee manuals or developed as a separate document, many organizations develop a set of *conflict-of-interest* policies. The potential for conflict of interest arises when members of the board or staff might find themselves in a position to benefit themselves, family members, or other organizations with which they are associated by virtue of their position within the nonprofit organization. It should be pointed out that in many cases the action by the nonprofit organization might be entirely appropriate—as, for example, when the organization chooses to engage the law firm of one of its trustees to undertake a complex real estate transaction or defend the organization against a lawsuit. However, in all cases, conflict-of-interest policies should suggest:

1. That an individual with a conflict fully disclose his or her relationship to the individual or organization benefiting from the decision
2. That the individual with a conflict not participate in the decision in which the conflict exists, which might mean:
   - Not participating in the vote
   - Not entering into the discussion prior to the vote
   - Absenting himself or herself from the room during the discussion and the vote

The documents just described provide the trustees with a mechanism for setting broad policy on the internal structure and operation of their organization, and they can develop other policies from time to time that further help bring clarity to these areas. By developing these policies, they also protect the organization and themselves considerably from legal exposure, because these policies demonstrate that the group took reasonable care to ensure that the organization would operate in a manner that would appear reasonable to "an ordinary prudent person in a like position" (the standard that most states' attorneys general would by law adopt in judging the actions of trustees).

PLANNING

The second major responsibility of the trustees is to engage in planning both for the short term (the next year), the medium term (the next five years), and the long term (the next decade). Planning involves the setting of broadly stated goals and specific objectives. To establish goals, the board must decide on directions for the organization and determine what they want to see accomplished. For example, a goal of the Compton Community Center might be to provide a rich variety of sports-related opportunities for at-risk schoolchildren in the city. To establish objectives, the board must be much more specific. Objectives are time bound, usually quantitative, and measurable. Thus for the goal of providing a rich variety of sports-related opportunities for at-risk schoolchildren in the city, an objective might be to provide at least one hour a week of supervised physical activities to 850 children, aged eight to eighteen, from low-income families.

Objectives, once set, allow for two additional activities to take place. One is the drafting of an action or implementation plan by which the objectives will be achieved. Generally, the implementation plan is developed primarily by staff and is reviewed by the board. It lays out the actual schedule of activities, use of resources (both human and financial), and logistics. The second activity that should follow the development of objectives is the establishment of an evaluation process to determine whether the organization actually achieves the objectives in the time allotted. Unfortunately, evaluation is one area that is often neglected by trustees. But it should not be. The trustees are responsible for keeping the organization on track. They should do so partially by tracking the effectiveness with which plans are actually carried out and objectives met.

Although planning will be discussed in more depth in chapter 9, it is important to outline at least some activities that a board should generally consider in the planning area. These include:

- Appointing a planning committee to develop the planning agenda for the organization
- Holding periodic planning retreats at least once every two years (and more frequently during the development of a long-range plan)
- Developing a written plan at least once every five years
- Establishing goals and objectives in advance of every new year
- Reviewing the operational and financial consequences of these goals and objectives

FISCAL RESPONSIBILITIES

"The executive director really knows about the budget. Let's let him develop the numbers, and we will simply approve what he comes up with."

"The staff is honest; let's not make their life complicated by insisting on cumbersome check-signing and cash-handling procedures."

Many trustees either make statements like these or make decisions that indicate that they believe them. In doing so, they are not only abrogating their responsibility to preserve the public trust by neglecting a fiduciary (or fiscal/financial) responsibility, but they are making themselves personally liable for legal action. Many trustees are under the mistaken notion that while a corporation can be sued, an individual who serves on its board is immune and cannot be sued. This is not the case. Corporations do offer certain protections, but if it can be proven that the trustees showed negligence in financial matters, they can be held personally liable. It is very unusual that creditors would have standing to sue trustees if the organization failed to pay them.[3] However, the federal government has standing to sue for the nonpayment of withholding taxes, and there are other cases where the personal assets of the trustees could be at risk. For example, in a trustee dispute one group of trustees could, on behalf of the organization, hold another group liable if it could be demonstrated that these individuals provided inaccurate financial information in the case of an important financial decision that adversely affected the organization. Even if the case had no merit and the judgment was for those accused, the defending trustees might find themselves bearing heavy legal costs.

The best way for trustees to avoid such situations is to exercise financial responsibility. This involves developing and monitoring budgets on the one hand and establishing fiscal controls on the other. In the area of budgets, the trustees perform several functions. One is a planning function. The preparation of the annual budget must be accomplished with the involvement of board members (a finance committee is often assembled for this purpose), and these individuals must satisfy themselves that revenues will be adequate to meet projected expenses. If there is a deficit at the end of the year, the trustees bear as much responsibility as the staff. It is simply not sufficient to say, "The executive director was incorrect in his projections." The trustees must be prepared to admit, "We did not ask enough probing questions." (Chapter 6 details the steps involved in the budgeting process.)

Preparation of the budget is only part of the trustees' oversight responsibility in this area. The two additional trustee functions are approval and monitoring. The approval step, which must be completed before the budget period begins, is an official action on the part of the trustees that carries the force of an endorsement. It says to the staff, "We have reviewed this budget and are satisfied that revenues and expenditures appear reasonable and achievable. We will take responsibility in helping you meet your revenue targets." Obviously, if such a statement indicates that there are projected revenues based on fund raising, the trustees have implicitly made a commitment to assist in this area.

Approving a budget is not enough. The trustees are responsible for monitoring and, if necessary, amending the budget throughout the year. Financial statements must be prepared for every board meeting that show how the actual revenue and expense figures compare with what has been budgeted (see figure 2.1). The example in figure 2.1 was taken from the first year's operation of the Compton Community Center as an independent corporation. The move to the new building had not yet taken place, and the budget was still modest. In spite of these factors, the trustees of the Compton Community Center received some surprises when they reviewed the financial statement for the first three months of the fiscal year.

The left-hand column of figure 2.1 shows the actual approved annual budget figures, the center column shows receipts and expenditures up to the closing date on the statement, and the right-hand column shows the difference between the first two columns for each budget category. At this point in the year, the trustees had an opportunity to assess the various budget estimates and adjust the original budget based on the up-to-date information given in the financial statement.

The trustees were not pleased with what they saw on this statement. For example, the revenue category called Grants showed only $1,000 of income after three months even though $10,000 had been budgeted for the year. One trustee asked whether the original figure was realistic. If not, she suggested that a more modest projection of income be inserted into the original budget; expenditures would then have to be adjusted downward as well. Similarly, the expense categories of Telephone, Utilities, and Office Supplies appear to have been considerably underbudgeted given the fact that nine months remained in the fiscal year. To her surprise, Mary Clarke was asked by the board to make adjustments.

Monitoring the budget is an important responsibility of the trustees, one that establishes certain important financial controls.

Figure 2.1. Compton Community Center Three-Month Financial Statement (September 1, 2011–November 30, 2011)

	Budget	Year to Date	Balance
Revenues			
Membership	$22,500	$ 6,212	$16,288
Admissions	6,500	2,431	4,069
Contributions	5,000	1,100	3,900
Grants	10,000	1,000	9,000
Total	$44,000	$10,743	$33,257
Expenses			
Salaries	$21,000	$ 5,250	$15,750
Fees/honoraria	5,000	2,000	3,000
Rent	4,000	1,000	3,000
Telephone	1,000	512	488
Utilities	500	333	167
Office supplies	800	612	188
Sports equipment	2,200	1,000	1,200
Benefit expense	2,000	0	2,000
Educational program	7,500	3,333	4,167
Total	$44,000	$14,040	$29,960
Net income (or loss)	0	($3,297)	

Source: Compiled by the author.

Other controls can be set through financial policy development. The board must determine such things as:

- Who will approve invoices and sign checks?
- Will individual staff members who are responsible for finances be bonded? Will the treasurer be bonded?

- Will there be a petty-cash account, and what controls will be put on its use?
- Should the organization allow first-person checks that are not countersigned?
- Should the books be audited by an outside examiner? If so, a group of board members must assist in the selection of this individual, review his or her report, and address any deficiencies that are revealed by the examination (or audit) itself.

More information in each of these areas is given in chapter 7. It is sufficient to say at this point that there are standard fiscal operating procedures for nonprofit organizations. These are generally known by most accountants, and thus it is appropriate that such an individual should serve on the board so that he or she can assist in developing appropriate fiscal policies. In this way, the trustees can assure themselves that the organization's financial house is in order.

FUND RAISING

No group of people should display a greater commitment to a nonprofit organization than its trustees. These individuals, who have agreed to serve the organization in a variety of ways, must set the tone for others—people in the community, funders, constituents, audience members, and clients. Trustees must support the organization in spirit, encouraging others to be as enthusiastic about its programs and activities as they are, and they must support the organization more tangibly with money, demonstrating that those closest to the organization, its trustees, are 100 percent committed to it. Put quite simply, everyone who serves on a board of trustees must contribute some cash every year to his or her organization. How much they contribute is another matter, but there should be no ambiguity about the requirement of some sort of annual cash gift.

It is not unusual for a potential funder to ask, "What percentage of your trustees contributes to your organization?" This question is a quick way for a donor to gather information on board commitment. If 100 percent of the trustees are contributing, and if 20 percent of the total monies raised from individuals is coming from the board, then the donor sees a level of commitment that allows him or her to say, "I see there is support from the core group, which gives me confidence to invest in the effort." On the other hand, minimal support can make a donor somewhat suspicious. "If the board is not contributing, why should I? What do they know that I don't?"

In some organizations, the matter of trustee donations is controversial because the trustees are recruited from community groups representing the lower end of the economic scale. The statement that "some people cannot afford to make a donation" is generally a ruse to avoid tackling the issue of required trustee donations head on. There is practically no one sitting on a board of trustees who cannot afford to come up with $10 once a year, and most people can probably come up with $50. If special exceptions have to be made from time to time, they can be considered on a case-by-case basis; this should be no excuse for the absence of a stated policy on board contributions.

How much should trustees be required to give? There is no correct amount and each organization must try to arrive at a formula that seems right and fair. In some organizations, there is no minimum contribution; people simply give what they can, but everyone must give something. In other organizations, a guideline rather than a requirement is offered. For example, "This year, our twenty-member board will be expected to contribute $10,000, or an average of $500 per trustee." In still others, a minimum level is set, anywhere from $100 to $10,000 per person. Finally, some organizations set a minimum level, say $300 per person, and state that only half or a third must be contributed in cash and the rest may be contributed in some other form, such as help in the office, donated equipment or food, or other forms of volunteer assistance. Keep in mind, though, that trustees are already expected to contribute time to the organization, and if volunteer hours are to be counted toward a donation, these should very clearly be "over and above" hours.

In addition to giving money, trustees must help raise money. Each trustee, in fact, should assist in some way with the fund-raising effort. Some will feel uncomfortable doing direct solicitation; however, as we will see in chapter 8, there are many other tasks involved in fund raising—prospect identification, list development and maintenance, letter writing, planning of events, and proposal writing—and every member of the board should be assigned some task related to one of these activities.

In selecting trustees, it is important to recruit people who have contacts in the funding community, such as businesspeople, wealthy individuals, and prominent citizens. Some of these people will recoil from the idea of fund raising. "I couldn't possibly ask my friends for money" is a typical refrain. However, these same people may be willing to do other things that are equally valuable. For example, while they may not want to ask their friends for money directly, they may be willing to make appointments for other people in the organization to do it. Or it is likely that they will at least share their knowledge of these friends' philanthropic interests, which is valuable information as the organization plans how and when to ask them for money. Trustees from the business community may not be willing to solicit their peers but may be willing to give a lunch on the organization's behalf at which contacts can be made, or they may be willing to make a phone call to set up an appointment for the executive director, which will ensure that the request gets past a lower-level employee. Trustees who can open doors in this way can be as valuable as those who actually do the fund raising.

Ultimately, an organization's list of trustees can itself be part of a fund-raising strategy. While people should not be selected for name value alone—a blue-ribbon name list can be put together as an advisory committee if window dressing is called for—a well-balanced group of influential trustees says something to funders about the importance of the organization in the community. If Mabel, John, and Sam (all prominent citizens) are willing to give their time and their names to this organization, it must be worthy of attention. If, in addition, they are willing to solicit funds on the organization's behalf, it must be worthy of support.

HIRING AND WORKING
WITH THE CHIEF EXECUTIVE

The character of almost every nonprofit organization is set in large measure by its chief executive. This is because the chief executive not only speaks for the organization publicly but also hires the staff that deals on a day-to-day basis with the organization's constituency. The public's impression of the organization is very much in the chief executive's hands. Consequently, the selection of this person is a very great responsibility. In selecting the chief executive, the following rules should be followed:

- Trustees should agree on what their expectations are. They should decide what kind of person they are looking for and what special qualifications the person should possess before they look at a single resume.
- Trustees should document what the job entails. There should be a clear job description (see chapter 4) that lists both general responsibilities and specific tasks.
- In talking to serious candidates, trustees should be honest about organizational problems. They should not pretend things are fine when they are not. If there are financial problems, staff problems, or even trustee problems, there is nothing to gain in the long run by hiding them.
- Trustees should be clear about how the chief executive's performance is going to be evaluated. If there is a formal review process, it should be described. If there is not, the person should be told what criteria will be used to determine how successfully he or she is performing in the job.
- In many cases, trustees may wish to utilize the professional experience, expertise, and contacts of an executive search firm. Although there may be substantial costs involved, the trustees may decide that such an investment is worthwhile in order to find, recruit, and select the best person for the job.

Evaluation. Regular evaluation of a chief executive is also an important responsibility of the trustees. It is an excellent way to foster good communication about perceived successes, failures, and expectations for the future. Evaluation should take place at least once a year, at some time immediately prior to the negotiation over salary for the upcoming year. Although chapter 4 gives general advice on personnel evaluations, one special feature of the chief executive's review should be mentioned here. Unlike most staff members, the chief executive works for more than one person. He or she works for all of the trustees. Thus the evaluation of a chief executive is not quite as straightforward as regular staff evaluations. Whatever system is set up, there should be some way for the full board to have input into the process.

One system that seems to work well is for the president of the board to circulate a questionnaire to trustees asking specific questions about the chief executive's performance during the past year. It should have several categories in which the performance can be reviewed that follow the responsibilities laid out in the job description. It should also include some general categories, such as how the person relates to the staff, the trustees, and the community. After the responses are collected, the board president can then summarize them for the chief executive, soliciting his or her reaction. Once the performance review is completed and general job performance objectives are set for the following year, the results can be summarized and circulated to the full board for review. After the process is completed, salary negotiation can begin.

Sometimes a board of trustees is faced with the unpleasant task of having to fire a chief executive. Occasionally, although the occasions are few, the individual has done something illegal or so blatantly offensive that immediate termination is the only alternative. More often, the situation is a judgment call, which makes the decision particularly sensitive and difficult. In spite of this fact, it is always better to bite the bullet and address the problem directly rather than to let it fester and hope it will go away. Trustees should never feel guilty about initiating a process of evaluation that may lead to termination. Those who resist doing so are not exercising their responsibility to the organization they are serving.

The *performance review* is a convenient first opportunity to alert the chief executive that the trustees are dissatisfied with his or her performance. The more specific the criticisms at this stage, the easier it will be for the board president to communicate them and develop a procedure whereby the executive is given some time to try to improve job performance. At the time that the board president speaks to the chief executive, board concerns should be communicated in writing, and written performance objectives should be set for a fixed probationary time period (preferably not more than three months). For example, the board may be concerned that fiscal management is sloppy and that financial statements are always late and inaccurate. A specific performance objective might be that the chief executive provides monthly financial statements to the board no later than two weeks after the close of each month. These statements can be checked by the board's treasurer. Along with specific job objectives such as this, the president should outline the criteria that will be used to judge whether the executive has been able to improve his or her performance on the job. After all of this is explained, the chief executive is given time to evaluate the situation, to try to improve, and to explore other employment opportunities. If, at the end of the period, the executive has not resigned and the board is still unhappy with job performance, a final opportunity for a resignation should be offered before the board resorts to the more extreme measure of formal termination. A very public firing is often a cue to the community and to funders that something is amiss.

Developing a Good Working Relationship. The relationship between the board and the staff of a nonprofit organization is critical to its successful operation. Much of the tone of that relationship is set by the chief executive and the board president. When these two individuals work well together, many potential problems between staff and board can be averted. When the working relationship is strained, a "we/they" atmosphere can permeate the internal operations of the organization.

Many of the problems in this area result from a fundamental misunderstanding of the limits of trusteeship on the part of particular board members. Some examples are:

- Board members may attempt to involve themselves in detailed administrative tasks that are the responsibility of staff. For example, a board member might visit the site of an activity sponsored by the organization and take it upon himself or herself to correct or try to supervise a staff person when this task is the responsibility of the chief executive.
- Board members may make programmatic decisions without consulting staff in areas where staff expertise would have been helpful. For example, a group of board members might decide to proceed with a fund-raising event without consulting the chief executive and the staff fund raiser.
- Board members may interfere in personnel issues. For example, they might invite unhappy staff members to bring complaints directly to them rather than to work through the chief executive.

These kinds of problems can surface in any organization, but they are most common in newer ones, especially those that are just beginning to hire professional staff. Board members who performed many stafflike functions on a volunteer basis as the organization was being formed often find it difficult to give up some of their authority. It is not uncommon for these individuals to continue to want to play an active role in the administration of the organization even after it is no longer appropriate to do so.

But this overstepping of board roles undermines the authority of the chief executive and can lead to an untenable working relationship with the board. Because chief executives are hired by their boards and must report to them, they are not in a position to reprimand those trustees who are out of line; they must rely on the president of the board to do so.

THE COMMUNICATIONS LINK

Many nonprofit organizations are the best kept secrets in town. Others go about their business without the benefit of any input from those they are supposed to be serving. In both cases, the fault lies partly with trustees who do not understand that part of their responsibility is to promote their organization's activities widely and to seek opinions and observations about the organization from a variety of people. Trustees should make regular appearances on behalf of the organization, speaking to community and business groups as well as to friends and associates. Some trustees may be better public speakers than others, but every trustee should take responsibility for telling people about the organization's activities and its importance to the community. At both formal functions and informal get-togethers, trustees should attempt to set up the two-way communications link with the public, they should provide free publicity and advocacy on behalf of the organization, and they should also get feedback from people to find out how others feel about what the organization is doing. Consider the following case.

CONCERTS FOR SCHOOLS, INC.

During a Rotary Club luncheon, a trustee of Concerts for Schools, Inc., a local music education organization, gave a short talk about the upcoming activities for the year, gently suggesting that the Rotarians might wish to make a modest contribution to the program. During the question-and-answer period, several members of her audience chided her about the seemingly elitist attitude of her program. Why did the group present only classical music? Weren't jazz and folk music art forms too? Why were all the performers from out of state? Didn't their state have any good musicians? After hearing the reactions of the Rotarians, the trustee discussed the experience with her board. Several substantive changes were made in the program. The following year, the trustee went back to the Rotarians to thank them for their suggestions that had resulted in major changes in the program. The result was a $1,000 donation from the Rotary Club.

Because part of the responsibility of trustees is to provide a communications link with the community, it should be clear why it is so important that a diversity of backgrounds be represented on the board. When all segments of the community are represented, each group sees the organization as its own, and this increases support in many tangible and intangible ways.

BOARD COMPOSITION

The responsibilities of trustees suggest those skills and areas of knowledge that a board must collectively possess. A practical listing might include the following areas of expertise:

- Nonprofit trusteeship
- Organizational planning
- Financial/accounting
- Fund raising (including business/corporate, individual, public agency, and foundation)
- Personnel management
- Legal matters especially relating to nonprofit corporations, contracts, and personnel
- Public relations

Various trustees should also be familiar with the programs and activities that the organization sponsors, and all trustees should support the organization's mission. They should represent a variety of backgrounds as well as various segments of the community, including different minority and ethnic groups that will give the board a broad vision and understanding of the true meaning of community and public service. In addition, specific nonprofits may require trustees with other types of expertise and representation. For example, if a nonprofit corporation owns a facility, operates a building, or maintains extensive grounds, it may be desirable to have an architect or a contractor on the board.

The purpose of having trustees with specific expertise is not to encourage encroachment on day-to-day activities that are staff responsibility, but to provide a monitoring capability for the board. Such trustee expertise helps the board in formulating policy, reacting to staff recommendations, and choosing from among alternative courses of action.

When choosing fellow trustees, the tendency is to say, "My friend John is interested in what we do, and he has served on the governing board of our church. I think he would be excellent." But this approach is not systematic enough and does not give enough consideration to the kinds of specific expertise that the board requires. An interest in an organization is not sufficient. For this reason, the development of a skills inventory chart is an excellent and simple mechanism to force the board (through its nominating committee, and with the staff, when appropriate) to analyze its needs. A skills inventory chart lists specific skills down the left-hand margin and lists existing and potential board members along the top axis.

Figure 2.2 is an example of a skills inventory chart. In this specific case, it is clear, first, that none of the existing trustees (Jones, Smith, Brown, Fox, and Evans) brings expertise in the legal field, in corporate fund raising, or in personnel. As the organization looks for new trustees, people with skills and experience in these areas should be sought. Second, we can see that Jones does not appear to be pulling his weight according to the skill areas listed. He may be on the board for other valid reasons, but the organization should analyze carefully what these reasons are. Third, while Smith (the organization's treasurer and a certified public accountant) brings considerable expertise in the financial/accounting area, her term is due to expire. If she is not reelected to the board, it will be necessary to find someone with similar skills to replace her.

Figure 2.2. Skills Inventory Chart

	Jones	Smith	Brown	Fox	Evans	etc.
legal						
accounting		X				
corporate fund raising						
public relations			X			
music performance				X		
personnel						
facility management					X	

THE DEADWOOD PROBLEM

Regardless of how hard a nominating committee may work, there will always be some board members who are not pulling their weight, are not active, and are not contributing either financially or otherwise to the organization. While this *deadwood problem* will almost always exist to a certain extent, there are things that can be done to minimize it.

Limiting Terms of Office

No trustee should assume that he or she is going to serve the organization indefinitely. Limits should be placed on terms of office and on the number of times a trustee can be reelected. One system that seems to work well is to have a three-year term with one opportunity for reelection. After three years, a trustee comes up for reelection; after six, he or she must go off the board for at least one year before being invited to serve again. Trustee rotation offers a process for replacing weak board members with enthusiastic and committed trustees. Because continuity on the board is important, though, it is desirable to stagger the terms of trustees so that only one-third of the board members should be reaching the end of their terms in any one year.

In recent years, the difficulty of recruiting strong, active trustees has become even more severe for many nonprofit organizations, and there has been a temptation to relax the term-limit requirement in order to keep trustees. The fear is that once trustees come to the end of their limit of years on the board, they will jump to other organizations and be impossible to recruit back. One way to counter this risk is to invite former trustees to other key activities including service on committees or as incorporators, overseers, or advisors, as will be discussed later in the chapter.

Attendance

Nothing undermines the effectiveness of a board more than absence from meetings. Indeed, regular attendance at meetings is one criterion that could be used in a legal case to judge whether a board member had exercised reasonable care and diligence in exercising his or her trustee responsibilities. Participation by everyone is necessary if the board is going to operate effectively. Thus it should be a stated policy of the organization that attendance at board meetings is required. Beyond this, the board might adopt a policy that two unexcused absences in a year constitute an automatic resignation. If a trustee has a legitimate problem, such as an illness or a death in the family, the president can excuse that trustee from a meeting. However, the policy should be clear that, without such a legitimate excuse (and without approval of the president), the trustee is expected to be at all board meetings. A slightly more liberal policy might be developed for attendance at committee meetings.

Financial Commitment

Previously it was pointed out that a nonprofit organization should insist that every trustee make an annual cash contribution. This contribution requirement, as well as the other obligations of trusteeship, must be clearly articulated to potential trustees as part of the recruitment and invitation process. The *pocketbook test* is, in fact, one excellent way to separate those trustees who will demonstrate commitment to the organization from those who will not.

The Trustee Manual

The deadwood problem is most prevalent when trustees lack a thorough understanding of the responsibilities of trusteeship and when they have the impression that serving on a board is more of a social function than a business function. To combat this problem, every organization should develop a trustee manual. Such a manual should be presented in loose-leaf form so that it can be updated regularly. The manual should include the following sections:

- Articles of incorporation with mission statement (The actual incorporation papers are less critical than the language that defines the nature and function of the organization.)
- Bylaws (usually divided into sections, each of which should begin on a new page to facilitate scanning for specific information)
- List of current trustees with business affiliations, business and home addresses, phone numbers, and term expiration dates
- List of committees and their respective members
- List of staff members with titles and areas of responsibility
- Brief (two- to three-page) history of the organization
- Description of roles, responsibilities, and requirements of trustees (a summary of the kind of information contained in this chapter relating to general trustee responsibilities as well as the specific requirements—attendance, financial contribution, and committee responsibility—that will be expected of everyone)
- Minutes of current fiscal year meetings
- Specific planning documents if available (a series of goal statements is often included here)
- The annual report from the last completed fiscal year (generally includes the audited financial statement; in lieu of an annual report, a promotional booklet can be submitted along with the financial statements for the most recently completed fiscal year.)

Recruitment and Orientation

Related to the need for a trustee manual is a complementary need for both a clear recruitment procedure (that spells out the roles and responsibilities of trustees) and an orientation session for individuals who have agreed to join the board. A suggested process follows:

1. A nominating committee is set up (with members either elected by the board or appointed by the president). The president should be an ex-officio member though not necessarily the chair. Individuals on the committee should collectively have a broad knowledge of the communities from which prospective candidates will be recruited.

2. The committee analyzes board needs, evaluates the performance of trustees up for reelection, solicits names of other prospective trustees, and reviews a prospective slate with the full board.

3. After tentative and initial approval of the slate, appointments are made with prospective trustees. Each individual is visited by at least one member of the board (often the president) who is sometimes accompanied by the executive director. At the meeting, the roles, responsibilities, and requirements of trusteeship are described. A copy of the trustee manual is left with the person so that he or she may study it in detail before making his or her decision. (If the person elects not to serve on the board, the trustee manual should be returned.)

4. No more than one week after the visit, the prospective trustee should be asked for a final decision. If the answer is yes, then the individual will have to be officially elected to the board according to the process set out in the bylaws.

5. Once a year, the board should hold an orientation session. If held at the organization's office, the session can provide new trustees with the opportunity to meet the staff and observe the daily operations. The president, executive director, and committee chairs often lead a series of short and informal discussions, and in some cases, an outside expert provides a pep talk on trustee roles and responsibilities. An orientation session is sometimes arranged to coincide with an event sponsored by the organization.

Evaluation and Dismissal

Some organizations have a formal review period at the end of each year at which time trustees evaluate one another's performance. It is usually the president who determines the evaluation process. Among the options available are informal discussions with each trustee or anonymous written statements. Whatever the process, the objective is the same: to identify ineffective trustees. If the president discovers that a trustee consistently receives poor evaluations from fellow board members, it is time to take action. Dismissal, through a majority vote of the board or some other procedure, is an action that should only be taken in the case of gross misconduct. However, other more moderate methods may lead to the same outcome. For example, a strong president can often counsel a trustee to resign by suggesting that he or she is overcommitted or seems to have lost interest.

It should be remembered that a good rotation policy, through limited terms of office, often makes the issue of trustee dismissal and forced resignation moot. Because terms are limited, most boards can live with a do-nothing trustee for a year or two, or even three. On self-perpetuating boards, however, where terms are not fixed, evaluation, dismissal, and resignation become more critical.

COMMITTEES

When a nonprofit organization reaches a certain size and its operation becomes more complex, the board usually finds that it is difficult to carry out all of its responsibilities efficiently without dividing up into smaller groups. These groups, or committees, allow for a detailed analysis of specific areas, such as fund raising, planning, budgeting, or programs before they are discussed by the full board. A committee structure offers several advantages. First, it allows for a division of the workload. Second, it promotes a more informal discussion of the pros and cons of various issues before they come to the board for a formal resolution. Third, it allows an organization to bring experts into the deliberation process without putting them on the board. For example, a fund-raising committee might include representatives from the business community willing to help on an occasional basis but who do not have the time or the inclination to be trustees. Fourth, a committee is an excellent testing ground for prospective trustees, allowing an organization to assess commitment and performance. In general, a committee should be chaired by a trustee, and the majority of committee members should be board members, but outside resource people and staff members can and should be included because they are often assets. The following committees are common in nonprofit organizations:

Executive. This committee is generally empowered to act for the full board in matters that require immediate action or do not involve major questions of policy or funding (this should be spelled out carefully in the bylaws). It is also the chief coordinating committee for the board, mapping out how the board's business should be conducted, setting agendas, and organizing the activity of other committees.

The executive director will often use the executive committee as a troubleshooting group, bringing to it problems needing rapid resolution. Generally the corporation's officers serve on this committee along with a few other members of the board, some of whom may be chairs of other committees. The executive committee should be small enough to function effectively (seven or eight members is common) and should be made up of individuals who do not live or work so far away from the organization's home base that they are unable to come to meetings on short notice.

Finance. This committee is empowered to study and make recommendations regarding all financial procedures and controls, assist in the preparation and presentation of budgets, and review all financial statements. This committee reviews audit results and recommends the retention of the auditor. An accountant is invaluable on this committee. In some large organizations there are separate committees for finance and audit.

Development. This committee, sometimes called the fund-raising committee, oversees the planning and coordination of fund-raising efforts. This will certainly include ongoing annual fund raising for operations and solicitations of larger gifts. It may also include planning for fund-raising events and for capital campaigns, although these are sometimes handled by separate committees in larger organizations.

Nominating. This committee identifies, screens, and recommends prospective trustees. Members of this committee can also assist in the recruitment and orientation of the trustees.

Planning. This committee coordinates long-range planning. Its function is described in detail in chapter 9.

Buildings and grounds. For organizations that own or manage facilities or property, this committee will monitor their condition, recommend maintenance and repairs, and plan renovation projects. It is advisable to have an architect, contractor, or someone with similar expertise on this committee.

Marketing/public relations. A marketing committee (see chapter 5) oversees how an organization communicates its message and its brand. For those organizations that sell a service or a product, the committee can also weigh in on a sales approach. It is often useful to have someone from the media or from a public relations firm on this committee.

Events or benefits. Organizations planning special events generally delegate responsibility for them to a special committee. Fund-raising events, such as benefits, should be handled by this committee if they are not handled by the development committee.

Program. This committee is organized to review the program activities of the organization and plan for the future. Because this committee has to work very closely with staff, its members must take care not to meddle in areas better left to staff management.

Personnel. This committee develops personnel policies (see chapter 4), recommends salary ranges to the board, may evaluate the executive director and recommend a specific salary level for that individual, reviews benefits packages, and handles grievances when board involvement is necessary.

Investment. For organizations that own significant assets that require investment (such as endowment funds), a special committee oversees the management of these funds. This may involve the evaluation of investment managers (with subsequent recommendation to the full board about which managers to retain), or it may involve investment decisions by the committee itself. Because of the fiduciary responsibilities associated with management of the organization's assets, the committee (and the full board) should make sure that there is adequate expertise on this committee and that its decisions seem prudent and do not involve excessive risk of the corporation's assets.

Few organizations will have all of these committees, and some organizations will have committees not listed here. Because there is almost always staff work associated with committees, they should only be formed if and when there is a need for them. Committee meetings, like board meetings, should have tight agendas and should not waste people's time.

OFFICERS

State laws vary but most generally require that a nonprofit corporation's board of trustees include at least three officers: a president (or chairperson), a treasurer, and a clerk (or secretary). Some organizations include additional officers, such as vice presidents or an assistant treasurer. The organization's bylaws will specify how many officers there must be, their titles, powers, and duties. The bylaws will also state the process by which they are elected and the frequency of the elections. (In this connection, it is common practice for the board to elect officers from among its ranks at the annual meeting of the corporation.) The selection of the right people to fill officer positions is an important task. Only the most qualified trustees should be considered for the regular officer positions. No one should be appointed to any of the three crucial positions (president, treasurer, and clerk) simply as an honor. It is an acceptable practice for an organization to create honorary officer positions such as "honorary chairperson" or "president emeritus" (in the latter case to honor a past president who is no longer active) so long as it is clear that these people have no special powers.

President (or chairperson). The president should be a person of authority who is respected by the board, the staff, and the community and has plenty of time to devote to the job. He or she should serve on the executive committee for at least a year before assuming the presidency in order to become thoroughly familiar with the operation of the organization. A good president can set the work standard for the board that keeps the deadwood problem to a minimum and keeps the trustees on track with their tasks in board and committee work. A good president can serve as a buffer between disgruntled trustees and the executive director, mediating tensions and resolving differences. A weak president, on the other hand, may allow various factions to secure for themselves too much authority and control. Personal agendas may then take precedence over organizational priorities. No one should be appointed to the presidency who is afraid to deal firmly with those who are getting out of line.

Today in many organizations, there is a trend toward calling the chief staff person "President." To avoid confusion, some of these organizations prefer that their boards be led by a chair (or chairperson) with one or more vice-chairs. In other organizations, one can find boards with both a chairperson and a president. This structure can be advantageous in larger nonprofits where the fund-raising function and other functions of the board leader need to be split up. Typically, the chairperson will be the board representative who leads the fund-raising effort. A person with the necessary prestige and name recognition may well be too busy to also work with the executive director, lead board meetings, chair the executive committee, and undertake the liaison work with other trustees. These latter functions would be the responsibility of the board president.

Treasurer. The treasurer must be someone with a good deal of financial experience, preferably related to the operation of nonprofit organizations. Accountants and businesspeople are generally preferred for this job; however, many of these individuals who have only profit-sector experience are not sufficiently sensitive to the special characteristics of financial management in the nonprofit sector, which are discussed in chapters 6 and 7. It is advantageous to find a person with some board experience in another nonprofit organization who also has financial expertise to fill the role of treasurer.

Clerk. The clerk (or secretary) must be well organized and have the ability to record information accurately. The clerk's task is important to the extent that he or she is responsible for maintaining the official records of meetings. For each meeting, the clerk must send out the agenda and keep the minutes. Unless meetings are tape-recorded, the minutes will be the only official record of board deliberation, and consequently they must reproduce the actual words of motions, who made and seconded them, and how they were voted. It is less important to keep a record of extended discussion on any particular issue, and the clerk should focus primarily on the decisions themselves. Once minutes are written, they should be circulated so that the trustees have a chance to review them in preparation for approval at the subsequent board meeting. If corrections are needed, a board member makes a motion to amend a certain section. After all the corrections are complete, the trustees vote to accept the minutes. With this vote, the minutes become part of the corporate records. The importance of the minutes cannot be overstated. Once they are approved, no board or staff member can claim that "things really did not happen that way at the meeting." They constitute the official and binding record of board decisions.

BOARDS OF INCORPORATORS/ OVERSEERS/ADVISORS/FRIENDS

The ideal board is one that is large enough to secure the expertise and volunteer hours to carry out its essential work but small enough so that everyone feels as if he or she has a role to play. In recent years, effective boards can be found that are as small as nine people (odd numbers of trustees are recommended to avoid the possibility of tie votes), though a more common minimum number is eleven. On the upper end, boards tend to get unwieldy when the number of trustees reaches thirty.

So what is to be done when the organization wants to involve more than thirty people in its essential work? Given the fact that people are more likely to volunteer if they are given recognition and are meaningfully involved, limiting the size of the board of trustees can prevent an organization from securing the commitment of key potential supporters.

The answer, for many organizations, is to set up a second group, often called a board of incorporators (or overseers or advisors or friends). This is a group that has *no legal authority to make binding decisions for the corporation.* Typically, however, individuals are invited to come to at least one special meeting each year, serve on the organization's committees, and participate in large joint meetings with the board at which major organizational issues are discussed (including planning retreats). They are also generally expected to contribute time or money in exchange for the recognition they receive.

In many nonprofit corporations, the incorporator (or overseer) structure is described in the bylaws. Often, there is no limit to the number of individuals who can serve (or the limit is a very large number like one hundred). There is also no term limitation. However, terms should be for a set period with a requirement that people be invited to serve subsequent terms. That way, if someone does not work out, they are not invited to serve another term. Nominations are made by the nominating committee and approved by the full board.

The advantages of this structure are:

- It provides a way to involve more people in the organization's activities without adding to the size of the board of trustees.
- It offers a place to put trustees who are coming to the end of their board terms but wish to stay involved.
- It gives the organization another mechanism for recognition of active supporters.
- It provides a place to put donors who cannot be active enough to be trustees, as well as volunteers who might not necessarily be trustee material.

- It offers a "testing ground" for potential trustees. By starting them in a less critical role, the organization can assess their level of commitment.

BOARD LIABILITY

Accountability is an important concept in trusteeship, and many board members ask, quite properly, whether they are legally liable for their actions and whether the corporation should carry liability insurance for itself and for the trustees individually. The issue is of particular concern to individual board members who worry that their own financial assets might be at risk in cases where there was proven negligence on their part.

The subject of board liability is complex, particularly because it involves state laws, which vary from state to state. Legal advice should be sought, particularly by those who sit on the boards of organizations engaged in hazardous activities or close-care services where risk may be higher. Some generalizations can be made, however, to give guidance in this area:

- The standards that are established for the actions of trustees of nonprofit corporations are found in the area of corporate law, not trust law. What this means is that the requirements governing trustee behavior are much less stringent and allow considerable opportunity to delegate authority and decision making and to rely on the expertise of others. Effectively, trustees are only liable for gross negligence and, according to the language of many statutes, need only exhibit "such care as an ordinary prudent person in a like position would use under similar circumstances."
- In general, trustees cannot be held liable for business judgments or financial decisions if these are informed, show no conflict of interest, and do not appear highly irrational. A financial decision that has an undesirable outcome or one that involves a high degree of risk is not sufficient grounds to hold trustees liable. Nevertheless, if trustees never attend meetings, if they approve major decisions involving the corporation's funds without soliciting any background financial information, or if they engage in any illegal financial activity, they can be held liable.
- Trustees are liable when conflict of interest is involved—especially

where a trustee's personal financial interest is put ahead of that of the corporation. Using corporate property for personal purposes, taking advantage of a financial opportunity at the expense of the corporation, or any kind of self-dealing without proper disclosure is generally not permitted by law.

- The trustees are liable for making sure that the corporation is carrying out its mission as articulated to both the state and federal governments. Donors, in particular, should be able to expect that their funds are used for the purposes for which the organization is established and/or that particular gift restrictions are honored.

- Trustees can be held personally liable for damages in the case of personal-injury cases. While it is generally the corporation that will be held liable, trustees can also be held liable if it can be demonstrated that the injury resulted from gross negligence on their part, although they would ordinarily be entitled to indemnification from the corporation.

- Trustees of nonprofit organizations are expected to make sure that their organizations comply with the rules and regulations set by federal, state, and local governments. The organizations must file financial reports with the IRS and with the state office handling public charities. They must fill out tax forms for employees, deduct taxes from paychecks, and deposit these funds periodically (trustees can be held personally and financially liable for noncompliance with tax requirements). In some cases, trustees can be held responsible for the organization's compliance with laws limiting lobbying activities; where a building is involved, they can be held responsible for making sure the organization is complying with building codes. It is essential to remember that as stewards of the public trust, the trustees are responsible for overseeing compliance with legal requirements.

Even though the instance of lawsuits is relatively infrequent in the nonprofit world, trustees do get sued, and, to a much greater extent, they become involved in threatened lawsuits that can require the expense of an attorney or a financial settlement even though these lawsuits might be without merit. Thus board members are rightly concerned about the risks associated with trusteeship. While laws generally favor trustees of nonprofit organizations, the cost of mounting a successful defense in a lawsuit can be very high. This is why many states are enacting laws to limit the kinds of cases that can come to court in this area. Nevertheless, the exposure to risk will never be reduced completely by state or federal statutes, because trustees, in the end, must be held somewhat accountable for their actions. In addition, since the assets of trustees are often considerably larger than the nonprofits they serve, those wishing to receive financial benefit from lawsuits will often target the trustees.

Securing Protection

There are several ways that trustees of nonprofit organizations can be protected from legal exposure:

- Nonprofit organizations can indemnify their trustees. This does not protect the trustees from legal action. But it does mean that the organization will pay for all costs associated with such action directed against the trustees, including the cost of settlement. The downside of indemnification is that it transfers risk from the trustees to the organization and puts the organization's assets at risk. Another problem is that in certain cases the organization may sue one of its trustees and, if successful, would not be responsible for paying the costs associated with indemnification.
- Indemnification insurance reimburses the corporation for expenses associated with the costs of indemnification as outlined above.
- Directors and officers (D & O) insurance protects both against indemnification costs and any other costs incurred by trustees that would not be covered by the corporation.
- Because all of these measures protect only the trustees themselves, the corporation should carry sufficient liability insurance to protect itself in the case of a lawsuit.

Should organizations take any or all of the steps outlined above? In the case of most nonprofit organizations, failure to carry liability insurance for the corporation is a mistake. When legal action is contemplated, it is well known that the law will greatly favor actions taken against the corporation over actions taken against the trustees.

Thus, from the point of view of the likely success of a lawsuit, it is the corporation that needs the greatest protection.

How much protection to afford the trustees is less clear, though increasingly nonprofit organizations are finding that offering full protection to trustees may be an indispensable step in recruiting prominent people to boards of directors. This is particularly true since in many cases potential trustees are likely to be successful in their own right and thus often have substantial personal assets to protect. In the case of nonprofit organizations engaged in hazardous services or those involving the care of patients, students, or infants, there is little choice. However, even in small organizations involved in seemingly low-risk activities, the trend appears to be toward offering full protection to trustees in what has become a very litigious era.

Five years after Mary Clarke had assembled her first board of trustees, she decided to find out why she was having such problems with the group. She went to one of her mentors, an experienced trustee from another organization, and asked for his views on trusteeship. After getting a long briefing on the roles and responsibilities of trustees, their various obligations, the commitment of time and money they should be expected to make, and the legal risks associated with trusteeship, Mary asked, "Why would anyone want to serve on a board?"

The answer to Mary's question is that trusteeship is a form of public service that often carries with it status in the community. Many established nonprofit organizations find people vying for the chance to become trustees. These are the lucky ones. For many of the newer, less prestigious organizations, finding committed trustees is more difficult. Nevertheless, these organizations should not compromise and turn the board into a social group with minimal responsibilities, because eventually, as the organization grows in prominence and importance, weak trustees become a tremendous drawback. It is better to take great care and to move slowly and carefully, even if it takes several years to achieve the full complement of trustees. In the long run, the safe and prudent course is to build soundly for the organization's future.

CHECKLIST QUESTIONS FOR CHAPTER 2

1. Have the articles of incorporation and the bylaws of your organization been reviewed by the board within the last five years? If changes are appropriate, has the board formally voted on amendments?

2. Has your board engaged in a comprehensive long-range planning process within the last five years? Does your board approve specific goals and objectives each year?

3. Is your board (or a subcommittee of the board) involved in the process of developing the annual budget? Do the trustees formally approve the budget? Do they compare financial performance to budgeted figures throughout the year?

4. Has your board developed and approved proper financial controls that meet generally accepted practices for nonprofit organizations?

5. Are all board members required to make a financial contribution? Is there a system that ensures that they will do so?

6. How active is your board in raising money? Are all trustees active in fund raising?

7. Has your board developed a process for evaluating the performance of the chief executive? Have your trustees given some thought to how they will recruit and hire a new chief executive when the time comes?

8. Does your board play a leadership role in promoting your organization in the community?

9. Is the process for identifying and recruiting new trustees effective; that is, does it result in a collection of trustees with the necessary skills and diversity of backgrounds? Is there a proper orientation process for new trustees?

10. Is there a trustee manual in your organization that spells out the requirements of trusteeship? Is there a clearly documented conflict-of-interest policy?

11. Have sufficient numbers of committees been developed in your organization to accomplish the work of the board effectively?

12. Has your organization considered a board of incorporators (or overseers, advisors, or friends)?

13. Is there a process that ensures that appropriately qualified people become officers in your organization?
14. Has your board considered the question of trustee liability? If appropriate, has your organization secured proper protection for the trustees, including insurance protection?

THREE

Assembling the Workforce

Sandra Harris is the executive director of Parent/Child Stress Services, a nonprofit organization whose mission is to prevent child abuse through parental counseling. The organization, which was founded thirty years before she took over, grew substantially and was undergoing a shift toward increased professionalism when she was hired. Sandra Harris finds herself facing several dilemmas. One is that she needs to decide on the types of people to hire for particular jobs. Her own background leads her to favor those who have a strong empathy for the field of child abuse, but many of her board members are urging her to hire individuals with specific management expertise. A second dilemma she faces is that she does not want to lose the loyalty of her volunteers, although increasingly she finds it necessary to replace many of them with professional staff.

The purpose of this chapter and the next one is to analyze the challenges associated with assembling a workforce. These include putting together the right mix of people who can provide maximum productivity and at the same time utilizing organizational resources most effectively. This chapter will discuss the philosophical principles that should dictate the hiring of staff, and it will suggest how organizations should combine salaried staff members, volunteers, and other kinds of workers most effectively. Chapter 4 will analyze how nonprofit organizations can clarify their personnel policies in order to develop a positive work environment for their workforce.

MATCHING THE RIGHT PERSON AND THE JOB

Sandra Harris' first dilemma has to do with identifying the right person for a new job. The board has authorized the hiring of a new director of resource development to oversee organizational fund-raising efforts. After an extensive search, she has narrowed her choice to two candidates. The first is a man who has worked for ten years in fund raising at a private school. His references are excellent. In his previous job, he was credited with working effectively with both the headmaster and the trustees, coordinating the annual fund drive, and running a small capital drive. He writes well and has experience writing foundation proposals. However, he has no background in the child-abuse field. The other candidate has worked in child-abuse organizations for twenty years. Originally attracted to the field because she herself was a victim, she has been primarily a counselor working directly with parents. She is personable and has excellent references.

In the interviews, Sandra finds herself leaning toward the second candidate. Although the woman has never been involved in fund raising (or in any management-level position), she says she is willing to accept a lower wage until she has proven herself. She understands the basic needs of Parent/Child Stress Services and talks easily and familiarly with Sandra about mutual acquaintances. She knows the acronyms associated with other service providers, government agencies, and national organizations. While the first candidate brings an appropriate set of skills to the job, Sandra is concerned that he lacks adequate familiarity with child abuse and prevention. Sandra likes him, feels he is talented and energetic, but worries about his ability to be credible to others in the field.

The dilemma faced by Sandra Harris is not unusual in the nonprofit environment, and like many of her peers, she is naturally gravitating toward hiring someone who is creative, enthusiastic, and has considerable training and background in her organization's field. *But this training is not related to the task that the candidate will he asked to perform.* Like many people with an abiding interest in the field, the second candidate is willing to accept low wages and learn a new skill on the job. Unfortunately, while this prospective employee may bring enthusiasm, creativity, and the willingness to learn, she lacks key management skills that can help her succeed in the job. Like any nonprofit organization, Parent/Child Stress Services needs experienced managers with business, financial, marketing, fund-raising, and even legal skills; it needs clerical workers and data-processing professionals who are familiar with the workings of an office and the needs of administrators.

For people like Sandra Harris attempting to fill staff positions, there are some basic questions that need to be addressed:

- Should they favor candidates who are bright and may be able to learn quickly on the job, even if they're inexperienced?
- Should they hire people who have experience in the field in which the organization is active, even if it is not related to the job to be filled?
- Should they lean toward individuals with strong educational backgrounds (a PhD, perhaps), even if the training is in an unrelated field?
- Should they give serious consideration to an individual for a management job if the person's training and experience does not include administration?

In order to answer these questions, it is first necessary to distinguish between program personnel and management personnel. Obviously, if a mental health center is hiring a psychiatrist, it will look for one who is well trained and knowledgeable in that field; if a theater troupe is hiring actors for a stage production, the people selected must have dramatic talent; if a school is hiring a teacher, a strong educational background is a primary prerequisite, if not the paramount consideration. In staffing the programmatic side of a nonprofit organization, direct training, experience, and skill in the field of activity are the sine qua nons by which people should initially be judged.

However, on the management side, the issue is not so clear. Might we speculate that an accountant with knowledge of biology will do a better job of keeping the books for a hospital than someone without such knowledge? Will a clerk-typist who is also a painter be expected to perform better than someone with strong secretarial skills if the employer happens to run an art gallery? More generally, should recruitment procedures in nonprofit organizations give preference to those whose backgrounds are somehow related to the programmatic activity of the organization? *The answer to all these questions is probably no.* If Sandra Harris is looking for a fund raiser, she should hire a fund raiser. Unless she is prepared to spend many months teaching someone without proper background and unless she is willing to take the risk that that person may not have the proper aptitude for the task, she should hire someone with an appropriate set of skills. Indeed, it is possible that she herself doesn't have the depth of knowledge to teach

someone anyway, and given the many demands of the executive director role, it certainly is not the best use of her time.

Similarly, when looking for a bookkeeper or an administrative assistant, the most important consideration is the person's skill *at that
job*. In some cases, at the clerical level, it may even be preferable to hire
someone without a special interest in the organization's field of activity
because there is less likelihood that the individual will feel frustrated
in performing menial tasks. It is also less likely that the employee will
possess a driving ambition to move up or out to a more interesting,
program-related job. The controversy surrounding this point among
nonprofit administrators is keen. But more often than not, experienced
executives tend to favor entry-level and middle-management personnel
with strong backgrounds in administrative areas.

Hierarchies and Expectations

There are other, more subtle reasons why people with management
backgrounds may be preferable choices for administrative tasks in
nonprofit organizations. Many people who consider working in nonprofit fields think of the organizations they might work for as places
full of interesting people who work in a loose administrative structure.
While this may attract creative people, it also tends to attract those
who are less comfortable with organizational hierarchies. Individuals
who come from management backgrounds, on the other hand, tend
to be more familiar and comfortable with hierarchically arranged
organizations. Often they have worked for profit-making concerns
where pyramidal authority chains are firmly established. As nonprofit
organizations grow in complexity and size, they must also move toward increasingly hierarchical structures. If they are staffed primarily
by people who believe in collective decision making or who feel that
all supervision should be informal and unstructured, then dissension,
frustration, and unhappiness can quickly set in.

Another major misconception about nonprofit organizations is
that administrative jobs within them tend to be more interesting
than comparable jobs in the profit sector. By and large, this is not the
case. An unsuccessful candidate for political office should not look
to a bookkeeping job in a university's public administration graduate
school as a way to work off his or her disappointment and frustration.
An unemployed musician or painter who looks to an arts organization

as a way to satisfy his or her creative needs is likely to be equally un-happy. "Administrative jobs," says one nonprofit executive, "involve the art of pushing paper. If you enjoy doing that task well, if you like inventing better systems for making the paper pushing more efficient, you can get great satisfaction from your job." In addition, many jobs carry management responsibility (that is, supervising other people), and that too requires special skills.

Finally, it is not true that a nonprofit organization is a haven from the real workaday world dominated by profit-motivated corporations, big government, and a largely impersonal, insensitive, and inflexible work environment. While there is a grain of truth here, it is remarkable how rapidly nonprofit organizations have become integrated into the world they are supposed to be unlike. Nonprofits that find themselves compet-ing to sell a service or a product, to influence public policy, or to secure funding find the going very competitive and the pressure at times tre-mendous. Nonprofit organizations must work with government agencies at the local, state, and federal levels to preserve tax exemptions, secure funding, and handle personnel issues, to name just a few such interac-tions. Nonprofit organizations are very much a part of the corporate/government structure as some employees discover to their unhappiness.

Creativity/Flexibility

It would be misleading to suggest that the best nonprofit employees are nose-to-the-grindstone management types without any sensitivity or interest in their organization's activities and without any imagination. Obviously, all other things being equal, an executive should certainly give preference to an applicant who, along with administrative and management skills, brings a knowledge, aptitude, or interest in other fields, particularly those related to the organization's mission. Even more important, however, may be the quality of imagination and flex-ibility that the person brings to the organization that allows him or her to grow in the job and help shape it and make it more productive.

Unlike large corporations that are highly structured and in which roles are carefully defined and largely unchanging, many nonprofit or-ganizations are small enough and sufficiently understaffed that a single person may be called on to fill a number of roles and perform a variety of tasks. In addition, because the administrative and management needs of the organization can change quickly through rapid growth or equally rapid constriction, a person hired to perform one constellation of tasks may be asked to consider a reassignment of responsibilities. Volatility and change is common among nonprofits, and as a consequence, flexibility in employees is an asset. Nonprofit organizations, with the exception of the oldest and most established, are not places for people who want to know that the job they are taking today will be the same job ten years hence. Rather, they are good places for people who see organizational change as an opportunity to learn new skills and possibly to secure rapid job advancement.

It is here, in the area of creativity and flexibility, that someone with a broader educational background and varied experience may have a substantial advantage over someone with fairly narrow training and experience in management. In many instances, it will be advantageous to have a person who has, in addition to some administrative skills and experience working with other people, an interest in growing with a job and shaping that job into something exciting and challenging. This is not true in every case, of course, because many jobs in nonprofits are routine. However, the nonprofit executive should consider searching out people who appear to have the special spark of curiosity, energy, and creativity even when their management skills are not fully developed.

To summarize, the nonprofit executive must look for several qualities in prospective employees. In order of importance, these may be summarized as follows:

1. Administrative skills related to the job to be performed
2. Management skills in working with others, especially when some supervisory requirements come with a job
3. Character traits that reflect creativity, flexibility, an enthusiasm for solving problems, and an ability to work with others
4. An understanding of the need for authority in an organizational structure
5. Knowledge, sensitivity, and enjoyment of the nonprofit field in which they will be employed

SETTING THE ORGANIZATIONAL PARAMETERS

Many organizations are anxious to begin recruiting and hiring staff before they have set basic organizational parameters. Both new organizations filling positions for the first time and older organizations replacing departing staff should not rush into the hiring process. Whether it is the trustees hiring the executive director or the director hiring other staff,[1] organizational parameters have to be set in two areas by:

- Determining specific tasks
- Distributing those tasks among salaried employees, volunteers, independent contractors, and outside organization service providers

Determining Tasks

On a regular basis (perhaps annually), or when there are significant changes requiring a reshuffling of personnel, the executive director or staff member most associated with oversight of personnel (with the input of the board or a board committee) must systematically outline everything that needs to get done in the organization. Objectivity is important, and those working on this effort should not simply be guided by the way things have been in the past. Rather, they should ask themselves the following series of questions:

- What tasks are being performed now and are they absolutely necessary?
- What tasks are not being performed that should be?
- What new activities are being added that will require additional work?
- What specific tasks are associated with the new activities?
- Are there tasks that are redundant and can be eliminated? Are there activities that will be eliminated that will make certain tasks unnecessary in the future?
- Do existing tasks need to be redefined or reshuffled in order to address staff concerns over job assignments?

In large organizations, this step, together with the ones that follow, may be carried out by a human resources or personnel manager or with the help of an outside consultant. A consultant brings a kind of objectivity to the process that can be refreshing. Whether or not a consultant is used, employees should be interviewed throughout this process because they have the most expertise about the jobs they perform. Keep in mind, though, that it is natural for an employee to feel threatened when there are many inquiries about his or her job responsibilities, so it is important to reassure staff that the process is not the same as a performance review.

Distributing Tasks

Many people make the mistake of assuming that all of the important tasks in a nonprofit organization need to be done by salaried staff. Often this is the most expensive way of getting jobs done and is not always the most efficient. There are actually four groups that make up a nonprofit organization's workforce—salaried staff, volunteers, independent contractors, and outside organization service providers.

Salaried staff will answer an organization's need for people who will provide ongoing services for important tasks and functions. An organization can expect them to meet high standards in their work and can subject them to more careful supervision and evaluation than other kinds of workers who may be occasional or hired for a specific task at a specific time. Because staff members have a continuing relationship with an organization, state and federal laws require that they be provided with various kinds of protection—unemployment coverage, social security protection, and various other benefits. In many nonprofit organizations, salaried staff forms the core of the workforce, promoting a sense of accountability and stability both internally and externally.

Volunteers are a source of free labor and can be of great value to nonprofit organizations. However, because they do not get paid, an organization has to devise other kinds of rewards that will keep them motivated and interested in offering their services. This may mean finding challenging tasks for volunteers when what the organization really needs is help with more mundane jobs. Furthermore, the process of recruiting, training, and retaining volunteers is not always easy, and their interaction with paid staff must be carefully orchestrated. Nevertheless, without volunteers, many nonprofit organizations would simply not be able to function; they are an important component of the workforce mix.

Independent contractors are individuals who are not members of the regular staff but are hired for a specified period of time or on an occasional basis, often to perform a discrete set of tasks. A nonprofit organization pays them a fixed rate for the job, does not withhold taxes from their fees for service, and does not extend employee benefits to them. When an organization is looking for special expertise to handle a particular job or is looking for an individual to offer a service for which there is not a continuing need, independent contractors often provide the most cost-effective solution. It should be noted that the federal government and different states have varying definitions of what constitutes an independent contractor, and it is important to check on these before assuming that someone fits the category, as will be described in more detail later in the chapter.

Outside organization service providers also provide a discrete service on a fee basis and in many respects are the organizational versions of independent contractors. Many of these organizations specialize in a single functional area and can offer their services at very competitive rates. Efficiencies of scale or access to special equipment or trained personnel often give them a competitive edge. Organizational service providers are especially common in areas where routine functions are the norm—payroll services, equipment maintenance, cleaning, food services, and so on.

In assigning tasks among salaried staff, volunteers, independent contractors, and outside organization service providers, there are generally a variety of options, each with its particular set of advantages and disadvantages. For example, consider three nonprofit organizations of roughly comparable size that are faced with the need to maintain their financial records:

- Organization A has put a bookkeeper on staff, at a salary of $25,000, who records all transactions, reconciles the bank statement, prepares financial statements for the board, computes all withholding taxes, issues the payroll checks, and prepares W-2 forms for employees and 1099 forms for independent contractors. This employee is costing the organization a good deal more than $25,000. In addition to her salary, the organization is paying its share of her social security taxes as well as her medical and disability benefits, sick time, holidays and vacation days, workers' compensation, and state unemployment insurance.

Finally, it provides her with office space and furniture. Thus the real cost of this employee is close to $32,500.

- Organization B has hired a bookkeeping service at $20,000 a year. The service not only completes all the tasks that Organization A's bookkeeper performs, but it also readily generates customized reports (using its sophisticated software) that the executive director and the board can use for budgeting and reporting purposes. The service constantly monitors all changes in tax laws, updates its accounting procedures as the laws change, and provides free advice that is quite useful. The service requires no office space from Organization B—payroll records and other reports are picked up and delivered—requires no employee benefits, and its employees are entitled to no unemployment benefits from Organization B (hence Organization B is not liable for unemployment insurance). The work of the bookkeeping service is reviewed by Organization B's treasurer who is a volunteer.

- Organization C has taken care of its financial operation in still a different way. One of the trustees, a retired accountant, has agreed to serve as treasurer. He volunteers his time to the organization, writing checks, preparing financial statements, and helping the executive director with budgets. A staff member, who costs the organization $26,000 a year ($20,000 in salary and $6,000 in benefits, allocated office space, and so on), spends about 20 percent of his time assisting the treasurer with the paperwork, filing, and record keeping. Finally, at the treasurer's request, the organization has contracted a payroll service to handle all of the payroll-related activity, including the collecting of W-4 forms, the computation of deductions, the issuing of checks (as well as automatic depositing into employee accounts where this is requested), and the preparation of W-2 forms at the end of the year. Organization C's total cost is approximately $13,000.

As can be readily seen, Organization A, by opting to assign a full-time staff member to the bookkeeping tasks, chose the most expensive alternative. Under certain circumstances, this choice might have been justified if people felt that it was desirable to have someone in the office all the time who was fully conversant with financial matters. Nevertheless, in other cases it probably would have been desirable for the board of trustees and the executive director to have chosen other alternatives. Some combination of outside organization service bureaus, volunteers, or independent contractors would certainly have been less expensive and might have provided greater expertise.

Special Issues Relating to Independent Contractors

Many organizations are tempted to hire individuals as independent contractors because it is simpler and less expensive than hiring regular employees. It is true that there is far less paperwork associated with independent contractors. No withholding taxes are required, independent contractors receive no benefits, and organizations are only required to file forms with the IRS at the end of the calendar year, and that only if the contractor earns more than a certain amount.

But it is not legal to hire people as independent contractors when their working patterns indicate that they should really be categorized as members of the regular staff. Someone who works in the office on a continuing basis should be treated as a salaried employee even if he or she works only part-time. Indeed, several governmental agencies including the IRS and states' Division of Employment Security can, and sometimes do, apply a test to determine whether independent contractors should have been categorized as salaried employees. If the work they do is short-term, and if the individuals enjoy more independence than other regular employees, the governmental agencies may well be satisfied. If the individuals do not meet these criteria and do not fit the definition of an independent contractor, the nonprofit organization can be forced to pay back taxes as well as unemployment compensation. For this reason, the advice of an accountant or a lawyer in the hiring of independent contractors is useful.

It is always desirable to have a written contract (or work agreement) with an independent contractor that specifies the task to be accomplished, the start date, the end date, and the compensation level. The contract usually does not specify the place where the work will be performed, unless this is crucial to a description of the task, nor does it describe the work hours or any other conditions that would suggest that this person is being treated like a regular employee. A sample work agreement is given in figure 3.1.

This work agreement grew out of Sandra Harris' need to find someone to work on a short-term project at Parent/Child Stress

Services. The organization had received funds from the State Department of Youth Services to analyze phone calls associated with its counseling program. The analysis required the creation of categories of calls and callers, types of caller problems, times of calls (by day of the week, time of day, holidays, and so on), and it also required looking for correlations between these various pieces of information.

It was clear to Sandra Harris that some specialized expertise and help would be needed and that it wasn't necessary or even desirable to add someone to the permanent staff. She considered using a volunteer to assist on the project, but in the end, she could not find anyone she could count on who had the proper set of skills and who could guarantee the time and help when it was needed. Wisely, she chose an independent contractor, hiring an individual for a specified number of days at the specific time when the project needed him.

After Sandra Harris had the work agreement drawn up and checked over by the organization's attorney, she sent two copies to the independent contractor so that he could sign and date them first. This is the preferred procedure because an organization wants to withhold its final signed commitment to an agreement until after the independent contractor has reviewed the agreement and accepted its terms in writing. Once the two forms were returned by the contractor with his signature, Sandra Harris signed and dated the documents, which made them fully executed and legally binding copies of the work agreement. One copy was returned to the independent contractor; the other was retained as the organization's copy.

Figure 3.1. Sample Independent Contractor Work Agreement

This agreement, dated March 21, 2012, is between Parent/Child Stress Services, Inc. (hereinafter, the "Organization") and John Doe of 25 Compton Road, Compton, California (hereinafter, the "Contractor"). The period covered by this contract is from May 1, 2012 to December 31, 2012.

The Organization and Contractor hereby agree as follows:

1. The Contractor shall assist the Organization on a research project being carried out by the Organization under contract to the State Department of Youth Services. The Contractor shall provide up to fifteen hours on the project per month. He shall provide an analysis of phone calls associated with the Organization's counseling program. Specifically, the Contractor will:
   - Create categories of calls and callers, types of caller problems, and timing of calls
   - Find correlations between these variables
   - Provide an interim and final report
   - Provide all data and analyses

2. Contractor will be paid $50/hour and may bill monthly. No additional payments will be made.

3. This agreement shall be executed by both parties on or before April 15, 2012, or it shall be null and void. Changes to this agreement shall require an amendment signed by the Contractor and by an authorized official of the Organization. This agreement may be canceled by either party provided 45 days' notice is given in writing to the other party. The Organization will be obligated to pay for all work satisfactorily completed by the Contractor prior to termination.

4. This agreement shall meet all standards specified in the State Department of Youth Services' General Provisions dealing with Fixed-Price Contracts, a copy of which is on file with the Organization.

5. Contractor acknowledges that all written materials, documents, reports and other results of his services performed under this agreement (the "Materials") are specially commissioned by the Organization as works made for hire for it, as such term is interpreted under the copyright laws of the United States. The Organization shall be the author and owner of all right, title and interest in and to the Materials, including, but not limited to, all copyrights in the Materials with the right to edit, change, and use the Materials in any manner that it may determine. If any of the Materials is determined not to be a work made for hire, Contractor hereby irrevocably assigns to the Organization, as of the time of the creation of the Materials, all right, title and interest, including without limitation all copyright, in and to said Materials.

6. This agreement shall be governed by the laws of the state of California, applicable to agreements made and performed therein, and each of the Organization and the Contractor agrees to submit to the exclusive jurisdiction of the applicable federal or state courts located in said state for the resolution of any disputes between them arising from this agreement.

In witness whereof, the parties have signed below.

Accepted and Agreed:

Contractor

_____ Date: _____
        (Contractor signature)

_____
Social Security No. or Taxpayer ID

The Organization

By: _____ Date: _____
President, Parent/Child Stress Services, Inc.

VOLUNTEERS

By the fifth year of Sandra Harris' tenure as executive director of Parent/Child Stress Services, she had assembled an excellent team of salaried staff, independent contractors, and outside organization service providers. She and her board were pleased. But now there was a new set of challenges that she had not anticipated, and it concerned her volunteers. Parent/Child Stress Services had been established by a group of individuals, and in the early days they contributed their time in running the organization. Many of these original founders continued to provide their services to the organization for free. But as Parent/Child Stress Services grew, some of these people had to relinquish their jobs to paid workers, and the transition was not always handled gracefully. A number of the volunteers who had worked in the office were not happy about being displaced by paid staff (many of whom they found arrogant and uninformed about the organization's history) or by independent contractors (who, they believed, brought no new skills to the organization). They resented the fact that all of these people were now being paid for what the volunteers had always done for free. Deep down, some wondered whether their many years of volunteer efforts had even been appreciated.

At the same time, Sandra Harris had identified many new kinds of activities for which volunteers were needed—fund raising, phone counseling, and basic data collection for research projects. But many of these areas required people with particular abilities or specialized interests, and she did not know whether to try to convince the existing volunteers to undergo some retraining or to attempt to locate other individuals who were already sufficiently motivated and knowledgeable to move into these areas.

Part of the problem was that Sandra Harris had been so focused on the needs of her organization that she had not thought about the volunteers themselves. If she had done so, she might have been better prepared to handle the psychological needs of her existing volunteers, and she might also have been better equipped to recruit and retain new people who would be enthusiastic about working for her organization for no money.

Recruiting Volunteers

A generation or two ago, many affluent women tended to stay at home and as they got older and their children moved away, they provided a steady stream of volunteers for nonprofit organizations. Retirement patterns, too, favored volunteerism since many men retired at 65 years of age or earlier, often with guaranteed pensions. But in recent years, all of that has changed. Most women work, and, increasingly, guaranteed pensions are a thing of the past. Today economic demands require both spouses to be in the workforce, and people work longer and longer into their careers. These trends have significantly reduced the potential volunteer workforce and require organizations to be much more aggressive in pursuing volunteers from a shrinking pool.

Recruitment begins with understanding the basic motivations behind volunteerism. Why do people volunteer? Volunteers themselves have provided a host of reasons:

- *Sense of self-satisfaction.* Many people like to use their free time in ways that bring them personal satisfaction and allow them to develop a positive self-image. Some volunteer because they want to feel needed, others like to keep busy in a way that is useful, and still others want to earn the respect of their peers and friends while doing something useful for the community.
- *Altruism.* Many people from all economic strata believe that helping others is a necessary part of a complete and good life. Often this impulse grows out of religious beliefs or family traditions and upbringing. In some cases, where individuals have little cash to spare, volunteering provides the only way to express such altruism. In others, volunteering may be combined with the giving of cash.
- *Companionship/meeting people.* Another important reason why individuals volunteer is to meet and mix with other people. Volunteering can allow them to widen their circles of acquaintances and develop personal bonds that can spill over into other parts of their lives. Individuals who move to new communities, older people who have lost a spouse, even adolescents and young professionals looking for a more active social life may all look to volunteerism as a way to widen their circles of friends.
- *Learning about a field.* Some individuals who have an interest in a particular field see volunteering as an excellent way to learn more about it, particularly if training and learning opportunities are built into an organization's volunteer program. Those who want to learn about foreign countries, current events, religious traditions, the arts, or a host of other fields can do so through volunteerism.
- *Creating/maintaining an organization.* Some volunteers are entrepreneurs who devote their energies to creating nonprofit

organizations and helping them grow and thrive. Pride in their organizations' success and continued expansion is often a prime motivating factor in their volunteer activities.

- *Developing professional contacts.* In some organizations, volunteering can put one in touch with important members of the community. Some people use volunteer jobs as a way to make contacts that may lead them to clients or other kinds of business or professional associations and opportunities.
- *Getting ahead in a career.* Many profit-sector corporations view employee volunteer service as an important way for the company to make a contribution to the community. Young executives and other company representatives are encouraged to volunteer; those wanting to move up the corporate ladder know that a volunteer position can be a real asset on a resumé.
- *Getting training/experience.* For some individuals, a volunteer position is a route to finding a paying job. Young people, people who have been out of the labor force for some time, or people wishing to change professions will sometimes use volunteer opportunities as a way to further these personal goals. They may learn a task, gain a marketable skill, or secure a recommendation for future employment.
- *Providing entry to a particular organization.* For some people who have a strong interest in working for or serving on the board of a particular nonprofit organization, volunteering provides an important entry point to becoming involved. Volunteering may be the necessary first step on a ladder that eventually leads to a paying job or a seat on the board.
- *Social panache.* There is much prestige associated with certain organizations, and their volunteers represent an elite group within the community. Associating with these volunteers carries a certain degree of status and marks a person as being part of a desirable social group.

What this means is that recruitment strategies need to align with the motivations for volunteerism. One organization may work primarily in corporate environments, focusing its efforts on young executives; another may work through local churches and civic organizations; still another may provide social occasions with socially prominent groups of community leaders who themselves volunteer. And in almost every case, members of an existing pool of volunteers can be used as a recruitment force, extolling the benefits and pleasures through a recounting of their own experiences.

Meeting the Needs of Volunteers

Board members and staff of nonprofit organizations must consider the motivations of prospective volunteers if they want their help. In some cases, both are so focused on their organizations' needs that they do not do so. "We need door-to-door fund-raising volunteers." "We need someone to donate legal help." "We need volunteers to read to patients." "We need people who will help learning-disabled children with their reading." This identification of volunteer jobs is important, of course, and a detailed description of what is involved in each task will make the actual assignment of volunteers a great deal easier when the appropriate time comes. What is lacking is an understanding of volunteer needs and a clear concept of how particular tasks can fulfill those needs.

Why should an organization focus on the needs of volunteers? Very simply, if it wants to be able to recruit and retain people to work for no money, it must figure out another means of providing them with satisfaction and fulfillment. In the case of Parent/Child Stress Services, Sandra Harris failed to think about this, and she was chided by one of her trustees who told her, "Volunteerism is a quid pro quo business. The organization gets something, but we don't get it for nothing—we have to give something back. A volunteer wants meaningful responsibility and wants to be taken seriously. The minute we take a volunteer for granted, we are in trouble."

Sandra Harris had been so focused on the needs of her organization that she failed even to provide recognition to those volunteers who had worked so long and so hard and whose jobs were now being taken by paid staff and independent contractors. Awards luncheons, mention in the organization's annual report and press releases, framed certificates of merit, or other clear indications of the organization's appreciation would have gone a long way toward meeting these individuals' need to feel appreciated.

Other nonprofit organizations have found a variety of ways to meet the needs of volunteers. Two interesting examples show how diverse the approach can be:

THE ART MUSEUM

An art museum in a large city needed volunteers to serve as guides for two special visitor groups—deaf visitors (who required guides who could use sign language) and foreign visitors (who required guides fluent in their language). At first, the volunteer coordinator had a difficult time finding volunteers. As she recalled, "I put notices in specialized publications and websites and printed up some brochures that were distributed at local professional conferences where there were many individuals who had the signing skills or the foreign language skills. Some of the inquiries I got as a result of these recruitment efforts were from people who were interested in paying jobs, but few wanted to volunteer. Those who did had work schedules that prevented them from giving us the required number of hours. Some balked at the amount of time they would have to commit to learning about the collection.

"Then, after talking to some of my other volunteer guides, I realized that I had been using the wrong approach. Some of my most loyal volunteers told me that their original motivation for getting involved had been to learn about the incredible collection we have here at the museum. For people with the slightest interest in art, our volunteer training program is a wonderful opportunity to learn from recognized experts—curators, conservators, artists. So I changed my approach in recruiting volunteers, and I even dropped the word *volunteer* from my pitch entirely. Instead, I said that the museum was starting a series of free seminars on the collection taught by noted authorities. The seminars would have extremely limited enrollments and would only be open to those who had the necessary skills to serve as guides for the hearing impaired or for foreign visitors. I set fairly rigorous eligibility requirements, including a minimum number of hours required per month. Of course, this just happened to be the same number of hours of training we require of all our volunteers, but I didn't say anything about that.

"Within three weeks, we had more volunteers than we could use, and I had to start a waiting list. And those we got were extremely motivated by the seminar. The irony is that we have always required that our guides go through this training because you cannot be a guide unless you know a great deal about the collection. But this was the first time that we referred to the training program as a *seminar* and promoted our staff as the *faculty* in our recruitment efforts. Now instead of people complaining about the requirements that we impose on them, they respond with enthusiasm, because this is clearly meeting their desire to learn about art. The lesson is that it is extremely important to think about the motivations of potential volunteers before you try to recruit them, and it is equally important to meet their expectations once they have agreed to come on board."

HIGH SCHOOL HEALTH CORPS

The High School Health Corps is a United States–based nonprofit organization that sends high school volunteers to Central America during the summer to assist on public health projects in rural areas. The organization is not affiliated with any religious group, and it attempts to stay apolitical in offering volunteer assistance to countries where young Americans will be welcome and safe. According to one of the volunteer recruiters for the program, meeting the needs of the countries is essential, but meeting the needs of the young volunteers is just as critical. Not only is it an important strategy in recruitment, but it becomes an even more important strategy in retaining volunteers once the rigorous six-month training phase begins.

"Our initial recruitment is done through schools and churches. We have a large group of ministers and principals who know the High School Health Corps and support it. They urge students to consider our program and to come to an informational meeting to find out more about it. They talk positively to the kids about our program. It is described as an exciting challenge and an adventure, a trip to exotic lands, an alternative to a boring summer. But the adults describing the High School Health Corps also say that the program meets the needs of young people in other ways. Kids can develop language skills, they can learn about the health field by actually working beside health-care professionals, they can involve themselves in an extracurricular activity that may help them with college admissions. By the time kids come to one of our informational meetings with their parents to learn more about the program, they are usually convinced that volunteering will do a lot for them.

"Even so, we do not leave anything to chance. We constantly emphasize the good points of the program but begin to shift our emphasis somewhat. We understand that the parents usually need some convincing too. They are concerned first and foremost about safety, and we have a good track record there. But we develop a pitch that will convince both parents and kids that the program will meet the most basic need of a young person—the need to be taken seriously and treated as an adult.

"In fact, at this meeting, we tend to talk less about the fun of world travel and more about the rigor and long-lasting impact of our training, the challenge of working in a foreign land with a different culture and language, and the genuine discomforts of living in a third world country. In a way, we are doing two things. We want to discourage those who are not serious and never will be. But for the others, we want to convey the message that the challenges of this program are precisely the reason that many young people should want to participate. The program gives them more responsibility than they have ever had before. We tell them that it will not be easy but that they will get tremendous positive reinforcement when they meet the challenge. Often, the person who conveys this message is another young person who has already served in the program."

The Volunteer Coordinator

At Parent/Child Stress Services, Sandra Harris admitted to her board that she had failed to address the needs of her volunteers. But she had a valid excuse. She simply had too many other things to do. She also had to confess that in her own mind volunteers were a lower priority in organizing the workforce than other groups—paid staff, independent contractors, outside organization service providers.

Sandra Harris' attitude is not unusual, and this is one reason that in many nonprofit organizations there is someone who serves as an advocate for volunteers, helps the chief executive understand their importance, and ensures that there are times when he or she can meet, greet, and thank the volunteers. In larger organizations or in organizations where volunteers constitute a large proportion of the workforce, the individual in this position is a member of the paid staff and may go by various titles such as volunteer coordinator or director of volunteers. In smaller organizations or ones requiring fewer volunteers, the volunteer coordinator may be uncompensated. In either case, a volunteer coordinator, whether paid or not, should have access to the chief executive, because a significant part of his or her job has to do with shaping the director's attitude toward the role of volunteers in the organization.

Indeed, a volunteer coordinator must be integrated into the operation of the organization at the highest levels and must be given the full cooperation of any department or staff person who will be working with volunteers. When the volunteer coordinator is a member of the staff, it is important to consider where he or she should be placed in the organizational structure. In the art museum described earlier, the volunteer coordinator was placed in the department of education, because 90 percent of the volunteers worked in that area. While the department had eighteen paid staff members, the volunteer coordinator was one of only three who reported directly to the director of the department and periodically met with the chief executive of the museum itself. In the High School Health Corps, which had a full-time paid staff of only seven, the volunteer coordinator reported to the executive director of the organization.

While the volunteer coordinator plays an important advocacy and educational role, sensitizing senior staff to the important place of volunteers in the organization, he or she has many other responsibilities. The volunteer coordinator is to the volunteers what a personnel director is to the paid staff. He or she has the overall responsibility for finding and placing volunteers and mediating between their needs and the needs of the organization. The full range of responsibilities in the job generally includes oversight of the following tasks:

- Establishing and constantly updating written policies on volunteer procedures, responsibilities, supervision, placement, restrictions, reporting, evaluation, recognition, and termination
- Developing volunteer benefits including free or low-cost use of organizational facilities or programs, access to organizational resources (e.g., library and dining facilities), opportunities to attend conferences, cash for travel and other expenses, letters of recommendation for subsequent job searches, and so on
- Determining where volunteers can be used most effectively in the organization
- Creating job descriptions for volunteers
- Developing recruitment procedures, including identifying organizations and individuals who will promote the volunteer opportunities, maintaining contacts with the media, using existing volunteers and staff for informational meetings, and designing appropriate print and website material
- Interviewing, selecting, and placing volunteers in appropriate jobs
- Developing orientation and training programs for volunteers
- Evaluating the performance of volunteers and reassigning or terminating volunteers in cases of unsatisfactory performance
- Organizing recognition events and opportunities to honor volunteers
- Helping to formulate and evaluate the structure and function of separate volunteer groups such as guilds or friend organizations
- Responding to the needs of designated representatives and officers of these volunteer groups
- Acting as an advocate of volunteer needs and interests with staff and others in the organization
- Training staff in how to work with volunteers, including supervision, evaluation, and recognition
- Responding to problems and complaints from or about volunteers and mediating conflicts among volunteers or between volunteers and staff

It should be noted that one of the most important responsibilities of the volunteer coordinator has to do with the termination of an unsuccessful volunteer placement. The old adage that a volunteer is someone who works for no pay and therefore can't be fired is not true. What is true is that the situation has to be handled with great finesse. The first step is for the volunteer coordinator to get all the facts and quietly evaluate the complaints. Sometimes the volunteer in question was not properly trained, did not receive adequate supervision, or was not told early enough that there was a problem. In such cases, it may be appropriate for the volunteer coordinator to remedy these problems and give the volunteer another chance. Alternatively, the volunteer can be reassigned to a less demanding or more appropriate position. In extreme cases, the job can be eliminated for a time or the volunteer can simply be told that his or her services are no longer needed. Such actions are difficult, but a skilled volunteer coordinator cannot shirk this responsibility.

It is obvious that in large organizations, no one person can be expected to actually carry out each and every task associated with the volunteer coordinator responsibilities listed above. In some cases, the volunteer coordinator may supervise several other paid staff members who will collectively attend to these tasks or he or she may work with a formal volunteer organization to help with the various aspects of organizing the volunteer program.

Volunteer Organizations

In some nonprofit organizations, volunteers have created separate formal organizational structures with their own boards, officers, and committees. These groups can help formulate volunteer policy; they can be active in recruitment, training, and supervision of volunteers; and they can be responsible for specific fund-raising projects or other kinds of special events. Often, the president of the volunteer organization sits on the parent organization's board of directors and represents the interests and needs of the volunteers at that level. The volunteer organization may have its own paid staff; however, more commonly, it interacts with the staff of the parent organization, especially with the volunteer coordinator.

The structural relationship between a nonprofit organization and its volunteer organization can vary. In some cases, the volunteer organization is called a committee and its operation is strictly controlled by the parent organization's board. At the other extreme, volunteer organizations are legally and structurally distinct. They are separately incorporated, file their own financial reports to the federal government, and have boards of directors who are not accountable to the parent organization's board.

There is much to be said in favor of volunteer organizations. They give the volunteers their own sense of place and allow them a chance to advance within the volunteer structure itself—serving on a committee, on the board, or as an officer. Just as important, volunteer organizations ensure that there is a formal vehicle by which the volunteers have a voice in policy development as it affects their ranks. Indeed, in most organizations that rely heavily on volunteers, such organizations are considered a necessity.

Nevertheless, from the parent organization's vantage point, tensions can arise over the issue of control. Particularly when a volunteer organization is separately incorporated, very clear rules have to be established to ensure that the goals of the two organizations are consistent. Where fund raising is involved, tensions can become particularly acute. If the volunteer organization has the legal right to dictate how its money is spent, much time can be wasted haggling over the transfer of funds. For this reason, most nonprofit organizations require that volunteer organizations are maintained as part of their own corporate structures.

Interviewing Potential Volunteers

Volunteers as well as paid staff may be involved in recruiting prospective volunteers. Once recruitment activities have begun, prospects have to be screened and placed. In most cases, interviews are the best way to accomplish this task. An interview has several purposes. First, it assures the prospective volunteer that the organization wishes to meet his or her needs and expectations. Second, it allows the interviewer to clarify the organization's expectations—often some kind of volunteer handbook is shared with prospects that outlines the goals, policies, and procedures of the organization's volunteer program. Finally, the interview provides an opportunity to assess a prospective volunteer's skills, temperament, and motivations and to begin to determine where that individual might fit into the organization.

Often the prospective volunteer is asked to fill out a form that provides basic information and can be a starting place for the interview. It might include some or all of the following information:

- Name, address, phone number, email address, date of interview
- Names and contact information for two references
- Previous volunteer experience, including names of organizations, dates of affiliation, responsibilities, and contact persons
- Time availability
- What the volunteer hopes to get out of the assignment
- Special areas of interest that might be relevant to job assignment
- Paid work experience, including present employer
- Specialized skills, including language, clerical/typing, and computer
- Education

In order to maintain consistency in the interviews, some organizations find it desirable to have a prepared set of questions. In addition, they may require that the interviewer keep a written summary of the conversation that, together with the information form filled out by the prospective volunteer, goes into a file and is maintained with other records by the volunteer coordinator. These records are invaluable.

Orientation and Training

Once volunteers are selected, they must be oriented and trained. Generally, orientation consists of all or some of the following:

- *An organizational packet.* This might include the organization's annual report, newspaper articles, brochures, flyers, reports, a list of board members, a staff organization chart, and an organization chart of the volunteer organization (if one exists) together with its charter and bylaws.
- *Background reading material.* In some cases, it is important to gather additional information about the volunteer assignment and responsibilities. In the High School Health Corps, described earlier, young people are required to read several books and pamphlets about the history and culture of the country they will be working in, health care in third world countries, as well as case studies based on the experiences of other volunteers.
- *A tour of the facility where the volunteers will work.* In some organizations, it is helpful for volunteers to tour the facility where volunteer services will be provided. For example, a church in a

major city offers daily meals to the homeless. It recruits volunteers to cook, set up tables, serve, clean up, greet and seat the homeless, and so on. New volunteers are required to come to the facility when it is empty and talk through the various tasks before being given an actual assignment.

- *A tour of the office and a meeting with the staff.* Where volunteers will be interacting regularly with staff, new recruits are often required to spend some time in the office before being given a specific assignment. They are introduced to staff members, shown where office equipment is located, and told how they are expected to fit into the general office work flow.

- *Films, slide shows, and demonstrations.* Often films or slide shows are the best way for volunteers to get a sense of the place where they will be volunteering before they get there. For example, the High School Health Corps shows films and slides of the countries where volunteers will be assigned so that they will be better prepared once they arrive. In other cases, films and slide shows are an excellent way to provide background on the organization, its history, and its volunteer activities. Films, slide shows, and demonstrations can also be used to show how particular volunteer tasks are carried out.

- *Group meetings and discussions.* Particularly in organizations where groups of volunteers come into an organization at the same time, group meetings provide an excellent way for basic orientation tasks to get accomplished. They also allow new volunteers to get acquainted with one another and get basic questions answered.

After the completion of general orientation (or sometimes combined with it) comes the training for the particular job the volunteer will be doing. Training varies depending on the complexity of the job and the background and experience of the volunteer. However, it should always begin with a discussion of the written job (task) description, which provides answers to some key questions:

- What is the job?
- Why is it necessary, what is its purpose, and how does it contribute to the overall operation of the organization?

- How is it done, what special equipment or expertise is involved, and what are the steps necessary for completion?
- With whom does the volunteer have to work and to whom is the volunteer accountable?
- How much time is involved, how many hours (or days or months) is the volunteer expected to work, and when is the job to be completed?

Training should also involve at least one preliminary meeting with the people with whom the volunteer will have to interact and, often, some practice or on-the-job training by a supervisor. Field trips, guided observations, and role-playing sessions may also be desirable in cases where the task is complicated or involves new skills.

It has been said that the single most important defining characteristic of any nonprofit organization is the people who work within it. The staff, volunteers, and other workers in the organization establish a tone, help to define its image, and determine the effectiveness with which the organization carries out its mission, its programs, and its activities.

Yet many nonprofit organizations operate under severe financial constraints, which make it difficult to get enough good people in their workforce. They cannot simply hire more employees whenever there is another job to be done. They cannot always pay more money to get the most qualified people for particular jobs. Instead, they have to maximize and stretch their scant resources. They must find committed workers who will work hard, often for modest pay, sometimes for no pay at all. They must make sure that everyone's skills are utilized to the fullest extent possible. And, perhaps most important, nonprofit organizations must create an environment where workers—whether paid or volunteer—know that their work is appreciated. For in the end, individuals are most likely to make the required extra effort when they feel their work is valued and contributes to the overall good of the organization.

CHECKLIST QUESTIONS FOR CHAPTER 3

1. Is the chief executive in your organization skilled in personnel work? Has he or she developed a system that ensures that each job will be filled by the best possible candidate?
2. Do employees come to your organization with the proper management skills related to the jobs they will perform? Do they seem to work well with others?
3. Has a proper assessment been made of all the tasks that need to get done in your organization? Has it been documented?
4. Are tasks in your organization appropriately distributed among salaried staff members, volunteers, independent contractors, and outside organization service providers?
5. Has your organization found effective ways to identify, recruit, orient, motivate, and recognize the work of volunteers?
6. Is there a volunteer coordinator in your organization? Are the coordinator's responsibilities clearly spelled out? Are this person's activities well integrated into the operation of your organization?
7. Is there a separate volunteer organization that is affiliated with your organization? Are issues of control and authority clearly resolved and documented?

FOUR

Personnel Policy

When John Sims of the Compton Community Center was hired as executive director, he was one of only five employees. The president of the board that hired him explained that there were no job descriptions for any of the staff positions because things were a bit "fluid"; it would be up to him to decide how to allocate tasks among the employees. Five years later, the Compton Community Center had a salaried staff of fifteen along with several teachers, coaches, and artists who were independent contractors. In order for the organization to run smoothly, there had to be very clear definitions of roles, responsibilities, and reporting relationships. The employees also had to know what they could expect from the organization in terms of compensation, job advancement, and other aspects of employer/employee relations.

Fortunately, John Sims had taken care of three things immediately on assuming the role of executive director:

- Preparing an organization chart showing reporting relationships and lines of responsibility
- Writing job descriptions
- Deciding on compensation levels and specific benefits[1]

Preparing the Organization Chart

As John Sims found, small nonprofit organizations such as the Compton Community Center often resist preparing an organization chart. This is probably acceptable when there are only two or three employees. But with five or more, an organization chart is a necessity. It establishes lines of authority, reporting, and accountability.

In a large organization, an organization chart is particularly important. Chief executives must delegate some of their supervising authority because supervision of each and every employee is not possible.

In delegating authority, chief executives must also delegate some accountability. The organization chart in figure 4.1, for example, tells us to whom the executive director has delegated supervisory authority and to whom one must speak if things go awry.

Consider what would happen in this organization if John Sims, the executive director, received a financial report that was full of incorrect information based on data incorrectly entered by the financial assistant. The director of administration would be called in to discuss the problem. She, in turn, would take up the problem with the financial staff. What the executive director should not do (unless the supervisor has been informed and approves) is deal directly with the financial assistant in trying to find out why the report was incorrect. John Sims might request a report on what the problem is, what was done, and what will be done to prevent it in the future—but he needs to have enough trust in his staff to handle the issue without his presence.

Given the fact that reporting and authority lines must be respected, they must be set up carefully. Supervisors must be capable of supervision; employees should not be expected to report to people who are incompetent. In addition, multiple supervisors should be avoided whenever possible. If an employee must report to two or more bosses and they do not agree, this puts the employee in an awkward position. In the organization chart in figure 4.1, for example, the program assistant carries out work for four people—the director of programs and the three coordinators (as indicated by the dotted lines). However, the principal reporting line is to the director of programs. This means that in instances where it is unclear whose work needs to get done, the program assistant can ask the director of programs to establish priorities.

Finally, when contracted personnel are employed by the organization on a regular basis, it is sometimes advantageous to place them on the organization chart so it is clear to whom they report. They are generally shown in boxes with broken rather than solid lines and are indicated as contractual. Figure 4.1 shows three groups of contractors all reporting to the appropriate staff coordinator.

Figure 4.1 Organizational Structure for the Compton Community Center

Writing Job Descriptions

A job description typically includes three components:

- A general description of the job
- A statement about whom the person holding the job reports to and whom he or she will supervise
- A list of specific responsibilities and functions

JOB DESCRIPTION

The financial assistant is responsible for the thorough and accurate maintenance of the program and financial records of the Compton Community Center. He or she is also responsible for the preparation of certain financial documents and forms and for the maintenance of related paper files.

Minimum Qualifications
- BA degree or equivalent
- One year of financial experience in a for-profit or nonprofit organization
- Working knowledge of basic accounting

The financial assistant reports to the financial officer. When volume is heavy, and at the discretion of the financial officer, the financial assistant may supervise a part-time clerk.

Responsibilities and Functions
- Prepares receipt and disbursement reports and general ledgers for all cost centers and accounts
- Reconciles monthly checking and savings account balances with bank statement
- Processes payables and receivables and generates checks following approval for payment and assignment of accounting codes by the director of administration
- Maintains paper files for all current and historic payable and receivable items
- Maintains computerized cost center, chart of accounts, and vendor files

- Maintains paper files for contracts, insurance policies, and other material pertinent to the fiscal administration of the Compton Community Center
- Other duties as assigned

Job descriptions generally begin with a brief overview of the job together with the expected minimum qualification of someone filling it. It outlines reporting lines and then lists in detail the responsibilities and functions. How much detail? A reasonable rule of thumb is that job descriptions should be able to be put on one or, at most, two pages with functions listed in order of priority. In order to leave some flexibility, a phrase like "Other duties as assigned" should be included in the list of responsibilities and functions.

Two additional elements should be clear in the job description:

1. *Whether the job is full-time or part-time.* Generally, if an employee works forty scheduled hours a week, he or she is considered full-time; less than that is generally considered part-time, though the organization has some flexibility to define what constitutes full-time or part-time for its own situation.
2. *Whether the employee will be paid a salary or wages.* Salaried employees are those whose salaries are generally computed on an annual basis (e.g., $50,000/year) and are guaranteed that minimum amount regardless of the actual number of hours they work. Wage earners are generally paid in hourly increments ($15/hour), and their total earnings are dependent on how many hours they work.

Occasionally, particularly in large organizations, job descriptions contain performance criteria that detail the minimum performance level expected of the employee for each task. For example, if the task is described as "Reconciles monthly checking and savings account balances with bank statement," the corresponding performance criterion might be "Minimum performance standards will have been met if employee presents reconciled statements to supervisor within two weeks of receipt of monthly bank statements."

Although performance criteria may be useful in very large organizations in which there are routine jobs with predictable tasks, they are usually cumbersome for smaller organizations. This is especially true as performance criteria may change while the basic job functions are less likely to change. Performance criteria are more useful in an annual performance plan drawn up with each employee that includes goals and the criteria by which those goals will be evaluated. This allows for evaluation of employee performance, which can be especially important if an employee is on probation.

Why have job descriptions at all? There are many arguments against them. They often take a long time to write and require extensive discussions with staff and several drafts. Furthermore, every time there is a staff reorganization with a shifting of responsibilities, the job descriptions have to be redrafted. Why not spend the time on something more productive and just explain to new staff what they are expected to do when they are hired? There are three reasons why it is important to have job descriptions.

First, the very process of writing job descriptions often reveals that the job responsibilities envisioned for a single person are unrealistic. For example, the executive director and the trustees may agree that one person should staff the development and pubic relations areas, but once each and every task is detailed in the job description, it may become apparent that no one person could possibly do all of them. In addition, once all the tasks are written down, it becomes easier to juggle responsibilities with a clearer sense of the total work needs of the organization and the time commitments of each staff member.

Second, job descriptions protect the organization's employees. Employees are able to refer to a document that outlines what is expected of them and provides the basis for an evaluation of their job performance. While technically they can be dismissed for not performing a task that was assigned orally by a supervisor but was not mentioned in the job description, it is far better to update job descriptions whenever a significant new responsibility is added. Commonly, an employee can expect to be consulted before significant changes are made in a job description, particularly if the change involves the carrying out of additional tasks. Similarly, the employee's supervisor owes him or her an explanation when tasks detailed in the job description are taken away and given to others. Finally, the employee can expect any job review, particularly one leading to salary adjustments, to be based on an assessment of performance of the tasks listed in the job description.

Third, job descriptions protect the organization. Like contracts, a job description outlines certain expectations in writing that, if not lived up to, offer grounds for dismissal. Without a job description, an employee can always say, "But no one ever told me I was supposed to do that." With the written document, there can be no disputing that the responsibilities were spelled out clearly. Similarly, as the supervisor assesses the job performance of an employee at the time of a performance review, he or she has a clear set of tasks and responsibilities on which to exercise valuative judgment. It helps the supervisor to be objective and to resist the temptation to give a good evaluation to an employee simply because he or she is quiet or pleasant and a negative evaluation to a less personable or less friendly member of the staff.

Many organizations have job descriptions that are out-of-date. Typically, an organization will write job descriptions (or hire a consultant to do it) and then forget that the descriptions need to be updated as new tasks and jobs are added and responsibilities change. Updating does not have to be difficult and should be done regularly. A certain time can be set aside, at least once a year, for the executive director or someone with specific personnel responsibility to oversee the review of all job descriptions and, in the case of those job descriptions requiring board approval, recommend changes.

Deciding on Compensation Levels

Deciding on salary levels and benefits for employees of nonprofit organizations often leads to controversy. On one side, there are many arguments to keep salaries low. Commonly, nonprofit organizations are faced with difficult financial obstacles because there is a limit to the amount of money that can be earned and raised. Furthermore, it is well known that many people may be willing to make financial sacrifices in order to work in the nonprofit sector—many have emotional investments in the organization's mission and activities—so it seems good business sense to take advantage of this situation. Finally, in the special case of a nonprofit organization setting the salary of a staff member who also sits on the board (often the chief executive), there may be arguments that an excessively high salary appears to circumvent the principles of nonprofit trusteeship discussed in chapter 2.

Half a century ago, many nonprofit organizations were staffed largely with volunteers and independently affluent people who were paid modest salaries. With increased professionalization, conditions changed, but nonprofit administrators are still, on average, underpaid for the kinds of jobs they do in comparison with similar positions in the for-profit sector. In some ways this is good for the organizations and their boards. Many organizations find themselves with plenty of applicants for jobs that pay far less than would comparable jobs in industry. But in other ways the situation is problematic. As large non-profits have discovered over the years, organized labor has made significant inroads in nonprofit organizations where collective bargaining is probably not the best way to negotiate wages and working conditions. The unions' successes grew in part out of workers' frustrations over inadequate wage scales. In addition, even where employees are unable or unwilling to bargain for better wages, talented people will generally work for inadequate pay for only so long. Eventually, they are lured by other opportunities offering new challenges and more money. While the nonprofit organization is usually able to find young, enthusiastic people to fill the places of departing staff, retaining the experienced employee is more difficult.

Nonprofit organizations are notorious for practicing false economy when it comes to staff salaries. For example, one organization may set the executive director's salary so low that it cannot afford someone with the kind of credentials and experience necessary to raise money and make the rest of the staff productive. The organization that pays its executive director $100,000 may be able to attract someone who can raise at least two times that in fund-raising efforts, while a $50,000 executive director may be unable to raise any money at all. Similarly, false economy is practiced in hiring untrained or unqualified people. It is not unusual to find an organization with two administrative assistants with minimal computer skills when a single, well-trained individual would cost far less, be more productive, and could supervise a couple of volunteers or work-study students for routine tasks.

How much to pay? The setting of compensation levels can be challenging, yet there are certain things an organization can do to make it easier. The first is to look for salary surveys of nonprofit industries that show the range of salaries paid for comparable positions. The second is to locate a number of similar organizations, then call or write them seeking information on employee compensation as well as the types and costs of benefits provided. Many organizations will be willing to share this on an exchange basis—so that they can benefit from learning the comparable data from your organization. This information should be summarized for the board, showing the lowest, highest, and average salary level for each staff position, together with the range of offered benefits. This helps establish norms for the industry (although local cost-of-living adjustments may be appropriate before compensation levels are set).

Next, the organization's budget should be studied for answers to the following questions:

- How much can realistically be expended on personnel?
- How much is necessary for non-personnel-related administrative costs (rent, telephone, postage, office supplies, and so on)?
- Is there enough left over for the organization to carry out its programs and activities, or is the ratio of administrative costs to total budget too high?

If it turns out that administrative costs are too high, the organization may face some difficult choices. Can the staff structure be reworked without compromising the level of service provided? Can some work be done by volunteers, by consultants, by work-study students or interns, or by other organizations? Can more money be raised?

There may well not be enough money to pay what reasonable people will believe they ought to be earning. Yet, because compensation levels are so crucial in determining the kind of individual who will ultimately work for the organization, the board should know what the ideal salary and benefit packages look like for each position. Some organizations prepare a budget showing personnel costs at industry-standard levels. A resulting deficit created by this higher compensation level is called the staff contribution to the organization, and it is the trustees' responsibility to reduce that number as much and as quickly as possible.

Before any final decisions are made about compensation levels, consideration must be given to whether the organization needs an especially qualified and talented person for a particular job. If having a good fund raiser is a priority, the trustees may decide to favor a high salary in the development area. If someone with experience in social media is necessary and there is a shortage of professionals in the area, it may be necessary to bring the salary of this individual up to a level more closely comparable to the level in the for-profit sector. Keep in mind, though, that when two individuals on the same level on the organization chart know they are earning substantially different amounts, this can undermine morale.

High salaries are controversial in nonprofit organizations, but they may be necessary to attract top-flight people. One device that some organizations use to justify the cost of expensive employees is to contract them out to other institutions on a time-available basis at a cost that earns substantial dollars for the organization. The employees must be willing, of course, and the employer should be careful that the organization's own needs are not compromised. Once the arrangement is finalized, it should be fully documented in the employee's job description. An example of how the arrangement might work follows:

The executive director of the Compton Hospital is an expert in hospital cost containment. His total annual compensation (salary plus benefits) is $225,000. Taking into account holidays, weekends, vacation days, and so on, the actual number of working days per year is 220; thus the director costs the hospital approximately $1,000 per day. Yet it turns out that other organizations are willing to pay a fee of $3,000 per day plus expenses for the director to come consult with them about cost containment. The hospital and the director have come to an agreement that he will consult on hospital time for fifteen days a year at a rate of $3,000 per day. The hospital takes in $45,000 for these fifteen release days, effectively reducing the $225,000 compensation package to $180,000. The hospital is responsible for contracting for the days and handling all billing and collections.

Once salary and benefits discussions have been completed, the trustees must set a salary range for each class of positions—executive director, assistant directors, program directors, coordinators, program assistants, clerical-secretarial, and so on. The top dollar figure in a range should be 15 to 30 percent higher than the bottom figure. If someone with relatively little experience is offered a job, he or she will probably be offered a salary near the bottom of the range but will be able to receive annual merit increases with more experience. Someone coming to the job with plenty of credentials and lots of experience will be offered a salary at a level nearer the top of the range. Ranges should be reviewed approximately every two to three years to ensure that they are still competitive.

Exempt versus nonexempt employees and overtime. Most employees will be covered by the Department of Labor's Fair Labor Standards Act (FLSA), which establishes minimum wage, overtime pay, record-keeping, and youth-employment standards affecting employees in the private sector and in federal, state, and local governments. One of its most important provisions relates to exempt versus nonexempt employees. Nonexempt employees are entitled to overtime pay. Exempt employees are not.

Some jobs are classified as exempt by definition. But for most employees, whether they are exempt or nonexempt depends on how much they are paid, how they are paid, and what kind of work they do. Most employees must meet all three "tests" to be exempt:

- *The salary-level test*—FLSA publishes an annual salary level under which employees must be paid overtime.
- *The salary-basis test*—Employees paid on a salaried basis cannot claim overtime.
- *The duties test*—These are some examples of responsibilities that would determine whether a job is exempt:
  - regularly supervises two or more other employees
  - has management as the primary duty of the position, and also,
  - has some genuine input into the job status of other employees.

In many nonprofit organizations the assumption is that people will work hard and that extra time they put in is an uncompensated part of their job. But this is not so, and some find themselves owing back pay to an employee who has been documenting hours and is nonexempt. Nor is the title of a job sufficient to ensure it is in an exempt or non-exempt category. Tests will be applied no matter what the job is called. It is best to carefully determine which employees are nonexempt, carefully keep records of hours worked, and either ensure that they do not work extra hours or budget for overtime pay.

Benefits. Today it is not uncommon for prospective employees to look as carefully at benefits packages offered by nonprofit organizations as at salary ranges. This is not surprising. With medical costs rising at a rate far higher than the inflation rate and with a number of factors making retirement seem more like a curse than a blessing, people want to know what the employer will do in these areas. Individual medical plans are expensive, so prospective employees will want to know whether there is a group plan available through the employer and what percentage of the cost the employer will pay. There will be questions about retirement benefits, disability insurance, life insurance, and other potential benefits. More prosaic benefits such as paid holidays, personal days, sick days, paid vacation, and so on will also need to be decided on by the board and documented for the employees.

In determining benefits, the first thing the trustees might do is set a target percentage-of-total-salaries figure on which to base the benefits package. For example, suppose the organization says that an amount equal to 15 percent of the total annual payroll will be paid to the employees in the form of extras. With that figure as a target, they can then determine which combination of benefits is best and how they should be allocated. In some cases, every employee will receive the same percentage of his or her salary in benefits. In other cases, the amount and percentage will vary depending on salary level, years of service, and other variables. Surveying similar organizations may be useful in attempting to come up with the best combination of benefits (published salary surveys that contain benefits information may be available from national service organizations). Keep in mind that nonprofit organizations have been slow to introduce adequate benefits packages, and newer organizations may want to err on the side of generosity in this area.

In budgeting benefits, it is important to leave some unallocated dollars for such employee-related expenses as workers' compensation and state unemployment insurance,[2] which are technically not considered part of the benefits package. Also, a percentage of the benefits package may be held in escrow for discretionary extras such as attendance at conferences, tuition assistance for work-related special courses, or other activities that may be made available to certain employees when they are requested and approved by a supervisor. Some organizations find the "cafeteria" model popular in which each employee is allocated a certain amount of dollar value that can be distributed among a variety of options.

In addition to querying other organizations, trustees may be able to get expertise about benefits options from benefits consultants, independent insurance agents, or the organization's accountant or lawyer. Reliable advice may also be available on the board of trustees, particularly from businesspeople. Larger nonprofit organizations in particular should seek specialized expertise since they may find themselves subject to specific legal requirements and language for nonprofit organizations. For example, employers with more than fifty employees are subject to requirements of the federal Family and Medical Leave Act of 1993. For these organizations, it is best to check with a specialist in personnel issues. However, for any organization, the complexity of the subject and the plethora of choices may make it desirable to make a special effort to recruit a trustee with relevant experience in this area. This same trustee might also chair a personnel committee, if the board decides to have one.

SETTING POLICIES AND PROCEDURES

After an organization has set the three basic parameters for personnel just discussed, the most important work is done. However, it is desirable to establish additional policies and procedures as follows:

- Employment and pay procedures
- Staff evaluation procedures
- Conflict-of-interest policies
- Termination and grievance procedures
- Sexual harassment policies
- General office practices and procedures

The clearer the policies in each of these areas, the less chance there is for misunderstandings. In addition, organizations that have documented policies in each of these areas are more favorably regarded by government enforcing agencies, prospective trustees, employees, and funders.

Employment and Pay Procedures

Most employees are interested in knowing as much as they can about an organization's hiring policy.

- How are employees hired and is there a formal process with public notice required?
- Are current employees given first preference for a job vacancy?
- Is there an affirmative action policy?
- Is hiring done solely on the basis of competence and qualifications?
- Is every prospective employee allowed to see a job description?

There is also interest in the question of what happens to an employee once he or she is hired.

- Is there an official training period?
- Do temporary or permanent part-time employees enjoy the same rights and benefits as full-time employees?
- How often are salary ranges and job classifications reviewed and by whom?

Another series of questions focuses on pay procedures.

- How often and in what form are employees paid?
- What opportunity is there for merit raises and are there periodic cost-of-living increases?
- Is extra pay available for extra work?

There are no right answers to these questions, but they do provide a kind of checklist of items that the board may wish to discuss and resolve. There are always a number of options and points of view. On the question of promotion from within, for example, organizational loyalty tends to be developed when employees view advancement as the reward for good work. Thus promotion from within can be a goal that the board and executive director decide to make into an explicit policy. On the other hand, a desire for fresh vision by top management may suggest that, in the case of the executive director's position and positions of senior staff, outsiders be given preference.

Documenting each and every policy once it is decided on is important. If the organization is vigorously attempting to attract minorities and other special constituencies onto the staff, for example, it is important to state this and have a clearly written affirmative action policy. The morale of employees can be badly bruised when such practices and preferences of the board are not made explicit. On the matter of training periods for new employees, many organizations and employees find them useful, as there is an understanding on both sides that the immediate performance expectations may be less rigorous.

Staff Evaluation Procedures

A prospective employee should be made aware of the process by which his or her performance will be evaluated, by whom, how often, and whether salary increases depend on a formal review process. In many organizations, an employee's supervisor meets with the employee once a year for a formal evaluation (the executive director's review, described in chapter 2, is conducted by the president of the board). A series of questions relating to the job description, performance, employee satisfaction, and supervisor satisfaction forms the basis of a discussion. For example:

- Which aspects of your job do you consider to be of highest priority and of lowest priority?
- Are there tasks that you are required to perform that are not in your job description, and if so, do you feel they should be added to the description or given to someone else?
- Are the demands on your time reasonable?
- Have there been aspects of your job that you have had to neglect for lack of time?
- How well do you feel you are getting along with your coworkers?
- What suggestions do you have about how you could be more productive?
- Do you get enough supervision or too much?
- Is this the right job for you? Which areas are most appealing, and which are least appealing?
- Which aspects of your job have you completed most successfully in the last six months, and which aspects least successfully?
- What do you hope to accomplish in the next six months in your job?
- Other comments, complaints, observations, and questions?

Many organizations follow a practice of employee self evaluation—that is, the employee submits a written draft of his or her evaluation (or the answers to the questions posed), and then that forms the basis for the supervisor/employee discussion. Then either the employee or the supervisor writes a final document (often the supervisor likes to write the final document as it gives him or her more control over what is written). In addition to discussing the employee's replies to the questions, the supervisor gives his or her impressions of the strengths and weaknesses of the employee's performance and discusses job objectives for the coming year.

Once a document is completed, both the employee and the supervisor review it, decide on any changes, and sign it. The executive director reviews the document and may decide to intervene if a problem seems to be brewing. Otherwise, the document becomes the basis for a decision regarding a merit increase in salary and ultimately becomes a part of the organization's personnel records.

Conflict-of-Interest Policies

Conflict of interest was discussed in chapter 2 in connection with trustees of nonprofit organizations, and it is also relevant in this chapter in regard to staff. Like trustees, if staff members are involved in a decision that could substantially benefit themselves, their family members, or others close to them, there can be an appearance that the decision was not arrived at objectively, that there was conflict of interest. In most cases, the benefit will be a financial one, though not always. If a staff person of a university sits on the university's admissions committee, he or she has a conflict of interest if involved in a committee decision to admit a child or other relative.

Because nonprofit organizations are so clearly mandated to have a broad public purpose and not to serve the parochial interests of board and staff, conflict of interest can have particularly negative connotations. For that reason, conflict-of-interest policies should be developed that state clearly how the organization will handle such sensitive situations.

The key to sound policies in this area is what is called *disclosure*. This is because it is not always inappropriate for people to be involved in decisions that may benefit them or a member of their families so long as the nature of the situation is clear to everyone else voting on the matter. Consider, for example, Joan Simons, the Information/ Technology Manager of the Compton Community Center. She has decided to purchase computer equipment from her husband's company. The company is extending a 35 percent discount, which is a better deal for the center than any other vendor in the city will offer. Thus no one questions the propriety of the decision. Nevertheless, it is important for Joan Simons to disclose the nature of her conflict of interest to her supervisor and seek approval before proceeding. In some cases, it may be appropriate for the supervisor to get the approval of the executive director or the board itself, particularly when large sums of money are involved. Conflict-of-interest policies do not necessarily prevent a financial transaction or any other kind of action from taking place, but they do ensure an objective review and decision on the issue based on a disclosure of all the facts.

There are times when a conflict situation can have a blatant appearance of self-interest. Suppose an organization had to decide whether to buy a piece of property from the executive director, who himself had purchased the property only one year before. In this situation, it is unclear whether the executive director acted in good faith in purchasing the property or whether his decision was based on knowledge that the organization would be interested in purchasing it later on. In such a situation, it may be appropriate for the organization's conflict-of-interest policies to indicate that an outside impartial review of such situations will always precede any kind of legal action. Because conflict-of-interest situations can vary so greatly in nature and because the appropriate response to them is not uniform, it is advantageous to secure the help of an attorney in drafting appropriate language for conflict-of-interest policies.

Termination and Grievance Procedures

Almost every organization is burdened at one time or another with an employee who simply does not work out. As unpleasant as it is to ask someone to leave, sometimes it is necessary for the good of the organization, the other employees, and the individual in question. By the same token, in any hierarchical organization, employees are somewhat at the mercy of their supervisors, and there must be organizational safeguards to protect them.

There are some offenses an employee may commit that are grounds for immediate dismissal. These include falsification of information given for personnel records, drug use during working hours, theft, violence in the workplace, and gross insubordination. In most cases where a supervisor is unhappy with an employee's performance, however, the situation requires a more moderate response because the problem is not as clear-cut. As soon as there are any grounds for concern, the supervisor must begin to keep detailed written records of problems, offenses, and discussions that include dates, times, and places. Without such a record, it becomes much more difficult to justify termination of an employee, and in some cases, such action may actually be illegal.

In addition to keeping written documentation, it is generally a good idea for a supervisor to ask for a preliminary meeting with an employee once it is clear that there is a problem. A verbal warning would be issued at this point with a note to the supervisor's file indicating that the discussion was held. The next stage is a more formal meeting with a written record, signed by both parties, and placed in the personnel file of the employee. The document should summarize the nature of the supervisor's criticism, the employee's response, and the specific job objectives and performance criteria to be used to evaluate that employee's performance in the future. A date should also be set for another meeting to review the employee's progress in the job. In cases where the performance of the employee is so poor that the supervisor thinks termination is a real possibility, the period between the first meeting and the second should be called probationary with the understanding that if performance does not improve, the employee will be asked to resign or be fired.

If an employee has a grievance regarding treatment, working conditions, or other matters, the complaint is usually taken up first with that employee's supervisor. If after an initial meeting, or series of meetings, the employee feels that the matter is not satisfactorily resolved, the employee can request a meeting with the person to whom his or her supervisor reports. (This meeting may or may not be with all three present.) In the case where the employee's complaint is with the executive director, the complaint is referred to the chairman of the personnel committee of the board or the board president. In all cases, it is the third individual consulted, the one with the highest position in the organization, who serves as the final arbiter of the problem.

Once an organization sets its policies on warnings, grievances, dismissals, and so on, it should follow them. Though under the concept of "employment at will" an organization can terminate employees at any time for any reason, it is the height of folly for employers to have a policy and not follow it. Policy language should use the word *should* rather than *must* to allow for the rare exceptions where policies are not followed. Given how difficult matters of termination can be and the various legal actions an employee might resort to (which, even if unsuccessful, can be time-consuming and expensive), it is sometimes preferable to offer an employee an opportunity to resign rather than begin what can be a long and unpleasant process leading to termination. A generous severance payment may be all that is required, and the resignation (which should be made in writing) prevents the employee from qualifying for unemployment insurance that, at the very least, would lead to higher premium payments.

Sexual Harassment Policies

While there is no federal legislation that requires nonprofit organizations to have a sexual harassment policy, several states do require it, and a series of Supreme Court rulings in the 1990s suggest that it is a good idea to have such a policy and to enforce it. A comprehensive and enforced policy provides employees with a mechanism and procedures for dealing with their complaints, using established company channels before going to the extreme of bringing a lawsuit.

Two types of harassment should be covered. The first is quid pro quo harassment—when a supervisor threatens a form of punitive action or suggests the possibility of special treatment in return for sexual favors. The second is hostile environment harassment—comments, jokes, or gestures of a sexual nature. A nonprofit organization can be held liable if a supervisor engages in either form of harassment. However, if the organization has taken reasonable steps to prevent it, it is generally on safe ground. For example, if the organization has a sexual harassment policy that is enforced, it will likely prevail in a lawsuit, especially if the harassed employee failed to take advantage of that policy, though most courts have held that there is a standard of "known or should have known" and that simply having the policy may not be sufficient (a sample written policy can be found at the end of the chapter).

General Office Practices and Procedures

There are a host of little details relating to day-to-day work life that should be spelled out for employees. Some relate specifically to in-office procedures; some are more general. For example, there may be:

- Specific rules about how the staff is authorized to make purchases (through purchase orders, petty cash, or on a cash-reimbursable basis)
- Guidelines governing travel (such as per-diem limits, times when air travel is permitted, and mileage reimbursement rates)
- Controls on personal use of the office telephone
- Rules governing the use and care of office equipment
- Limits placed on the organization's liability for personal property left on the premises
- Guidelines governing outside work, such as whether the employer has first refusal on publications and whether the organization permits leaves of absence to do outside jobs
- Other intellectual property and confidentiality issues
- Policies regarding working hours and conditions that address regular office working hours, flextime or overtime arrangements, and overtime compensation.[3]

THE PERSONNEL MANUAL

Once all the organizational parameters and specific policies and procedures have been set and voted on by the board of trustees, they should be collected in one place—put between two covers as it were—and made available to current and prospective employees. Those experienced in personnel matters sometimes counsel organizations to allow employees to review a new manual or a new policy before it is finalized—not for their approval but to make sure they understand it and if there are questions or circumstances that the writer has not taken into account—to allow for adaptation or modification. A personnel manual is an essential document for any nonprofit organization that has more than seven or eight employees or a budget in excess of $500,000. (Many smaller organizations have personnel manuals as well.) A typical personnel manual table of contents might look something like that in figure 4.2.

Personnel manuals are only useful if they are kept up-to-date. Like job descriptions, they should be reviewed at least annually by the executive director (with help from a trustee or the board's personnel committee if appropriate). A good, clear personnel manual contributes to positive staff morale and prevents the kind of procedural ambiguity that often leads to problems. By comparing personnel manuals from well-managed nonprofits, an organization can distill those elements it considers most important before putting together its own. A more detailed example of a personnel manual can be found in figure 4.3.

Figure 4.2. Table of Contents of a Typical Personnel Manual

Personnel Policies, Procedures, and Benefits

Foreword: A brief description of the organization, its philosophy, purposes, and programs

Employment
  Basic Policies
  Hiring Procedures
  Interim (probationary) period
  Types of employment (full-time, part-time, temporary)
  Maintenance of personnel records

Working Hours and Conditions
  Office hours
  Flexible time
  Overtime
  Absence reports

Salaries and Wages
  Salary structure through job classification
  Paydays
  Deductions
  Raises (merit and cost-of-living)

Employee Benefits
  Waiting period
  Vacations
  Holidays
  Sick days
  Personal days
  Maternity leave
  Paternity leave
  Leave of absence
  Other excused absences

(continued on next page)

Figure 4.2. Table of Contents of a Typical Personnel Manual (cont.)

Personnel Policies, Procedures, and Benefits

Insurance, Retirement, and Other Benefits
  Social security
  Medical insurance
  Life insurance
  Disability insurance
  Unemployment insurance
  Workers' compensation
  Education fund

General Policies and Procedures
  Outside work
  Promotions
  Office closing
  Telephone
  Travel
  Personal property

General Office Practices and Procedures
  Office coverage
  Smoking
  Use and care of equipment

Performance and Salary Review
  Timing
  Procedures
  Considerations

Problems
  Grievances
  Suggestions
  Warnings

Sexual Harassment Policy

Termination
  Resignation
  Retirement
  Release
  Discharge
  Final pay

Organization Chart

Salary Ranges by Position

Conflict-of-Interest Policies

Personnel Evaluation and Review Procedure

Note: Job descriptions are generally not included in the personnel manual.

SPECIAL ISSUES INVOLVING CHIEF EXECUTIVES

The chief executive[4] of a nonprofit organization is often the single most important person in determining the effectiveness and morale of the staff, establishing the quality of the work environment, and projecting the organization's image in the community. Among the many special challenges that can be faced by nonprofit organizations in connection with chief executives are two that deserve special mention: the issues surrounding a founder/director and the problems associated with codirectors.

Founder/Directors

Nonprofit organizations often encounter special personnel challenges with regard to founders who ultimately become chief executives. The challenges are generally of three kinds.

First, because a founder/director is usually completely committed to the organization he or she has established, there is less likelihood that pressure will be put on the board to provide adequate compensation, staff support, and acceptable working conditions. In this regard, founder/directors generally do not know how to insist on fair treatment and, as a result, often do not receive it.

Second, as organizations develop, board members are usually content to allow founder/directors to continue their strong leadership. This may turn out to be harmful to the organization in two ways: If the organization is driven primarily by a founder/director, board members may fail to get sufficiently involved in decision making, and such an organization may provide the opportunity for trustees to avoid exerting themselves in critical areas of board responsibility such as fund raising. It may also lead to a crisis if the founder/director resigns.

Third, it is often the case that the individual with the vision, imagination, and entrepreneurial energy to be a founder is not the best person to be an organization's chief executive after a certain number of years. Yet boards are often reluctant to take steps to remove a founder/director.

How should an organization deal with these challenges? In the area of compensation, staff support, and working conditions, a member of the board (or a personnel committee) should regularly interview or survey individuals who are knowledgeable about the organization's industry (representatives from national service organizations, funders, administrators, and trustees from similar organizations). These individuals should be asked what a fair compensation package should include (salary level and benefits) and should be asked specific questions about numbers of staff people, job responsibilities of the chief executive, and working conditions that they would expect to see in such an organization.

In the area of defining the appropriate respective roles for the founder/director and the board, it is often useful to bring in an objective outsider who can assess the organization's needs, interview both the director and the trustees, and make recommendations based on the experiences of other organizations. While it may be possible for those involved to redefine their relationship, unfortunately they are often so close to the situation, and the subject is such a sensitive one, that the discussion breaks down and results in hard feelings rather than productive solutions.

Finally, what happens when it becomes clear that the founder/director is not the best person to be the chief executive? In some instances, the solution may be quite straightforward, particularly when the individual in question has ability and a fundamental interest in the programs of the organization and is simply weak as a chief administrator and staff supervisor. In this case, it may be possible to shift the individual to a senior staff position in the organization—a position relating to programs—and bring in another individual to serve as the chief executive. To accomplish such a transition is not easy, but many organizations have pulled it off. To be successful, the founder/director has to welcome the move as an opportunity to focus on his or her area of interest, not as a slap in the face and a demotion. Otherwise, the new chief executive will have a very difficult time and a recalcitrant staff person undermining the effective operation of the organization.

Sometimes it becomes clear to boards of directors of nonprofit organizations that their founder/directors really must move on. This situation is awkward and unenviable. How do board presidents tell founder/directors that their organizations have grown beyond them, that their boards or staffs (or both) are dissatisfied with their performance, that their organizations require chief executives with different skills? And how can these founder/directors be properly rewarded for their substantial contributions even when they are being asked to step down from their positions?

These questions are difficult ones because, in most cases, a founder/ director has made a substantial emotional investment in his or her organization. In addition, while the founder/director may or may not have invested cash in the organization, it is almost a certainty that he or she has made a contribution by way of substantial donated time and by accepting a compensation package that was not competitive, at least in the earliest days of the organization's history. Board members, taking these things into account, often tolerate an untenable situation for far too long, sometimes putting an organization at risk and almost always undermining the morale of those connected with it.

Given the emotional and financial issues involved, the board should decide on a course that addresses both. First, a great effort should be made to secure a resignation with honor rather than a termination with acknowledgment of failure. Addressing the emotional side of the action, the board should be prepared to take certain steps that will ac- knowledge the founder/director's accomplishments and importance to the organization. The individual's name (with the title Founder) might be listed on all stationery and promotional material above the names of the board members. A special effort might be made with the media to do feature stories celebrating the fine work of the individual (at the very least, press releases should talk about the board's acceptance of the resignation with profound regret and a statement by the president of the board highlighting the important contributions of the founder/ director to the organization).

On the financial side, the board should be prepared to offer a gen- erous severance package. From the point of view of organizational self-interest, such a settlement often encourages a speedy and painless resignation by the founder/director. However, in a more generous way, it recognizes the financial sacrifices of the individual over the years. It is also likely that after many years of energetic commitment to a single organization, the individual will need some time to decompress and adjust before seeking other employment, and the additional compen- sation offers this opportunity.

Finally, some organizations take the step of placing a resigning founder/director on the board as a way of rewarding him or her and not severing entirely the connection between the individual and the organization. While this sometimes works well, more often than not it causes problems. The founder/director cannot step back from the day-to-day operational issues and often confounds and frustrates the work of his or her successor. This step, while certainly symbolically advantageous, is usually not practically worthwhile.

Codirectors

A second issue faced by some nonprofit organizations concerns the desire to have more than one chief executive. In some organizations, where there are two staff hierarchies, such a structure makes sense. For example, in a symphony orchestra, there is generally a music director (the conductor) and an executive director (who serves as chief of administration). The first makes all personnel decisions regarding musicians, while the second hires all other staff. Both individuals report to the board of directors, and each has a well-defined area of responsibility. However, in other organizations, the codirector structure causes problems. Consider the following case.

WILDERNESS SERVICE AMERICA

Wilderness Service America (WSA) is a national membership organization whose primary purpose is to provide information, funding, and a national advocacy voice to local organizations in the conservation field. Originally formed at the behest of and with funding from a national foundation, WSA was created through the merger of two national organizations with overlapping activities and mission. The national foundation, which was funding both, threatened to cut off its support unless a merger plan could be worked out. Consequently, the boards of the two organizations agreed to form a single organization, and it was further agreed that the two executive directors, who were friendly and shared a mutual respect, would serve as codirectors.

Initially the structure worked well, and the newly merged board felt itself lucky to have two individuals with such eminence in the field. However, within three years, a consultant's evaluation of the organization, based on confidential interviews, revealed several problems with the codirector structure:

- WSA's directors of marketing, fund raising, and programs

all complained that they never knew to whom to report. On paper, both of the codirectors were to be consulted on key decisions. But rarely were they both in the office at the same time, and when they were, they did not always seem to agree on important matters. Senior staff also confessed that they were beginning to learn how each codirector would react to certain questions, and they would go to one or the other depending on what kind of an answer they wanted.

- Board members complained that they never knew who was responsible for what. Said one, "Whenever I would ask one codirector for clarification on an important decision or action, I was referred to the other who, inevitably, was out of the office. Sometimes, when I finally reached the second codirector, he claimed that the subject I was interested in really wasn't something he was familiar with. I am losing confidence in the system."

- One major foundation representative complained, "Shared accountability is no accountability. If I am giving half a million dollars, I want to know who to call when I need to know about our investment."

In following up on these comments, the consultant found that there was a well-designed organization chart with functions and responsibilities clearly divided. But what existed on paper was not carried out in fact, and because the chief executive position was shared, ambiguity and opportunities for misunderstandings crept into the system.

In thinking about Wilderness Service America and other organizations that have experimented with codirectors, it is important to acknowledge that there are organizations that have been successful with various kinds of shared authority arrangements. There are even a few organizations—some that have survived for decades—in which all major decisions are made collectively by the whole staff. But these organizations are rare, and the number of instances of shared power arrangements that have failed far outnumber those that have survived.

It is generally the case that a conventional hierarchical structure will work best in most nonprofit organizations. When it comes to the chief executive, the outside world and the employees are looking for a single individual whose level of authority and accountability are higher than anyone else's on the staff.

THE VALUE OF EMPLOYEES

Nonprofit organizations can be very special places to work, and their employees are often especially committed people. Many could earn more money in other kinds of organizations, but they may be attracted to the nonprofit because of what it contributes to the quality of their lives and the lives of others.

Therefore, it is important for the organization to state explicitly in the personnel manual that it regards its employees as one of its most valuable assets. This attitude should also be demonstrated by the interest and compassion that the trustees show toward the staff. It is the trustees' responsibility to set policies that contribute to a harmonious and productive work environment. It is also the trustees' responsibility to praise work that is well done and reward employees who give generously of themselves. Clear and fair personnel policies themselves are only a part of the organization's obligation to the employees. The other part is a positive and caring attitude that reflects the respect and admiration that the employees have earned. In nonprofit organizations particularly, this latter obligation must never be forgotten.

Figure 4.3. A Detailed Example of a Personnel Manual

Compton Community Center Personnel Policies, Procedures, and Benefits

Foreword

The Compton Community Center is a nonprofit corporation designated as a 501(c)(3) tax-exempt organization by the Internal Revenue Service. It was founded in 1966 to provide recreational opportunities to young people in the Compton community.

The Compton Community Center considers its staff its most valuable asset. Furthermore, it believes that a clear understanding of the working agreement between the Compton Community Center and its employees is the basis for a harmonious and productive environment. This document has been developed to explain, in as specific a manner as possible, what the Compton Community Center offers to and asks of its staff.

Policies are not immutable, conditions and attitudes do change, and there may be situations in which exceptions to these policies are appropriate. Suggestions are always welcomed. It is, furthermore, an underlying assumption of this manual that special and unique situations may be resolved through the cooperative efforts of all concerned.

Working Hours and Conditions

Overtime/Compensatory time: In most circumstances, the Compton Community Center does not recognize overtime for exempt employees. There may be some circumstances in which time off will be granted to exempt employees in recognition of the unusual amount of time required by a project or undertaking. All requests for compensatory time must be made in advance to an employee's supervisor. Overtime for nonexempt employees will be provided in accordance with legal requirements.

Absence reports: If, owing to an unforeseen emergency, an employee is unable to be at work, he or she should notify his or her immediate supervisor by 9:30 AM on the first day of absence. If the absence extends beyond one day, the supervisor should be kept informed. An employee should attempt to estimate the likely duration of his or her absence.

Each employee should keep his or her supervisor informed of any planned future absences (vacation, holiday, personal day, leave, and travel). In all instances, provisions should be made to ensure that office deadlines are met and requests from clients are covered.

Salaries and Wages

Payday: Employees are paid by check on the fifteenth and final day of each month. If a payday falls on a weekend or holiday, payment will be made on the preceding workday.

Advance payment of salaries is not made except in the case of a vacation paycheck.

Deductions: The federal and state governments require employers to withhold income tax from each employee's paycheck. Employees, therefore, must complete W-4 forms in order to indicate the number of exemptions claimed and to authorize the Compton Community Center to make the appropriate withholdings. Any change in an employee's number of exemptions *requires the filing of a new W-4 form.*

Raises: Each employee is reviewed annually on the anniversary date of his or her hire. Raises will be based on formal and regular review of each employee's performance during the past year.

Employee Benefits

Waiting period: The first month of employment is considered a waiting period. During this time, employees are not eligible for certain benefits. These include the accrual of vacation time and medical insurance. After the interim period, employees are entitled to all the benefits outlined in this section.

Vacation: All full-time employees with less than two years of service will accrue vacation leave at the rate of one day per month up to a total of ten days per year. Full-time employees with two to ten years of service will accrue vacation up to a total of fifteen days per year; those with ten or more years of service will accrue vacation up to a total of twenty days per year. Vacation leave is credited on the last day of each month worked.

The Compton Community Center believes that vacations serve a purpose and that it is advisable for persons to take vacations regularly. For this reason, no employee may carry forward into any year more than one year's credit of vacation days.

Vacation may be taken at any time following three months of service provided that the timing is approved by the employee's supervisor. Vacations may be taken at any time during the year, but not in advance of being earned. However, because all vacation schedules must be approved and coordinated to ensure continued efficient work flow, it may not always be possible for vacations to be taken in a single unbroken period. The Compton Community Center will, however, attempt to meet all requested vacation schedules, but to do so, it is important that employees indicate their vacation preferences as far in advance as possible. Preference will be given on the basis of work schedules and requirements, and employee seniority,

Holidays: The following holidays are customarily observed by the Compton Community Center, and the office will be closed on these days:

New Year's Day	January 1
Martin Luther King Day	Third Monday in January
Presidents' Day	Third Monday in February
Memorial Day	Last Monday in May
Independence Day	July 4
Labor Day	First Monday in September
Columbus Day	Second Monday in October
Veterans' Day	November 11
Thanksgiving Day (and day after)	Last Thursday and Friday in November
Christmas Day	December 25
One Floating Holiday	Elective

If any of these holidays falls on a weekend, it will be observed on the Friday before or the Monday after, at the discretion of the executive director.

Holidays that fall during an employee's scheduled vacation entitle that employee to another vacation day at his or her discretion.

Sick days: Sick leave is to be used only in the event of actual sickness and not for personal days. Sick leave is available to each employee up to two months' leave, at the discretion of the executive director.

Personal days: Each employee is entitled to three personal-day absences per year. A personal day is a planned absence not chargeable to the vacation category. Personal days are available in half-day increments, are credited to each employee at the beginning of his or her working year, and are always subject to prior approval by the employee's supervisor. Personal emergencies, not involving employee illness, may be charged to the personal-day category.

Personal days may not be carried forward from one year to the next, nor do they constitute a monetary claim against the Compton Community Center if unused at the termination of an employee's service.

Maternity leave: An employee may be granted up to four weeks' maternity leave with pay and an additional eight weeks of unpaid leave provided that her immediate supervisor is given at least two weeks' notice of the anticipated date of departure. An employee's intention to return to work should also be verified at this time.

An employee may work for as long as she wishes prior to delivery, as long as her health allows her to fulfill her regular duties.

Upon return from maternity leave, an employee will assume whatever position, authority, and level of seniority she held prior to the leave. Regular benefits will continue to accrue during the leave.

After the first four weeks of maternity leave, an employee may apply whatever accrued vacation time she may have against the time she is absent. If during any portion of this leave an employee becomes sick or disabled, she will be eligible for regular sickness benefits.

Paternity leave: Under certain circumstances a father may wish to assume family duties following the birth of a child. The Compton Community Center, therefore, offers two weeks' paid and an additional two weeks of unpaid paternity leave. The same conditions apply to paternity leave as to maternity leave.

Leave of absence: A leave of absence is defined as an approved absence, without pay, of a limited and specified duration. It does not, therefore, constitute a break in service, although no benefits are accrued during the leave.

A written request for any leave of absence in excess of five working days must be submitted to the executive director at least one month prior to the beginning of the leave. Shorter leaves of absence may be approved verbally by an employee's supervisor.

Unused vacation days may be applied against an approved leave of absence.

Unless expressly stated otherwise in writing by the executive director, a leave of absence in excess of six months will constitute a break in service. A returning employee cannot be guaranteed his or her previous position although every effort will be made to provide a comparable situation. Benefits and seniority will accrue from zero beginning with the date of rehiring.

Jury duty leave is granted by the Compton Community Center with the understanding that any employee will clear such leave with his or her supervisor prior to departure. The Compton Community Center will pay the difference between the employee's juror fee and his or her regular rate of pay.

Medical insurance: The Compton Community Center currently participates in the Compton Community Health Plan, a local health maintenance organization. Full medical insurance coverage is part of every full-time employee's benefits. Employees are urged to read the prospectus of the Compton Community Health Plan carefully to learn precisely what coverage is available to them.

Social security: As required by law, the Compton Community Center participates in the social security system. The organization withholds a certain percentage of an employee's salary, which it matches with organizational funds. There are no additional retirement benefits offered to employees.

Unemployment insurance: All staff members are covered by the State Unemployment Insurance Program. Eligibility and waiting periods depend on the reason for termination of employment.

Workers' compensation: The Compton Community Center carries compensation insurance in accordance with the requirements of state law. This insurance provides benefit payments to an employee who is injured while working for the Compton Community Center or becomes ill or disabled from any occupation-related situation.

General Policies and Procedures

Office closing: If the office is to be closed because of inclement weather or other emergencies, each employee will be notified by email as early as possible. The closing decision will be made by the executive director, and it is assumed that employees will follow this decision.

Telephones: Compton Community Center telephones are necessary for business purposes. The number of phone lines is limited, and it is therefore requested that employees keep personal calls to a minimum.

Office coverage: It is essential that the office and the telephone be staffed at all times from 9:00 AM to 5:00 PM. Staggered lunch breaks should therefore be arranged among staff. Employees leaving the office should tell the person answering the phones where they will be and when they will return.

Smoking: No smoking is allowed in the Compton Community Center offices.

Performance and Salary Review

Timing: An employee's performance review takes place annually, on or near the anniversary date of his or her hire. Salary review takes place annually.

Procedure: The salary review process may result in three categories of determination:

1. An employee's work is found to be more than satisfactory and consistent with the objectives for the position. A merit raise may be recommended. All decisions on merit increases are made by the executive director based on a variety of factors such as general economic climate, normal salary range for the job, and so on.

2. An employee's work is found to be generally satisfactory but not wholly consistent with the objectives set for the position. The employee will be informed as to his or her areas of satisfactory performance and those areas that need strengthening. A specific plan for improving performance in the specified areas will be worked out with the employee's supervisor. A minimum merit raise or no raise may be recommended at the discretion of the employee's immediate supervisor.

3. An employee's performance is found to fall below satisfactory standards and not to approach stated job objectives. The employee will be warned of this situation by his or her supervisor, the specifics of the unsatisfactory performance will be discussed, and a performance-improvement plan will be implemented. No merit raise will be awarded.

Sexual Harassment Policy

Introduction: It is the goal of the Compton Community Center to promote a workplace that is free of sexual harassment. Sexual harassment of employees occurring in the workplace or in other settings in which employees may find themselves in connection with their employment is unlawful and will not be tolerated by this organization. Further, any retaliation against an individual who has complained about sexual harassment or retaliation against individuals for cooperating with an investigation of a sexual harass-ment complaint is similarly unlawful and will not be tolerated. To achieve our goal of providing a workplace free from sexual harassment, the conduct that is described in this policy will not be tolerated, and we have provided a procedure by which inappropriate conduct will be dealt with if encountered by employees. Because the Compton Community Center takes allegations of sexual harassment seriously, we will respond promptly to complaints of sexual harassment, and where it is determined that such inappropriate con-duct has occurred, we will act promptly to eliminate the conduct and impose such corrective action as is necessary, including disciplinary action where appropriate. Please note that while this policy sets forth our goals of promot-ing a workspace that is free of sexual harassment, the policy is not designed or intended to limit our authority to discipline or take remedial action for workplace conduct that we deem unacceptable, regardless of whether that conduct satisfies the definition of sexual harassment.

Definition of sexual harassment: The definition of sexual harassment is set forth as follows: *"sexual harassment" means sexual advances, requests for sexual favors, and verbal or physical conduct of a sexual nature when:*

(a) submission to or rejection of such advances, requests, or conduct is made either explicitly or implicitly a term or condition of employment or as a basis for employment decisions, or

(b) such advances, requests, or conduct have the purpose or effect of unreasonably interfering with an individual's work performance by creat-ing an intimidating, hostile, humiliating, or sexually offensive work environ-ment.

Under these definitions, direct or implied requests by a supervisor for sexual favors in exchange for actual or promised job benefits, such as fa-vorable reviews, salary increases, promotions, increased benefits, or con-tinued employment, constitute sexual harassment. The definition of sexual harassment is broad, and in addition to the above examples, other sexually oriented conduct, whether it is intended or not, that is unwelcome and has the effect of creating a workplace environment that is hostile, offensive, intimidating, or humiliating to male or female workers may also constitute sexual harassment.

While it is not possible to list all those additional circumstances that may constitute sexual harassment, the following are some examples of conduct that, if unwelcome, may constitute sexual harassment depending on the totality of the circumstances, including the severity of the conduct and its pervasiveness:

- Unwelcome sexual advances—whether they involve physical touching or not
- Sexual epithets or jokes, written or oral references to sexual conduct, gossip regarding one's sex life, comments on an individual's sexual activity, deficiencies, or prowess
- Displaying sexually suggestive objects, pictures, cartoons
- Unwelcome leering, whistling, brushing against the body, sexual gestures, suggestive or insulting comments
- Inquiries into an individual's sexual experiences
- Discussion of one's sexual activities

All employees should take special note that, as stated above, retaliation against an individual who has complained about sexual harassment and retaliation against individuals for cooperating with an investigation of a sexual harassment complaint are unlawful and will not be tolerated by this organization.

Complaints of sexual harassment: If any employee believes that he or she has been subjected to sexual harassment, the employee has the right to file a complaint with our organization. This may be done in writing or orally.

If you would like to file a complaint, you may do so by contacting [name of sexual harassment officer]. This person is also available to discuss any concerns you may have and to provide information to you about our policy on sexual harassment and our complaint process.

Sexual harassment investigation: When we receive a complaint, we will promptly investigate the allegation in a fair and expeditious manner. The investigation will be conducted in such a way as to maintain confidentiality to the extent practicable under the circumstances. Our investigation will include a private interview with the person filing the complaint and with witnesses. We will also interview the person alleged to have committed sexual harassment. When we have completed our investigation, we will, to the extent appropriate, inform the person filing the complaint and the person alleged to have committed the conduct of the results of that investigation.

If it is determined that inappropriate conduct has occurred, we will act promptly to eliminate the offending conduct, and where it is appropriate, we will also impose disciplinary action.

Disciplinary action: If it is determined that inappropriate conduct has been committed by one of our employees, we will take such action as is appropriate under the circumstances. Such action may range from counseling to termination of employment and may include such other forms of disciplinary action as we deem appropriate under the circumstances.

State and federal remedies: If you believe you have been subjected to sexual harassment, in addition to the above, you may file a formal complaint with government agencies. Using the company's complaint process does not prohibit you from filing a complaint with these agencies.

Termination

Resignation: An employee wishing to resign from the Compton Community Center should so indicate to his or her supervisor, in writing, at least two weeks prior to the date of resignation. It is requested that an employee who has resigned set aside at least one hour so that the executive director and the supervisor of the employee may discuss his or her reasons for leaving.

Discharge: Employees who are discharged by the Compton Community Center following warnings for inappropriate behavior or employees discharged without warning for serious offenses are not eligible for severance pay. Employees discharged owing to job elimination may be eligible for severance.

Final pay: Prior to the issuance of a final paycheck, an employee must return all keys, books, or other Compton Community Center property.

CHECKLIST QUESTIONS FOR CHAPTER 4

1. Does your organization have an organization chart that clearly and unambiguously shows chains of employee authority and accountability?
2. Are there job descriptions for all employees in your organization? Are they up-to-date?
3. Are compensation scales realistic and fair in your organization?
4. Are employee benefits comparable to those in other nonprofit organizations of similar size? If salaries and benefits are not adequate, is there a plan to address this issue?
5. Has your organization clearly documented its hiring and pay procedures? Is there a formal evaluation procedure for every employee in your organization? Have grievance and termination procedures been developed?
6. Has your organization developed conflict-of-interest policies for employees? Is there a sexual harassment policy?
7. Does your organization have a personnel manual? Is it complete and up-to-date?

FIVE
Marketing

Abbott Academy is a prestigious coeducational secondary school in New England. As a college-preparatory day school serving approximately two hundred students, Abbott was historically known for several things—its outstanding teachers, its demanding curriculum, its tough grading policy, its urban campus, and its requirement that all students spend a specified amount of time doing some form of public service.

In what one of its graduates called Abbott's "glory days," the *Simpson Guide to Private Schools* wrote glowingly of the school:

> *If you care about providing an outstanding education to your child, Abbott Academy should rank high on your list of secondary schools. Its graduates all are admitted to prestigious colleges: one year, almost a third of the class ended up at Harvard or Yale. The tuition is kept considerably below that of comparable institutions thanks to a large endowment and continuing annual support from its founder, Joseph Abbott. As a result of Mr. Abbott's generosity, parents are not asked to make contributions to the school as occurs in most comparable institutions. Some say that when a child is accepted at Abbott, he or she has gained a passport to success in college and later life.*
>
> *But don't get your hopes up. Abbott accepts only one in eight applicants, and the academic accomplishments of those who apply are remarkably high. Abbott boasts the highest "yield" rate of any New England secondary school—that is, once accepted, most applicants happily sign up for the four-year program. Minority students are favored in admission procedures, and because the academic program is so rigorous, the school has instituted a special tutoring program that is geared primarily to those minority students who have not had good academic preparation. Overall, Abbott Academy is among*

the top institutions of its kind in the country—it is one of those schools that seems to have it all.

At the time it appeared, the *Simpson Guide* article on Abbott Academy greatly pleased the school's trustees, all of whom had been friends of Mr. Abbott himself. For almost a decade, they congratulated themselves on their association with an institution that "had it all." Yet, over time, the school's fortunes began to change. There were fewer applications, and although this reflected the demographics of a smaller applicant pool and increased competition, the downward trend was even more severe than had been predicted. Of even greater concern was the falling yield rate (the number of students admitted to Abbott who decided to enroll). At its peak, Abbott's yield rate had been close to 85 percent, but it was below 50 percent only a decade later. Perhaps more alarming, college admissions among Abbott seniors was becoming much less predictable. While many students were still going to prestigious colleges, an increasing number of them had to be satisfied with schools that previous Abbott students would not have considered. Finally, there was the problem of the budget. When Mr. Abbott retired as the school's headmaster, he put the school on notice that his annual contribution would be declining. For the first time, the board had to consider a significant tuition increase, annual fund raising, or both.

At a board meeting, Charles Mayfield, the school's new headmaster, told the trustees that the situation should not be viewed with alarm. If the number of qualified applicants was dropping, then the school should just make do with fewer students for a year or two. The trends would change, and there would be plenty of applicants once the "pendulum swings back as it always does." Tuition could be raised a little to meet the income gap, and affluent parents might want to consider "throwing in a little extra" to help out. Mayfield conceded that the school could do a better job of convincing prospective parents of the superior merits of Abbott Academy once their children had been accepted. But he "eschewed unseemly promotional efforts such as those employed by our competitors" and suggested that sending out a copy of the *Simpson Guide* article was probably the most appropriate public relations effort the school could mount. As to the growing unpredictability of college admissions, Mayfield explained that Abbott's overall record had been very good over the years and that no dire predictions should be made based on one or two years of lackluster performance.

In time, Abbott Academy's trustees and headmaster could no longer ignore the ominous signs that things were getting worse. Applications were down to such an extent that the school was accepting more than half of the students who applied, a stark contrast to the one in eight applicants that had been reported in the *Simpson Guide* of several years before. Even by admitting such a high percentage of applicants, Abbott could no longer maintain a student body of 200 qualified students because so many of those accepted ended up choosing other schools. With only 178 students in the school, tuition revenue was down, and because fund raising was not very effective, the school was beginning to use principal from its endowment to cover operating shortfalls. The unpleasant and unpredictable trends in college admissions continued—in fact, for the first time in the school's history, two seniors were not accepted at any college. Faculty members complained that this was because the quality of students was slipping. Indeed, many of the most experienced teachers were considering alternative employment because their jobs at Abbott were "no longer rewarding." Finally, the percentage of minority students was also declining despite special recruitment efforts in the minority community.

A PROBLEM IN MARKETING

We will return to Abbott Academy at the end of this chapter and review this story's happy ending. But for now, given what we know, we can see that although the problems of Abbott Academy had been mounting for years, they had been misdiagnosed by the headmaster and the trustees. Charles Mayfield had behaved a bit like a doctor telling an elderly female patient with a ruptured appendix that she was really fine, no examination was necessary, and she might consider taking an indigestion tablet for an upset stomach. By electing not to do a comprehensive diagnosis, and by mistaking symptom for disease, Mayfield and the trustees failed to develop an appropriate strategy for identifying the school's predicament. Like the incompetent doctor, they did not delve beneath the surface to find out what was really wrong. Correct diagnosis, in the case of Abbott Academy, would have required several steps including the following:

1. Accurately identifying the school's multiple constituencies and monitoring their changing characteristics, needs, and perceptions
2. Conducting appropriate research to determine the school's strengths and weaknesses, its position relative to its competition, and its perceived value in the community
3. Considering how the school's program might be modified in light of the realities identified
4. Developing a sensible pricing strategy
5. Responding to a changing environment (including the physical environment—where the school was located) and assessing how that was making it increasingly difficult for potential clients to take advantage of what the school had to offer
6. Developing a strong brand for the school
7. Promoting the brand and the institution utilizing a variety of strategies.

In effect, the board did not approach the challenges facing Abbott Academy from a marketing perspective.

What is marketing? Marketing is the continuous diagnosis and analysis of the changing needs and perceptions of customers, clients, and constituents and devising strategies to meet these needs and perceptions. Marketing is the creation of an appropriate brand for a product, service, or organization. It is the analysis, planning, implementation, and control of decisions in the areas of product offering, distribution, promotion, and pricing.

In the nonprofit sector, marketing is the engineering of *satisfaction* among a variety of groups. The groups can include users of an organization's services, funders, trustees, regulators, and others who will have an indirect impact on the organization's success, such as the media and even members of the general public. At one time, mapping and implementing a strategy for each of these groups could be done at a deliberate pace. Today, that luxury no longer exists. Because the internet allows people to form judgments and express opinions instantaneously (and sometimes erroneously), the need for vigilance, expedited planning, and rapid response is crucial. But while the internet can be a worrisome challenge, its speed and power also offers extraordinary opportunities. Any organization, even a tiny one, can create a very strong and positive impression quickly thanks to the internet at a fraction of what comparable efforts might have cost before. Developing a variety of appropriate marketing strategies using multiple tools can help organizations succeed at what they set out to do, meeting programmatic and financial goals, satisfying the needs of their constituents, and telling a positive story over and over again to different people in a variety of coherent and consistent ways.

As we look at the case of Abbott Academy, we can examine the components of marketing in some detail and demonstrate how a marketing perspective might have helped the headmaster and trustees correctly diagnose problems and devise strategies to solve them.

THE ISSUE OF MULTIPLE CONSTITUENCIES (MARKET SEGMENTATION)

One of the most important aspects of marketing is called *market segmentation*. In the nonprofit sector, market segmentation refers to the various constituencies whose satisfaction must be addressed. In most cases, different strategies need to be developed for each group, but many nonprofit organizations do not correctly identify all their constituencies in the first place. This was certainly the case with Abbott Academy, which had stated publicly and quite explicitly that the single constituency to which it needed to address itself was its students. The school catalog had begun with the following words: "Abbott Academy was founded with the express intent of providing an outstanding education to young people. It is to our students, therefore, that we devote our attention, our resources, and our energies."

From a marketing point of view, students were not the only constituency whose needs had to be addressed if Abbott was to be successful. Other groups included:

- *Parents.* Parents generally played an important role in the choice of their child' school, judged whether the amount of tuition they were asked to pay was reasonable, and decided whether they might wish to contribute an additional amount voluntarily. Yet, Abbott actively discouraged parents from visiting (except when parents were summoned to a conference with a teacher or the headmaster). The school had no parent support organization and offered no social events for them. There were few forms of communication. Many parents felt isolated from the school and wondered whether they or their children had done something wrong. Afraid for their children and how they might be penalized, they never actually complained to the faculty, trustees, or headmaster that they did not feel a part of the school family.

- *College representatives.* It was college admissions officers and other officials who decided whether to admit Abbott Academy applicants and, in effect, determined Abbott's reputation as a college-preparatory school. Yet little was done to cultivate this constituency. Mr. Abbott had maintained good contacts at a few Ivy League schools during his tenure. However, once he retired, no new bonds were forged. Furthermore, Abbott Academy had had little or no contact with representatives of "lesser" schools, who were given the impression that their campuses were being used for safety applications by the Abbott students. As Abbott students cast a wider and wider net in their applications to colleges, the lack of a strong college network should have become increasingly obvious.

- *Potential applicants/prospective students.* By serving its enrolled students well, Abbott administrators felt that they were doing all they could to make the school an enticing place for prospective students. Yet, remarkably, there was little or no opportunity for those enrolled to influence those applying. Prospective students met only with adults (generally in the company of their parents). Their short visits to classes, during which they sat in the back row and were not drawn into discussions, often produced an impression that Abbott Academy was a school only for exceptionally bright kids, not for them. Because Abbott's playing fields were not adjacent to the campus, prospective students never saw them, and this confirmed their impression that the school consisted primarily of classrooms and hard work.

- *Minority representatives.* When Joseph Abbott founded Abbott Academy, he believed that a fundamental tenet of the school should be to offer young people of color an opportunity to gain an outstanding education. He also believed that a critical part of the education of white students was to come into contact with individuals whose backgrounds were substantially different from their own. But the school never really developed a strategy to court this minority constituency. Abbott himself had believed special efforts to be unnecessary inasmuch as the benefits of an Abbott Academy education were an obvious enticement. Gradually the school found itself losing minority candidates to other secondary schools whose faculties included more black, Hispanic, and Asian teachers, whose curricula included works by black and Latin American writers, and whose boards included several nonwhite trustees.

- *Alumni.* In most schools, alumni are an important source of dollars, and they also promote the institution and help recruit prospective students. At Abbott, this constituency was never invited to become involved. There was no alumni bulletin to keep them informed of school activities, there were no reunion functions or other opportunities to foster institutional loyalty, and there was no annual appeal for contributions. When Abbott Academy finally launched its first alumni fund-raising activity, few alumni participated.

- *Faculty.* Abbott Academy's faculty, like the employees of many nonprofit organizations, was overworked and underpaid. In the halcyon days of the institution, their satisfaction came from the academy's institutional prestige among secondary schools, the intellectual stimulation that came from working with bright students, and the repeated statement by Joseph Abbott that they were the most talented faculty in secondary education. But as Abbott Academy's problems mounted, the trustees forgot that this constituency was critical to Abbott's success. They cut the number of faculty members, increased teaching loads, froze salaries, and made the fatal mistake of second-guessing curricula and teaching methods. With the declining quality of the student body, a loss of pride in their work, and no financial incentives, there was very little to keep the best teachers at Abbott.

- *Trustees.* Trustees can bring prestige, money, and expertise to the operation of a school or any nonprofit organization. But Abbott Academy's trustees, most of whom were Joseph Abbott's friends, had never been expected or asked to do any of these things. When the school's fortunes began to turn, the new headmaster did not feel comfortable asking the trustees to become more active because, he felt, they were important, busy people who were doing the institution a favor by serving. He was also reluctant to admit that his administration was not as successful as his predecessor's. By not courting this group, he got from them precisely what he asked for: nothing—no support, no money, no commitment.

- *Other donors.* Like most nonprofit organizations, Abbott Academy relied on contributed income to balance its budget. Although it had an ongoing source of earned revenue—tuition—it could not charge a high enough price per student to support its expenses. For decades, there had been only one donor, Joseph Abbott himself. In this respect, the distinguished founder had been uncharacteristically shortsighted. Unwilling or unable to continue to cover the operating deficit of the school indefinitely, he was forced to put the school on notice that other donors would have to be found. But because they had never been courted, donors were hard to come by. Abbott Academy had never solicited money from alumni, parents, or foundations and had not appealed to wealthy individuals whose relatives had attended or taught at the school. The school had, in fact, not solicited funds from anyone. As a result, when Abbott Academy's fortunes began to change, there was no loyal group of donors to turn to for help.

Each of these constituencies could have been a vital link in helping Abbott Academy solve its problems, achieve its goals, and remain fiscally healthy. Yet, by focusing on only one group—its students—the school's leadership paid a very high price. They were unable to meet one of the great challenges that face every nonprofit organization—the challenge of identifying each of its constituencies clearly and accurately and developing separate, appropriate, and effective strategies to satisfy each one.

BRAND

Choose a nonprofit organization—perhaps one that you have strong opinions about and know well. Now go out and ask several people to share their impressions of it with you. The responses will give you some sense of the strength of that organization's brand. Its brand is, among other things, the sum total of beliefs, ideas, and impressions that people have about the organization, its activities, and the people associated with it. In the nonprofit world, a strong brand is a critical element in gaining patients, clients, students, or audience. It is also essential in gaining donors and broad community support. The message conveyed must entice, attract, and impress. But it also has to be rooted in reality. Developing and promoting a brand is essentially the same as making a promise or a pledge. It must be based on an ability to deliver.

What contributes to a strong brand?

Good branding emanates from accurate self-knowledge and an ability to learn about and shape perceptions. In an ideal world, those are things over which an organization has some degree of control. But the strength of an organization's brand is also shaped by events—both positive and negative—over which it has little or no control. On the positive side, imagine the impact on a university's brand when a faculty member wins the Nobel Prize or its basketball team wins the NCAA playoffs. Similarly, think of the opportunity afforded a hospital when it is ranked #1 in cancer treatment in a national survey or a zoo that is cited as among the Top 10 family destinations by a prominent magazine for parents. These are all fortuitous events that can enhance the brand.

Sometimes, events can have a negative impact on an institution's brand. If a university president is involved in an ethics scandal, if a labor strike at a hospital turns violent, if a symphony orchestra receives a spate of negative reviews, if the U.S. Congress decides to launch an investigation into unsavory or illegal practices of a nonprofit organization even though there is little evidence to support the claim, a previously strong brand can be tarnished. Trustees often assume that under these circumstances the public will forgive and forget, but this is a dangerous assumption. The proper course of action is to figure out how to protect the brand from negative events, statements, or impressions. Because a brand is based on many subjective beliefs and impressions that can spread virally over the internet, it is often necessary to make a quick and dramatic change (e.g., the resignation of the CEO or an errant staff member or the elimination of a controversial program). But in addition to this, the organization must attempt to change adverse opinion by launching a carefully designed campaign to create more positive impressions and press.

Certainly, when a precipitous event unfairly tarnishes an organization, it is crucial to diagnose the problem quickly and begin to mount a counterstrategy. If during a political campaign, a candidate for national office suddenly tries to tarnish a nonprofit civil liberties organization as un-American, the organization can mount its own counteroffensive to show that its activities are considered mainstream and it is the candidate who is "out of step with the American people."

What is more difficult is noticing when an organization's brand is eroding slowly and imperceptibly over time, particularly if this trend occurs during a period in which the trustees and staff believe the organization is flourishing. This is precisely what happened in the case of Abbott Academy. Abbott's image as reflected by the *Simpson Guide* article had suggested that the institution was among the best of an elite group of private secondary schools. But several things began to erode what had been a blue-ribbon brand. As Abbott Academy encountered its first difficulties with college admissions, rumors began to circulate that the school could no longer get its students into college. Although this greatly exaggerated the facts, the rumor worried prospective parents, many of whom began to assume that there was a connection between declining college admissions and the retirement of Joseph Abbott. They wondered what else the founder's retirement might portend. The rumor also had an effect on prospective students. Without a guaranteed passport to college, young people began to question the value of what the *Simpson Guide* had called a "rigorous" academic program. They did not want to attend what one prospective student called an "intellectual boot camp" and another called a "grind farm for turkeys and book lovers." While Abbott Academy could have taken active steps to reverse these assaults on the school's image, the changes occurred so slowly and imperceptibly that no one in the institution clearly understood what was happening.

THE MARKETING MIX

Why does someone choose to buy a product, purchase services, pay for programs, or even make a contribution to a nonprofit organization? What are the elements that contribute to that individual's decision? From a marketing point of view there are four critical elements, commonly referred to as the four *P*s, or the marketing mix:

- *Product*, or in the case of most nonprofit organizations, the programs and services offered

- *Promotion* of the products, programs, or services
- *Price*, or what it costs to participate
- *Place*, or where the products, programs, and services are available

Product

The most obvious elements in a customer's decision to purchase are the characteristics of the products, programs, or services being offered. Very simply, the customer must be satisfied that the products, programs, and services live up to or exceed expectations. In the for-profit sector, many resources are allocated to research and development of new products and product testing. Once a product is developed, the consumer has to be assured that it will deliver on its promise. Thus guarantees and the service accompanying the product are part of the product offering itself. Indeed, some companies have distinguished their products from those of their competition by offering money-back guarantees or a service fleet of trained professionals to keep the product in good working order.

In the nonprofit sector, organizations tend to be much less rigorous in developing and testing new products, programs, and services or updating and modernizing old ones. Evaluation is expensive, and few nonprofits have a line item for research and development. They offer few guarantees of program effectiveness to their constituents or funders, though often they make unsubstantiated promises. The issue is complicated by the fact that nonprofit organizations are not product-driven, but mission-driven. Whereas an automobile company must develop a popular car to be successful, the most respected theater troupe is not necessarily the one that produces the most popular play, especially if its mission reflects a concern for exploring new and experimental work. Indeed, many nonprofit organizations pride themselves not on designing products for consumers but rather on educating consumers' tastes and preferences.

But this point of view in the nonprofit sector often leads to a lack of rigor in examining and evaluating products, programs, and services, which is shortsighted. Consider, again, the case of Abbott Academy, a school that firmly believed that it knew what was best for its students and would not have considered inquiring about consumer preferences. In its early years, Abbott's product—its academic program—was considered conservative and traditional, but solid. It required students to take, among other things, three years of Latin, a year of Greek, a year of philosophy (including a semester of ethics), a year of ancient history, and a year devoted to the art of the Renaissance. Two decades later, such a program was seen to be anachronistic. Abbott offered no course in African American or Latin American literature, it provided no classes dealing with current events or the politics of the third world, and its computer and science equipment was not equal to that of the competition. Had Abbott Academy chosen to ask its constituents—prospective parents, college admissions officers, and minority candidates, among others—it would have discovered that its product was no longer competitive in the secondary-school marketplace.

Similarly, Abbott Academy offered nothing in the way of a guarantee of its product to parents concerned about college admission. While no school can guarantee college admission to all of its graduates, Abbott Academy's competition was able to boast about its expanded college-advising staff, its special tutoring sessions to prepare students for the college board exam, and its phone call follow-up of student applications by the headmaster in cases where parents and college advisors agreed it might make a difference.

Some nonprofit organizations can and do offer firm guarantees of their products, programs, and services, and this often makes a difference to their customers and constituents:

- A shelter for battered women guarantees confidentiality and police protection for its clients.
- A third world support organization guarantees that 90 cents of every dollar raised will go directly to people in the third world.
- A small liberal arts college guarantees that all of its students will be taught by regular faculty members (not graduate assistants as would be the case in a larger university).

Yet another aspect of the product, program, or service an organization offers is the manner in which it is packaged. Packaging includes not only the physical container that holds a product but also the aura that surrounds it. Thus, although the color, shape, and design of a box of cereal may influence potential buyers, a brand name may influence them even more. This prestige or name recognition is also important in the nonprofit sector and can enhance marketability. For example, art museums have discovered that blockbuster shows, geared to the name of a famous artist, will draw far more people than shows of comparable quality that feature a mixed group of well-known and lesser-known artists. The prestige of the sponsoring organization itself may also be an important aspect of packaging the product. Many students who apply to Harvard's graduate schools may be less influenced by the quality of the faculty or the courses and more influenced by the Harvard brand.

One other thing to keep in mind about product offerings is the seeming paradox of choice. On the one hand, consumers increasingly want to be able to customize what they purchase, whether it is the features on their cars or the music on their handheld devices. On the other hand, research shows that when consumers are offered too many choices, they often opt out of choosing altogether. Today, many seek expert advice to cut through this diversity of options that the internet provides at the push of a computer key. In this complex world of seemingly unlimited options, three things are true:

- First, in most cases, the greater the opportunity for consumers to choose the features of what they purchase, the better they will like it. Many symphony orchestras have learned, for example, that despite numerous subscription offerings, a "select your own" series will often be the most popular.
- Second, despite this desire to customize and have choices, it is important to limit offerings to a small enough number that it is not overwhelming if consumers are to be encouraged to act. A museum gift shop offering a seemingly endless array of nearly identical products with very similar price points over the internet may in the end discourage some purchasers.
- Finally, consumers will often flock to "experts" who will tell them what is the best product to buy or which organization is the best to do business with. Consumers are often hungry for someone else to make the choice for them. Becoming familiar with who those experts are and gaining entry onto their preferred lists can be extremely beneficial.

Promotion
Some nonprofit organizations can be categorized as the best kept secret in town. Their programs and services are largely unknown. If they

have an image problem, it is that they have no public profile at all. By failing to promote themselves and their activities, these organizations sail a dangerous course. For when potential constituents do not know of their existence or do not really have an impression of what they do, participation, sales, or support are hard to come by.

Nonprofit organizations can promote themselves in various ways. Certainly the internet has changed the rules completely, allowing even the smallest organization to develop a high-profile presence through websites, blogs, social media, and other electronic means. Free media coverage; organized word-of-mouth campaigns; and carefully organized opportunities for presentations at conferences, service organizations, clubs, churches, and chambers of commerce can all contribute to the arsenal of promotional strategies.

An organization may be promoting itself, its products, its programs, or its services. Or it may be advancing a particular political agenda, attempting to influence legislation, or seeking to gain the attention of public and private funders. Whatever the purpose and whatever the techniques, it is essential to remember that we live in a "noisy" environment with millions of entities and people vying for attention. Without being proactive in getting a message out there, organizations will find themselves drowned out.

In a for-profit organization, a great deal of money is spent on promotion. Well-staffed marketing departments allocate large advertising budgets, devise free giveaway campaigns, use mass direct mail, and work with large sales forces trained to promote products to potential customers. In the nonprofit world, there are generally fewer resources available. Even so, some small nonprofits can look very professional and achieve a wide reach in their promotion. Those involved in planning promotional campaigns must plan carefully and spend dollars wisely.

- Websites are one of the most cost-effective tools in promotion, and many excellent ones are designed for minimal dollars. One goal for a good website is to entice some of the visitors to make a purchase or a donation, so the home page must make the route to that option obvious, quick, and effortless. But the website also should entice visitors to stay on the site, getting as many page views as possible so the organization can make its case. While the purchasers or donors may be happiest with a quick and efficient visit, information seekers should be offered much interesting and interactive content to keep them entranced and connected. Often, a good site can enhance its own original content through links to other interesting content on the web.

- Capturing names and contact information, especially email addresses, should also be a major goal. While snail-mail addresses can be purchased, email addresses by law cannot be bought or sold without permission. So providing incentives for people to share their email addresses is important. Offers of free one-time admission to events, drawings (with a prize), or a free e-newsletter that promises advance notice of events and special discounts are just three devices to incentivize people to provide the information you want.

- E-news and e-blasts are also promotional vehicles that can be effective, though great care must be exercised in their use. If an individual is overwhelmed with email traffic, he or she may simply opt out of receiving more. Opting out (or requesting to be removed from an email list) is a major problem, but the request must be honored and the email address is no longer available for use. On the other hand, judicious use of such communication allows remarkably accurate targeting of messages. If a particular group of ticket buyers to a concert series always seems to come to concerts by pianists, this group can receive targeted emails (and other kinds of mailings) when such a concert is being offered. Similarly, they can receive a customized e-newsletter filled with background information on the pianist, the music, the types of pianos used at the first performance of each piece, and other related upcoming concert information.

- Blogs and social media sites are increasingly part of the tactical arsenal of a good promotion plan, and they offer the very appealing opportunity for consumers to be involved in the organization at multiple levels. They also provide a vehicle for viral messaging that can create extraordinary opportunities to spread the word, though it can also pose great challenges if the messaging is either negative or downright misleading. The care and feeding of media sites and blogs is time consuming, and nonprofit organizations need to be realistic about the extent of content and monitoring they can provide.

- Old-fashioned direct mail is still effective, especially as an acquisition tool. Because it is possible to purchase or otherwise barter for names and addresses, direct mail is often the best way to find new customers or donors. List brokers will sell names by the thousands in very specific categories (subscribers to a certain magazine, graduates of a specific college), or list trades can be arranged with like organizations (generally for one-time use).
- News releases should go out regularly to a list of media representatives and other key people on the organization's mailing list. Pitching feature stories to the media is also important, and they often come about from meetings with media people who should be constantly cultivated. When it comes to paid advertising, careful thought needs to be given to media buys so that placement aligns with where possible customers and supporters will see it. Media rates are always negotiable, and organizations should try to get the best possible deal. Media outlets are increasingly frank these days about the fact that local free coverage is linked to the willingness of organizations to invest advertising dollars.
- The telephone should be used as a public relations vehicle. Paying telemarketers to sell tickets or other services is still a common strategy, especially for larger nonprofits, while smaller ones can use carefully scripted volunteers. In addition to being a sales tool, the phone can be used to thank major donors, survey constituents about their opinions, and invite them to special events.
- Occasional public relations events should be planned and carried out by staff and/or volunteers. These can include award ceremonies, involve celebrities, or use any other device to create broader interest.
- Displays can be designed for high-traffic locations (such as malls) or for offices and institutions whose clientele might have an interest in the material (e.g., hospital weight-clinic displays and brochures in doctors' offices, and college displays in high school libraries). When appropriate, these display areas can be manned by volunteers.
- Convenings of field or community leaders around issues of current interest to participants demonstrate the important role the

organization can play in solving problems and facilitating dia-logue. They also reveal the level of respect the organization can command from other organizations and individuals.

There are several mistakes organizations make in promotion.

- One is to assume that the more you say in a promotional device the better. In fact, the opposite is true. Short, carefully selected messaging is always more effective. To paraphrase and adapt a quote from Mark Twain, "I didn't have time to write a short press release, so I wrote a long one." It is always best to take the time for the shorter version!
- A second mistake in promotion is missing the easy opportunities to acquire names, addresses, and other pertinent information. Point of purchase is an obvious place to capture such informa-tion—again, incentivizing people to provide email addresses and other information will be valuable in later sales and fund-raising solicitation. Websites are also important vehicles for information capture ("sign up here with your email address to receive a free gift.")
- Finally, a third mistake is the tendency to oversell a product or service. If customers or constituents have specific expectations about a product or service and these expectations are not met, they will be disappointed. Promotion based on exaggerated claims will generally lead to unfulfilled expectations. When a nonprofit organization oversells a program, the constituents' inevitable dis-appointment can be doubly damaging. They will cease supporting the program, and they will be critical when they describe it to others.

Indeed, overselling is precisely what occurred when Abbott Acad-emy chose to send out the *Simpson Guide* article as a promotional piece to prospective parents. The article, which had been written almost two decades earlier, described a different Abbott Academy of another time—a school that accepted only one in eight applicants and sent all of its students to prestigious colleges. But that did not continue to be a fair description of the school, and many parents and students felt misled. Many of those who chose the school were disappointed and angry. Some students left the school after one year; parents criticized the school publicly for its false advertising.

Price

Price is also a key element in the marketing mix because it helps establish a perceived value for a product or service. All other things being equal, if two products sit on a grocer's shelf, we will buy the cheaper of the two if we believe both to be exactly the same. But two brands of mustard or two kinds of hair spray are rarely seen as the same. The manufacturers go to great pains to make their products appear distinct. And one of the elements that contributes to that distinctiveness is price. We will often buy the more expensive of two products if we think it offers greater value. Because we usually do not have a well-developed system for assessing value, we will often assume that the more expensive product is the better product.

This close relationship between price and perceived value is nowhere more evident than in the competitive world of nonprofit organizations. It is often difficult to assess the "real" value of the various offerings of hospitals, day-care centers, universities, and theater companies. A consumer attempting to distinguish between two organizations in the same field may sometimes conclude that the one whose price is higher actually offers the better product or service.

Ironically, it was this psychology—the linkage of price and perceived value—that created a major problem for Abbott Academy. Joseph Abbott, the school's founder, had endowed the school heavily in the early years and made significant contributions to keep the tuition affordable for less affluent parents. Yet, over time, as competing schools raised their tuition charges to levels a third or more above those of Abbott, some people began to wonder if there was something wrong with Abbott Academy's academic program. In stark contrast, one of Abbott's competitors, long considered an inferior school academically, decided to price itself higher than any other secondary school in New England, hoping that this would create an image of quality (at the same time, they increased scholarship aid to compensate and made some other changes). Remarkably, after only three years, this school saw the number of its applicants surpass that of Abbott Academy for the first time. While other factors certainly contributed to this trend—the academic program was revamped, and the school increased promotional activities—incoming parents who were interviewed admitted that price played an important role in their determination of quality.

Another important consideration in the area of pricing for non-profit organizations has to do with the scaling of contribution levels. When asking donors for money, many organizations create a range of giving opportunities. In one organization's annual direct mail appeal, the categories of giving may start at a low of $20 and end at a high of $1,000. A similar organization may scale its categories of giving from $100 to $5,000. Other things being equal, the second organization often will collect more money *from the same group of people* because it has defined itself to be of greater value to donors.

Place

The final element in the marketing mix is place, the location at which the products, services, and programs are made available to constituents. The critical role place can play in the provision of a service by a non-profit organization is underscored by these examples:

- When a counseling center built on its success and moved its offices from an inner-city neighborhood to a more affluent location, its old clients ceased coming and the organization's mission of serving the poor was significantly compromised.
- A symphony orchestra continued to give concerts in its acoustically superior concert hall even though the urban neighborhood where the hall was located had deteriorated and its audience had largely moved to the suburbs. The result was a decline in ticket sales.

Place also turned out to play a major role in the decline of Abbott Academy's preeminence in the private secondary-school marketplace. In 1970, when the *Simpson Guide* wrote its laudatory article on Abbott, the school's urban campus was an attractive enticement to many young families who had chosen to move back to the city. In those days, downtown real estate was relatively inexpensive, and the city itself was going through a kind of renaissance. Abbott catered to a new group of young city families who believed in the importance of education and did not trust the city's public school system. But by the end of the twentieth century, the renaissance of the city had been so successful that downtown real estate prices had escalated tenfold or more. Young families with children could no longer afford to live in the city and were moving closer and closer to Abbott Academy's suburban competition. Whereas the idea of an urban campus had given Abbott an edge at one time, it put the school at a disadvantage a couple of decades later.

Many nonprofit organizations have come to understand that if customers, clients, or constituents cannot or will not come to the organization's headquarters, the organization must take the product or service to them. Indeed, developing a proper *distribution* system for products and services is as important in the nonprofit world as it is among profit-making companies:

- A drug treatment center that also provides clean needles to heroin addicts (in order to combat AIDS) found that addicts were reluctant to come to its designated locations for the needles. The organization now uses a mobile van.
- A church, whose historic cathedral was located in what had become a major business and industrial center, established two suburban satellite churches for its members who attended weekend services. The downtown cathedral is now used for short midday services during the week.
- A theatre troupe found that public schools could no longer afford buses to bring students to its theatre for youth programs. The theatre now sends small groups of actors to the schools.

In each of these examples, the organizations realized that no matter how good the products or services offered, constituents would not make use of them unless they were conveniently available.

MARKET RESEARCH

In order to develop an overall marketing strategy or plan, a nonprofit organization must have access to much factual information on how well it stacks up against its competition; how it is perceived in the community; how its programs, activities, and products are regarded; and how it might command a bigger share of customers, clients, funders, or other constituents. This is accomplished through market research. Market research seeks to:

- Analyze leading trends in the "community" in which the organization operates as well as trends in its industry
- Understand the perceptions of various constituents in regard to the organization's brand, its programs, its activities, and its governance and administration
- Assess constituent preferences in areas where the organization is, or seeks to be, active
- Analyze threats to the organization according to their potential severity and likely occurrence
- Analyze opportunities for the organization according to their potential and their probability of success

In light of the findings, market research can be expanded into a full marketing audit that identifies the organization's strengths and weaknesses in terms of external factors like public awareness, effectiveness of programs to meet constituent need, pricing, and strength of marketing efforts as well as internal factors such as effectiveness of staff, board, and volunteers and use of financial resources.

Some people think that one of the main purposes of market research is to help organizations invent new products or services to satisfy constituents. But this is not usually the case. Nonprofit organizations in particular often need to figure out how they stack up against the competition, how well their messages are being conveyed, how to better target their programs, and how to consolidate programs and activities, concentrating on those that most clearly relate to their missions and most appropriately meet the needs of their constituents. Good market research helps organizations to *focus* resources and energies.

The sequence of steps involved in market research is as follows:

1. *Define research objectives.* Decide very specifically the questions that need to be answered.
2. *Do preliminary research.* Collect any information that will help define the objectives more clearly, including existing statistics on the industry or the target constituency, completed research studies, a general survey of the organization's competition, and an assessment of constituent attitudes that could be revealed through a few preliminary interviews or small group sessions.

This preliminary fact-gathering phase could also include a management review or outside assessment of the organization.

3. *Design the formal research.* Develop the data-collection strategies (through web or intercept surveys, mailed questionnaires, interviews, or focus groups), decide on how the target group will be sampled (randomly, by zip code, by occupation), and choose the means of contact (email, telephone, in person, or snail mail).

4. *Do fieldwork.* Collect the data, making sure that the procedure is as free of bias as possible.

5. *Analyze the data.* Analyze, interpret, and report the results.

At the end of the twentieth century, nonprofit organizations were being advised to hire outsiders to conduct market research because survey design and analysis was simply too complex for most nonprofit staff. While it is still useful to have the assistance of an experienced, objective professional at least in designing the methodology, the internet has greatly changed the equation. It allows many organizations to conduct fairly sophisticated research themselves, using computer programs to systematically organize collected data, provide a fundamental analysis in a summary report, and export data for further analysis. It is still necessary to know something about survey design and how to ask good questions that will lend themselves to analysis, but it is not necessary to have a detailed knowledge of statistics for many simple surveys. Keep in mind, however, that it is all too easy for an organization's own representatives unwittingly to design market research that will confirm their own prejudices rather than uncover the facts. Working with a group to review the objectives, the approach, and the questions is often a safer way to go. In the end, whether internal or external resources are used, good market research is almost always a sound investment.

It had never occurred to the headmaster and trustees of Abbott Academy that the institution's problems could be analyzed from a marketing perspective. But then a new board member, who was a marketing consultant, offered to conduct a marketing study for the school free of charge. Ultimately, his fellow trustees declined the offer. They agreed with Headmaster Mayfield, who said that marketing was simply an inappropriate analytical or management tool at a place like Abbott. Mayfield, like so many who work in nonprofit organizations, fundamentally misunderstood what marketing was all about. First, he assumed that marketing was no more than simple promotion and advertising and that the Academy's problems should be solved in ways that were less crass. Second, he felt that marketing was inappropriate because it was oriented toward the idea of buying and selling, customers, and profit. Finally, he was offended by the idea of marketing because he found it so manipulative. He argued that if Abbott was doing a good job and providing services that were genuine and needed, then it should not be necessary to engineer customer satisfaction.

All of these arguments missed the point, of course. Market research would have allowed the headmaster and trustees of Abbott Academy to look systematically at the school's mission, its image, its constituents, its competitors, its resources, its strengths, and its weaknesses and then devise strategies to gain a more favorable position in its own competitive marketplace.

THE ROLE OF A MARKETING COMMITTEE

Many nonprofit boards, even boards of very small organizations, have marketing committees. Often they are helpful, but just as often they do harm—with members suggesting innumerable strategies that are neither feasible nor affordable and wasting a good deal of staff time. Members of a marketing committee can also involve themselves at a level of detail that is inappropriate—suggesting typefaces on posters or the colors in a logo. While a good staff member is always wise to seek feedback and opinions, such decisions should not be the purview of the committee whose role should be advisory in any case. The strong hand of a board chair and/or executive director is sometimes necessary to reign in a marketing committee whose members have run amuck.

Part of the problem is that almost anyone can fancy himself or herself an expert when it comes to marketing—if not in general theory, at least in the one or two things that he or she is convinced will result in more customers, better media coverage, or a strengthened brand. And as is so often the case, these individuals mistake their own personal and subjective predilections for objective and verified reality. Because the opinions are often not based on any firm data, the person with the most emphatic personality or persuasiveness wins the day. Especially dangerous are individuals who, by virtue of their work lives in larger corporations, convince others they are experts. The marketing strategies of large corporations trying to support an international brand, and the vast budgets that support them, are simply not relevant to the needs of even most very large nonprofits, and talking about what one or another of these corporations does to sell products or get media attention is generally irrelevant, counterproductive, or both.

Does this mean that nonprofit organizations should not have marketing committees? Not at all. First, a range of opinions is always valuable, so long as it is clear that it is staff who will make the ultimate decisions. Also, a marketing committee can play an important role in reviewing a marketing plan for the year, suggesting adjustments in overall strategy, and even suggesting implementation. Individuals on a marketing committee can be valuable resources in collecting reliable information for market research, such as serving as interviewers or bringing back information collected more informally in community settings. Finally, members of a marketing committee can serve as troops on the ground, carrying out the tactics that have been developed in a marketing plan—reinforcing the brand, talking up events, passing out material, and even representing the organization and providing opportunities for presentations with the many institutions with which they have affiliations.

Who should be on the marketing committee? Marketing committees, like all committees of the board, should have at least one trustee, but the committee should be augmented by nonboard members with expertise and assets they bring to the table, such as professional market researchers, media representatives, promotions people with retail outlets, and others with relevant experience.

GETTING IT RIGHT

In 2012, an Abbott Academy alumnus was checking the school's website, trying to decide whether to send a link to a prospective student and her parents. In the past, he had always found the school's promotional material an obstacle in recruiting. The staid graphics and the interminable, self-congratulatory prose had seemed off-putting to youngsters and their parents as was the front-and-center emphasis on the school's academic rigor. In most cases, the alumnus had started his recruitment pitch with a simple conversation.

But what he found on the website surprised and delighted him.

It represented a totally transformed image of the school, which now referred to itself simply as "Abbott" (the somewhat archaic word *Academy* had seemingly vanished, except in the small print). On the website's home page was a photo of a student and a short quote about how wonderful it was to be in a small school where you could make close friendships, be in small classes, get to design your own curriculum with your faculty advisory, and walk to the baseball park. There were links to stories by students about young alumni—one who had become a mayor in her twenties, another who was starting his second season as a Major League Baseball player, and a third who was a builder of solar homes. There was also a link to a photo gallery of student activities in the arts—a student play production, photos from an exhibition of student paintings and ceramics, and a link to a video of a student concert. On another web page was a series of photos of students and faculty, accompanied by short blurbs about "what Abbott means to me"—a variety of favorite things about the school.

Another thing that interested the alumnus was the way Abbott was now handling the issue of college admissions. It was hard to dispute that Abbott could no longer assure placement in elite schools as it once had. In previous promotions, the school had always started by listing the most prestigious schools and showing the number of the year's graduates who would be attending them. But with no students admitted to Harvard one year and none to Yale the next, the list was losing its luster. Now on the statistics page about the school, "Colleges and Universities" was downplayed. It was merely one of seventeen statistics provided, and it simply said: Number of Colleges and Universities that Students Have Matriculated to in the Last Five Years: 88. This new emphasis in the marketing materials indicated that Abbott would find the right place for its diverse student body. No matter what the profile of each individual student, he or she would be matched appropriately to a college or university.

In talking to a board member the following week, the alumnus congratulated her on the new website, saying how delighted the prospective students and parents had been in reviewing it.

"Yes," came the reply. "We finally bit the bullet. A board member had offered us free market research, and we had resisted. But with the declining enrollment, we knew we had to do something, so we agreed to have the research done. What we learned was a wake-up call that has landed us with a new headmaster, an expanded college advising staff, a new branding effort, a comprehensive and adequately funded marketing plan, and, this year, a major backlog of quality applicants that once again has propelled us to the top among private schools. Our marketing is carefully tailored to the various constituencies we serve. Our pricing is now more in keeping with our competition (we are no longer the least expensive private school among the top five) and this has allowed us to attract more minority students because there is more money for scholarship aid. All of this vitality has attracted a group of new trustees who understand that part of their role is to give and get money.

"We are still a very proud group—albeit somewhat more humble than we used to be. We are still Abbott Academy. We are still academically tough. We still feel we provide the best education in the city if not the entire region. But now, you know what? You would be surprised how many other people agree with us."

CHECKLIST QUESTIONS FOR CHAPTER 5

1. Has your organization accurately identified its various constituencies? Does it have an effective way to determine whether they are well served?
2. Is the organization able to assess the effectiveness of its brand in the community and among its various constituencies? Is there a strategy for enhancing and improving the organization's brand?
3. Does your organization offer products, services, and programs that are competitive in the marketplace? Are constituents satisfied (i.e., does your organization deliver on its promises)?
4. Does your organization promote itself and its activities to all of its constituencies? Are promotional efforts effectively targeted? Are sufficient dollars budgeted for public relations efforts, and are these dollars deployed wisely?
5. Are the products, services, and programs of your organization appropriately priced?
6. Has your organization conducted in-depth market research within the last five years? Have you made organizational decisions based on the results of this research?

SIX
Financial Management

When I am handed a budget or a financial statement, I feel my eyes glazing over. Numbers are just not my thing. Thank goodness there are others in the organization who understand money.

Financial management is, for many, one of the most forbidding aspects of the administration of nonprofit organizations. This is because they come into nonprofit organizations with little financial background and, in some cases, a numbers phobia. Often they have chosen to work as staff members or serve on boards because of a knowledge and commitment to education, conservation, child abuse, or some other activity. For them, the financial area—budgets, reports, and procedures—seems unrelated and dull, something for the "financial people" to deal with.

Even people who are more sophisticated about numbers can have difficulty with the finances in nonprofit organizations. For those who come from the business sector, certain terminology and concepts do not translate well. In addition, financial statements can be confusing, sometimes seeming to overstate or understate reality. It is no wonder so many people just throw up their hands.

But unfortunately, finances cannot be left completely to the experts. Budgeting, for example, is a critical part of overall organizational planning, and any board member who wants to be involved in setting priorities for the organization must take some interest in the budget. Similarly, analyzing financial statements is an important way to take a measure of an organization's health while at the same time protecting the organization's interests and those of the public. Sound internal financial procedures are necessary to stay within the law and to offer acceptable assurances to donors that their monies are safe.

Part of the reason that people become confused with financial management and draw away from it is because financial experts use a special language. There are many terms that serve as shorthand for basic concepts. The concepts themselves are generally not difficult; neither is the language, once you know it. However, many people were never taught what the terms mean, and some continue their involvement with nonprofit organizations remaining confused about important financial decisions. This chapter and the one that follows introduce some of the financial terms and procedures. It will become clear that financial management is generally logical. To some, the concepts may seem dull, but for the most part they are not difficult. This chapter deals with aspects of planning for the fiscal year, especially developing budgets and cash-flow projections. The following chapter explains how to keep financial records.

THE FINANCIAL OR FISCAL YEAR

We all make plans and keep records, and we usually have some systematic way of doing so. In financial management, planning and record keeping are set up according to fixed time periods, the most common of which is the fiscal year. Because *fiscal* is simply another word for financial, the fiscal year is the basic financial record-keeping (or accounting) period of the organization, the time frame in which all financial transactions are grouped together, added up, and reported on.

Individuals in their personal financial record keeping also have a fiscal year of sorts. It begins on January 1 and ends on December 31. This is the time period in which individuals group financial transactions for tax purposes. We can say that the fiscal year for individuals is the same as the calendar year. For nonprofit organizations, however, the fiscal year is not always the same as the calendar year. In fact, a nonprofit corporation can specify any dates for its fiscal year. It simply specifies in its articles of incorporation that "the corporation's fiscal year ends on [date] each year." That date could be the executive director's birthday or the anniversary date of the organization's founding, although neither of these choices is likely to be in the best interests of the organization.

How should a nonprofit organization choose a fiscal year? The following three considerations should be kept in mind:

- The fiscal year should roughly parallel the organization's program year. That is, one year's program activities should not fall into two fiscal years. If the academic year for a school runs from September to June, for example, it would be unwise to set the fiscal year to run concurrently with the calendar year and end on December 31. The result would be that the academic year would fall into two fiscal years, and it would be difficult to prepare budgets and analyze the financial performance of the school on an annual program-year basis.

- The fiscal year should end, whenever possible, just before a period of relative inactivity. There is a great deal of effort involved in closing the books at the end of the fiscal year. If an audit is involved, and in most organizations it is, an accountant needs to check financial records and review bank statements. Because this places a heavy burden on the staff, the audit should take place when other demands on staff time are minimal.

- The fiscal year-end may be chosen to coincide with a primary funder's fiscal year-end and resulting reporting requirements. For example, if a major portion of an organization's support is from the state government, the organization may select the same fiscal year-end as the state to simplify reporting on state grants.

It is an unfortunate fact of life that choosing a fiscal year for a nonprofit organization does not guarantee that its financial reports will all conform to the requirements of others to whom it must present its financial statements. The government and other public and private funding sources may require an organization to keep certain records according to *their* accounting periods, and often these do not correspond to the organization's fiscal year. For example, payroll records must be kept on a calendar-year basis in order to satisfy federal and state government accounting needs and to give salaried employees and independent contractors their W-2 and 1099 forms, respectively, for tax purposes. A state funding agency, on the other hand, may require financial reports for a year ending June 30 as part of the final report for a grant. However, careful selection of a particular fiscal year-end may reduce the number of different financial reports required.

THE BUDGET

A budget is a financial plan. It specifies how much money an organization thinks it will take in and how much it will spend. A budget is generally laid out in two sections, each of which is grouped under a main heading: the first is income (or revenue), and the second is expense (or expenditure) (see figure 6.1). Within the two sections, there is a further subdivision into specific income and expense categories. Each of these categories is placed on its own line with a dollar estimate listed, and for this reason, these categories are called line items. Another name for a line item is an *account*. Thus when someone refers to the salary account, the reference is to that line item in the budget in which all salary expenditures are grouped. All line items (or accounts) taken together are called the *chart of accounts*. This is the listing of all the budget categories. These categories are generally the same as those on an organization's income statement (see Income Statement in chapter 7).

Figure 6.1 Budget of the Compton School

Income		Expenses	
Tuition	$41,000	Salaries	$38,200
Bookstore sales	10,000	Benefits	4,000
Foundation grant	5,000	Honoraria	2,500
Business scholarships	5,000	Supplies and maintenance	5,200
Individuals	23,000	Equipment rental	3,400
Total	$84,000	Promotion	6,500
		Facility rental	20,000
		Contingency/reserve	4,200
		Total	$84,000

Source: Compiled by the author.

How does an organization decide what categories to include in its chart of accounts? After all, there are many ways to break down the same financial information. For example, a hospital could decide to lump all salaries under a single line item. Or it could subdivide salaries into many categories such as:

Salaries—physicians
Salaries—nursing staff
Salaries—administrative
Salaries—custodial

Every organization has to decide for itself on an appropriate chart of accounts. It must balance its need for detailed breakdowns of financial projections and records with the need to keep things simple. The best way to develop a chart of accounts is to look at the accounts of similar organizations that are well managed, approximately the same size, and have been around for some time. Compare the various listings of accounts. Look for commonalities and differences. Take into consideration your own special needs. Then begin to develop your chart of accounts based on the collective wisdom you have gained.

PROJECT BUDGETING

Project budgeting (also known as functional, departmental, or cost-center accounting when referring to record-keeping procedures) allows an organization to analyze the income and costs of its various activities on a project-by-project basis. This form of analysis can be useful for organizations evaluating particular programs for cost-effectiveness or for revenue-generating potential. How is the single-fund budget (as in figure 6.1) converted to this more complicated format (as in figures 6.2 through 6.5)?

- Generally, income that is program specific is allocated to the appropriate program categories (or *columns* of the budget). Thus a grant for an education program will be placed in the Education column of the budget as will tuition for educational workshops. Other income that is not tied to a particular program can be spread across the various columns as needed or desired. (A more detailed explanation of income allocation is discussed under Step 3 of the budgeting process and is shown in figure 6.5 later in this chapter.)
- Similarly, program-related expenses are placed in the appropriate columns. The salaries of teachers for the education program are placed in the Education column, as are expenses associated with educational supplies (as in figure 6.4).
- Administrative and fund-raising costs can be isolated in their own columns or allocated among programs (or some combination of both). Smaller organizations may decide that they do not need to allocate these costs to analyze the costs of particular programs. Larger organizations may wish to allocate costs included under

fund raising or administration to particular programs, but there will still be some fund raising and administrative costs that may not be attributable to any program and are isolated in their own columns.

In project budgeting, deciding whether and how to allocate fund-raising and management and support costs (administration) is often not a simple matter. Some people feel that the best way to accomplish the allocation of these costs is by some sort of formula. They may estimate the percent of staff time spent on a particular program in order to allocate salaries or calculate the percent of space used by each program in order to allocate rent expenses. For example, if the answer to the question "How much of our director's time will be taken up by the new technical assistance program?" is 10 percent, then 10 percent of his or her salary is allocated to that program. Or you might want to determine what percentage of the photocopier and postage expenses should be allocated to the technical assistance program. Again, the idea is to find a reasonable figure based on anticipated demand.

It is unlikely that all fund-raising, management, and support costs can reasonably be allocated to the various programs; expenses for which no reasonable basis of allocation exists should be included under Fund Raising or Administration (see figure 6.4). There is one cautionary note, however. Some people take cost allocation much too seriously. They count stamps, monitor conference calls, and keep logs of people's time. This may be useful for a day or a week to get a rough approximation on which a percentage can be developed for each program, but it can be overdone and can result in much wasted time and frustration.

Figure 6.2 Project Budgeting for the Compton Opera Company

	Version #1 (Note deficit in Touring project)			Version #2 (Individual Contributions have been shifted from Home Season to Touring to create a deficit in the Home Season budget.)		
	Home Season	Touring	Total	Home Season	Touring	Total
Income						
Ticket sales	$62,500	$0	$62,500	$62,500	$0	$62,500
Road fees	0	45,000	45,000	0	45,000	45,000
National Endowment	0	5,000	5,000	0	5,000	5,000
State arts council	10,000	0	10,000	10,000	0	10,000
Individual contributions	5,000	5,000	10,000	0	10,000	10,000
Total	$77,500	$55,000	$132,500	$72,500	$60,000	$132,500
Expenses						
Salaries	$56,000	$21,500	$77,500	$56,000	$21,500	$77,500
Living allowance	0	18,000	18,000	0	18,000	18,000
Travel expenses	0	8,000	8,000	0	8,000	8,000
Scenery, etc.	8,000	2,000	10,000	8,000	2,000	10,000
Truck	500	4,500	5,000	500	4,500	5,000
Promotion	2,000	2,000	4,000	2,000	2,000	4,000
Administration	11,000	4,000	15,000	11,000	4,000	15,000
Total	$77,500	$60,000	$137,500	$77,500	$60,000	$137,500
Excess (or deficit)	$0	($5,000)	($5,000)	($5,000)	$0	($5,000)

Source: Compiled by the author.

If one reason to do project budgeting is to determine cost-effectiveness, another is to offer flexibility in developing budgets for fund-raising purposes. For example, consider the Compton Opera Company's dilemma. It needs $5,000 to support its touring program activities (figure 6.2), but the director of the Friendly Foundation of Compton is more interested in supporting hometown activities, and these are currently breaking even. What to do? As one looks at the budget, $10,000 of unrestricted individual contributions have been split evenly between Home Season and Touring ($5,000 in each). When the director of the Friendly Foundation tells the director of the opera company that he is interested in making a $5,000 contribution to the company's programs in the local community, the opera company director must find a way to shift the $5,000 shortfall from Touring to Home Season. He can do so by preparing a new budget with all the individual contributions allocated to Touring. In this way, by shifting $5,000 of revenue out of the Home Season category into Touring, he creates the required $5,000 income gap in the Home Season.

Now suppose that the opera company director thinks there is a possibility that the foundation might give his organization even more money (perhaps as much as $10,000) if a financial need could be demonstrated in the budget. The director can prepare a budget that includes a Reserve Fund category (see figure 6.3). Income is shifted into the Reserve Fund, thereby creating the appropriate additional shortfall in the Home Season. The opera company director, sensing that the foundation may be prepared to give as much as $10,000 to the Home Season, shows a shortfall of exactly that amount *in that category* (see bottom line of Home Season column in figure 6.3). Meanwhile, the organization banks a healthy surplus for the year (bottom line of Reserve column).

Figure 6.3 Further Adjustments in Project Budgeting for the Compton Opera Company

	Home Season	Touring	Reserve Fund	Total
Income				
Ticket sales	$57,500	$0	$5,000	$62,500
Road fees	0	45,000	0	45,000
National Endowment	0	5,000	0	5,000
State arts council	10,000	0	0	10,000
Individual contributions	0	10,000	0	10,000
Total	$67,500	$60,000	$5,000	$132,500
Expenses				
Salaries	$56,000	$21,500	$0	$77,500
Living allowance	0	18,000	0	18,000
Travel expenses	0	8,000	0	8,000
Scenery, etc.	8,000	2,000	0	10,000
Truck	500	4,500	0	5,000
Promotion	2,000	2,000	0	4,000
Administration	11,000	4,000	0	15,000
Total	$77,500	$60,000	$0	$137,500
Excess (or deficit)	($10,000)	$0	$5,000	($5,000)

Source: Compiled by the author.

Note: In this budget, the organization created an even larger deficit position in the Home Season by shifting unrestricted ticket income to its Reserve Fund. Now it can legitimately ask for $10,000 of support for the Home Season budget (bottom line, first column). If a $10,000 grant is not forthcoming, the money allocated to Reserve can be put back into the Home Season, and the total cash requirement is only $5,000. This is why the actual total organizational deficit (as shown on the bottom line of the last column) is only $5,000.

People who work in nonprofit organizations are sometimes nervous about manipulating numbers in this way. They worry that the procedure may not be appropriate or even legal. Some think that nonprofits must lose money—or at best, break even—to meet legal requirements. This is a fundamental misunderstanding of the nonprofit concept. A surplus (that is, an excess of income over expenditure) is not only legal; it is desirable. If it were not, how would it have been possible for the established universities, churches, art museums, and other nonprofits to build such large reserves in the form of endowments over the years?

Although surpluses, reserves, and endowments are legal, profits are not. A profit is another name for *owner's equity*. In a for-profit organization, the organization's owners (or partners or shareholders) benefit directly when the organization makes money. They may take the profit in cash or the distribution may be deferred, but in any case, a direct benefit inures to the people who have the financial interest. Nonprofit organizations do not have owners, of course, and they do not have shareholders. They serve the public, and so any excess of income over expenditure must ultimately be used for a charitable purpose. The word *ultimately* is important here. The money does not have to be spent right away. It can be put away in some kind of reserve fund or into an endowment (which is simply a reserve fund that has specific restrictions on when and how the assets are to be used). This putting away process is highly desirable, and all organizations should strive to put some money away each year.

CONTINGENCY/RESERVE

Generating enough excess income in order to put money away can be facilitated through the budget process. A nonprofit organization should create an account called *contingency/reserve*, which should be listed on the expense side of its budget. The amount budgeted on this line should equal as much as 5 percent of the organization's total income. In figure 6.1, for example, a nonprofit organization that has a budget of $84,000 for the year has budgeted $4,200 (or 5 percent) for contingency/reserve and allocated only $79,800 for its regular ongoing expenses. This contingency/reserve amount may vary in other organizations, however, depending on the following factors:

- The size of the budget (larger organizations can allocate a smaller percentage)
- The predictability of levels and sources of income (the less predictable the income, the larger the contingency/reserve)
- The relative stability of the organization (the more unstable or new the organization, the larger the contingency/reserve)
- The extent to which expenditures are fixed in advance (the less fixed the expenditures, the greater the contingency/reserve)
- The experience of the current management (the less experienced the management, the greater the contingency /reserve)

What is the contingency/reserve line item used for? First, it can serve as a form of self-insurance in case some unexpected expense comes up during the year. This is the contingency portion. The Compton Opera Company experiences a bad storm on the night of the big *Aida* production, and single ticket sales come in $2,000 under budget—the contingency/reserve line item takes care of it. Or someone trips on the front stoop of the Compton School and takes legal action, which, even though the organization is insured, leads to an unexpected attorney's fee of $1,000. Once again, the organization has a pocket of uncommitted money from which it can draw.

If at the end of the fiscal year there is still money left over after all contingencies have been taken care of, the line item contingency/reserve becomes simply a reserve. In other words, the unallocated money can be put away in some kind of savings instrument—a savings account, money market fund, or stock—as determined by the board of directors on the advice of a financial professional. Each year, funds should be set aside in this way until such time as the organization has 50 to 100 percent of an entire year's budget in reserve (including board-designated endowment).

Why preach such fiscal conservatism? Anyone familiar with the statistics on the plight of nonprofit organizations knows that a great number go bankrupt within the first decade of existence. Ambitious programs get designed with inadequate financial reserves. Inflation, higher costs, reduced income, and other factors lead to larger and larger cash shortfalls. Prudent planning demands that an organization put away reserves to carry them through tough times.

Another reason to put money in reserve is related to fund raising. Many funders do not wish to be alone in their support of a project or a capital purchase. Others do not like to be the first to contribute. Reserve funds speak to both of these problems in the following way. Suppose a recreation organization wants to buy a new piece of equipment for a town park. It will cost $10,000. The organization wishes to secure ten $1,000 gifts from wealthy individuals in the community. The board knows how difficult it will be to get the first contribution. So, board members agree to guarantee $3,000 of the required amount from the reserve fund. The executive director is now ready to make his first call. He tells the donor that the organization is trying to raise $10,000 and that $3,000 is already in hand. The psychological effect is much more positive than telling the donor that he or she would be making the first contribution. In the end, if the whole $10,000 is raised in contributions, the organization simply does not draw on the reserve funds.

Consider, alternatively, that you wish to embark on an exciting new training program for disadvantaged youth and the U.S. Department of Labor has agreed to give you $25,000 on a matching basis. Because the project is a new one, you cannot find any corporation, foundation, or group of individuals to provide the matching funds. However, you and your board of directors are convinced that the project is important and will ultimately be entirely fundable by outside sources. You decide to draw the matching funds out of your reserve fund. After a year, the project is deemed successful. Now with favorable press material, a positive outside evaluation, and other critical acclaim, you can approach the same funding sources without having to draw on the reserve fund.

Finally, there is another reason why the reserve fund is so important. Most nonprofit organizations experience cash/cash flow problems at some time during the fiscal year, as is discussed later in this chapter. Put another way, these organizations find that they need to pay bills before there is adequate income to do so. Often salaries and programmatic expenditures place heavy cash demands on the budget early in the year while funding sources are slow to come through with the cash (some operate on a reimbursement basis only). It is embarrassing to find the organization in a position where it cannot pay bills or meet its payroll, especially when the board has approved a balanced budget. One alternative is to borrow money, but this is usually expensive unless the organization can draw on the largess of a wealthy friend or board member who will make an interest-free loan. On the other hand, with an adequate reserve fund, the organization can borrow from itself. That is, it can take money from the reserve fund early in the year and replenish it later when the projected income is finally received. It is important to remember, though, that even this procedure has a real cost. By taking money out of a reserve fund, the organization is foregoing certain income by forfeiting interest. It is important to keep this in mind so that the staff does not become cavalier about drawing on the reserves. It is always better to maximize a good cash flow position by doing adequate cash flow planning several months before the beginning of the fiscal year (see Cash Flow, later in this chapter).

Reserve Funds Functioning as Endowment

Some nonprofit administrators and board members are concerned that too large a reserve fund can be a disincentive for funders inasmuch as it looks like the organization may not need money. The fear is that a foundation, corporation, or government agency will look at financial reports that show a healthy reserve and conclude that such funds could be used to support the activities that the organization is seeking support for. This is particularly true in cases where organizations, through prudent fiscal management, allow their reserve funds to grow very large.

While this is less true than it used to be, since funders increasingly recognize that having a cash reserve is an indication of a healthy, stable organization, one way to address this issue is for the board to designate a portion of the reserves as "board designated reserve" or "funds functioning as endowment." An endowment is a reserve fund with special rules and restrictions as to its use. Generally, endowments consist of invested funds (principal) that must be left intact (only income from the investment can be utilized by the organization). While these funds will still be classified as unrestricted on financial statements, a note indicating that they are acting as "board designated reserve" or "funds functioning as endowment" can serve to notify a funder that these funds are not available to cover current expenses.

A second reason to impose an internal restriction or designation for these funds is to assure that these funds are not expended without careful examination of the conditions requiring their expenditure. Excess cash is quite easily expended in the course of daily business, and it is important to assure that the cash reserve only be drawn upon when truly needed. In truth, the board can undesignate the endowment or reserve restrictions that it originally imposed and restore these funds to unrestricted cash reserves at any time. Nevertheless, from the point of view of the presentation of the finances to outsiders and from the point of view of internal financial controls, the organization may be in a better position when some of the reserve funds are designated in this way.

THE BUDGETING PROCESS

If budgeting is a form of financial planning, then it is important to know what specific procedures are involved in doing it effectively. There are two important considerations:

- Budgeting should always be related to the overall planning process of the organization. No one is in a position to plan for the future without a clear sense of what the available resources are. Conversely, sensible budgets, or financial plans, cannot be put together without knowing where the organization is going. Simply allocating money is not enough. Using it strategically is what the budgeting process ideally should be about.
- Trustees, often through a committee, should be involved in both the budgeting and general planning process. Because board members must set long-range goals for the organization, decide on program priorities, and ultimately assume fiscal accountability, it is important that they be involved in the budgeting process both in the forecasting stages and later when the budget is monitored.

Beyond these general considerations, there are eight steps that an organization should take to complete a successful budgeting cycle.

Step 1: Make a Wish List

The first step in budgeting has nothing to do with numbers or dollars. It concerns an annual review of what trustees and senior staff want the organization to accomplish in the year to come. At the beginning of the budget cycle, they should consider a number of questions about the upcoming year:

- What should the organization be doing in the next year?
- What core activities are essential?
- What additional activities might be undertaken if cost were not an object?
- What staff needs are associated with these activities?
- Are there special one-time expenditures that might be considered for things such as equipment, the improvement of physical facilities, and outside consultants to assist with evaluation or marketing or development?

This step is essential because it forces people to think systematically about the organization's activities, its mission, and its programs. It provides an opportunity to review the purposes for which the organization was formed, its long-range goals and plans, and its short-term objectives. Making a wish list is fun because it does not require a close monitoring of costs. It is the last time in the budgeting process that such an opportunity presents itself.

Step 2: Cost Out the List

How much will it cost to carry out the activities listed in Step 1? Obviously, there are some basic costs that have to be covered just to keep the organization going. There is the office, core staff salaries, and expenses related to the basic programs that were done last year and that will continue. Each of these must be carefully costed. In addition, the expenses associated with new activities will also have to be evaluated.

Determining how much things will cost is not an easy process. There are two approaches commonly used:

- The first approach, called the *incremental budgeting* method, leans heavily on information contained in previous years' actual expenses and income. If an organization is carrying out an activity that it has done for several years, then the easiest way to prepare a budget for the coming year is to add a percentage increment for inflation and other factors to the figures contained in the previous year's financial statement (referred to as "actuals") or the current year's budget.

- The second approach, called *zero-based budgeting*, requires that each line item of a budget be calculated anew. Staff members are told that any item in the budget will be zero unless they can provide a full justification for some other figure.

Obviously, some combination of these two approaches is desirable in the budgeting process. The previous year's expenses together with projected expenses for the current year will be immensely helpful in estimating not only the next year's expenses but also income for the period. On the other hand, each item in the budget should also be examined carefully without reference to another year's figures. An assessment should be made, item by item, of whether the expenditure is required and if so, how large it should be. In addition, new projects and activities require estimates for which the previous year's actuals and budget are not very helpful.

In costing out the wish list developed in Step 1, two things are important to remember:

- Costs should always be estimated on the high side. Add at least 5 percent to all expense figures. Those people who budget expenses at a level they think will be correct (with no percentage added) are almost always underbudgeting.
- As you consider the costs of *new* programs and activities, remember that they will add to your central administrative costs. It is not enough simply to estimate how much you will actually spend on a new program. The simple addition of the program puts an added burden on the core staff, space, office equipment, and so on.

COMPTON HOSPITAL'S INVISIBLE EXPENSES

As an example of how a new activity almost invisibly seems to increase central administrative costs, consider the case of Compton Hospital, which decided to undertake a prenatal education program. Staff members costed out all anticipated expenditures connected with the new program. However, they forgot that the hospital published the *Information Bulletin,* in which each hospital class was given a one-page description. By adding the prenatal class, the hospital was required to add a page to a publication that was paid for out of its central administrative budget and hire a designer to spend some time adding to the organization's website. It is crucial, as the costing process goes forward, that realistic overhead increases such as these are built into the budgets of new initiatives.

If project budgeting (see earlier discussion) is being used by an organization, projected expenses should be allocated to proper categories (see figure 6.4).

Step 3: Allocate Income

Using the same list of activities developed in Step 1 and costed out in Step 2, it is now time to consider how much income can be expected from each activity. Again, last year's actuals and the current year's updated budget projections can be helpful. However, this step has some built-in complications because it is likely that there are certain funds specifically earmarked for particular activities and other income that has no such restrictions and can be put anywhere.

Here it is important to differentiate between unrestricted and restricted funds. Unrestricted funds are monies received with no particular instructions or limitations as to how they are to be used. Admissions, memberships, earned income from publications or a shop, and general donations are all examples of unrestricted funds. Restricted funds, on the other hand, are those received with special conditions placed on their use. The conditions can apply to the time period during which they are to be used, the purpose of their use, or both. A grant for a new piece of equipment or a contribution to a scholarship fund can only be used for the purpose that the donor specified. Similarly, a grant for the fiscal year beginning July 1, 2012 cannot be used before that date or after June 30, 2013. An organization can always request that the person or organization that imposed a restriction lift or change it. However, until such permission is given, restricted funds must not be used for any other purpose.[1]

Figure 6.4. Compton Museum Project Budgeting

Expense Projections

	Education Program	Permanent Collection	Travelling Exhibitions	Membership	Fund Raising	Administration	Total
Salaries	$22,500	$18,000	$9,000	$10,000	$25,000	$20,000	$104,500
Benefits	3,375	2,700	1,350	1,500	3,750	3,000	15,675
Fees	16,000	2,000	0	0	5,000	4,000	27,000
Supplies	2,700	500	500	1,100	800	3,000	8,600
Telephone	300	600	600	500	200	2,000	4,200
Travel	0	50	700	100	2,000	2,000	4,850
Printing	2,000	2,000	2,000	2,000	2,000	2,000	12,000
Equipment	1,000	1,500	500	500	500	2,000	6,000
Shipping	0	500	2,000	0	0	0	2,500
Utilities	600	1,500	300	300	300	600	3,600
Insurance	800	11,000	5,000	200	200	1,000	18,200
Total	$49,275	$40,350	$21,950	$16,200	$39,750	$39,600	$207,125

Source: Compiled by the author.

Once restricted funds and unrestricted funds have been separated, the process of allocating income is as follows (see figure 6.5):

1. Put all restricted income into the proper program activity or category. That is, any income clearly attributable to a specific project should be put into that category and marked. Later on, if the budgeting team begins cutting back programs or reallocating income, it is important to remember that these funds cannot be transferred from one program category to another.
2. Cover all of the most basic administrative costs with unrestricted income.
3. Allocate the balance of unrestricted income across all the programs and activities listed. You may want to allocate it on a percentage basis as was discussed in connection with expenses in the section on project budgeting. Or you may want to use a simpler method and divide the money up on a roughly equal basis among programs. The first method, although more work, does help you assess the relative cost-effectiveness of programs.
4. Understate all income estimates by at least 5 percent. Just as you left some margin for error on expenses, so must you be equally conservative on income forecasting.

Step 4: Compare

This is often called the read-it-and-weep step. It should be clear by this time that some activities must be given up if the budget is going to balance. There is simply too much expense and not enough income. In fact, if income is adequate to cover expenditures at this point in the budgeting process, there should be great concern that the organization is not reaching far enough or being ambitious enough. Put another way, if the organization can pay for all of its wishes *at this point in the budgeting process,* people are not wishing hard enough. The organization's reach should exceed its grasp so that it can continue to grow in its ability to provide services and programs to the public. However, the board is not acting responsibly when it ultimately undertakes more than it can pay for. Many projects should be considered even though only some will be undertaken immediately. The examination of a potential activity one year is valuable in planning for that activity another year.

Figure 6.5. Compton Museum Income Projections with Restricted and Unrestricted Funds Separated

	Education Program	Permanent Collection	Travelling Exhibitions	Membership	Fund Raising	Administration	Total
Membership	$0	$5,350	$0	$16,200	$7,500	$7,500	$36,550
Admissions	10,000	0	0	0	15,000	15,000	40,000
Rental fees	0	0	14,000*	0	0	0	14,000
Tuition	28,500*	0	0	0	0	0	28,500
Museum shop	0	0	0	0	7,500	7,500	15,000
Individual donations	0	30,000	0	0	9,750	9,600	49,350
Government grants	0	5,000	2,500	0	0	0	7,500
Corporate grants	2,500†	0	0	0	0	0	2,500
Foundation grants	2,000†	0	0	0	0	0	2,000
Endowment income	4,000†	0	1,000	0	0	0	5,000
Total	$47,000	$40,350	$17,500	$16,200	$39,750	$39,600	$200,400

Source: Compiled by the author.

Note: Only unrestricted funds can be switched from one column to another. If there is a decision to eliminate the education program, for example, only the $10,000 of unrestricted income from admissions can be switched. The funds with a dagger in that column will be lost as income unless restrictions are lifted by donors. The asterisked funds in that column ($28,500 in tuition fees) will be lost revenue and therefore cannot be reallocated.

*Income generated by program
†Restricted gift

In evaluating one program activity against another, the board should be careful about using the exclusive criterion of cost-effectiveness. There are certainly appropriate questions that can be asked. Which activities come closest to paying for themselves? Which have the highest cost relative to the income that they bring in? But these are the kinds of questions that are more compelling in profit-making companies. While they are certainly of more than passing interest to any nonprofit organization, it is important to remember that nonprofit organizations are not in business primarily to make money. Their missions may dictate that they *should* carry on certain activities that are not cost-effective. How would we feel, for example, if the only activities engaged in by a certain church were its profitable rummage sales and bingo games? We (and, most likely, the IRS) would be concerned that a more fundamental mission of the church was not being fulfilled. Thus cost-effectiveness, while one major criterion, is only one; the primary criterion should relate to the mission of the organization—its purposes, goals, and objectives.

Step 5: Set Priorities

Any board member or staff person who has sat through a budget balancing session knows how traumatic it can be. Everyone seems to have a pet project. Every expenditure appears to have its defender. Yet at the same time everyone knows that the organization must be more fiscally restrained. In the end, a priority-setting session must relate not solely to dollars and cents but to a fundamental assessment of the organization's reason for being. It is too easy in the heat of the moment to argue for or against a proposed expenditure on its own merits or on cost-effectiveness. But it is important to ask questions such as the following ones:

- Is this activity really central to what the organization is about?
- Does it help the organization get where it should be in a year, in two years, in five years?
- Might it be more important to build a reserve to protect the organization over the long term than engage in a new activity area?

These are difficult questions, but in asking them, the trustees are fulfilling a fundamental role in deciding what course is best for the organization and most clearly in the public interest.

Step 6: Adjust and Balance

Once activities have been put in some semblance of priority order, a little negotiation is still possible as the budget is adjusted and put into balance. If the Compton Museum's travelling exhibition program is a high priority but there is simply not quite enough income to cover it, perhaps some money can come out of the acquisitions budget. If the program is dropped instead, monies that were allocated to it can be moved to other areas if those monies are unrestricted. One must be careful, obviously, not to move monies that can only be used for the travelling exhibition program itself. For example, if there is a grant for that program or if there was income projected from exhibition rentals, that income is now lost to the organization.

There is one other danger at this point in the budgeting process, and that is going back and exaggerating income in order to avoid making the hard budget cuts. Consider the following case:

> ## THE BUDGET SESSION OF THE COMPTON YMCA
>
> The finance committee of the Compton YMCA had spent three evenings trying to balance the budget for the coming year before presenting it to the full board. The group had arrived at an impasse. They could find no more cuts, and expenses still exceeded revenues by about $70,000 on a budget of $1.3 million. The contingency line of the budget had already been cut from $65,000 to $30,000, which was the precise amount of income projected from two questionable grants that were written into the budget. As the third evening's meeting was coming to an end, the head of the committee said, "Let's just increase the line of the budget for Individual Giving by $70,000. It will mean everyone will have to work a little harder this year." In order to balance the budget, the fatigued group agreed to increase the line for Individual Giving to a figure that was 50 percent higher than that recommended by the development committee.

Was this a responsible step for the budget committee to take? Probably not. While the budget numbers were now in balance, they were based on unrealistic income projections. The development committee had made its best estimate of contributed income, and the finance committee had exceeded it by a large margin. Such action simply increases the risk of a deficit at the end of the year.

The budgeting process, as discussed so far, has guaranteed that figures will be skewed conservatively. Income has been understated, expenses overstated, and up to 5 percent of total income has been put in the contingency/reserve category. Even though the budget is balanced on paper, it would appear that there is far more money coming in than going out. Careful budgeting, however, requires this approach. It is almost always the case that certain expenses have been forgotten and certain anticipated income will come in short. In the event that the actual financial picture results in income far exceeding expenses, the board has the enviable task of deciding what to do with the additional money.

Step 7: Approve

Now that the budget has been worked out, it is necessary for the full board of directors to discuss and approve it. This is more than a mere formality. In voting through a budget, the board exercises its fiduciary responsibility in setting financial limits and boundaries for the staff. The board is also implicitly agreeing to meet the projected revenues through a commitment to fund raising. A board of directors should never approve a budget based on a wish and a prayer that projects unrealistic fund-raising goals. If such a budget is approved and the funds are not raised, it is the trustees who must take responsibility. Thus a good question to ask during the approval process is, "Do we really know how every projected revenue dollar will be earned or raised, who will be responsible, and whether the targets are realistic?"

On the expense side, a responsible board member should ask how estimates were determined. For example, if the line item for Postage is $2,500 and the board member is told by staff that the number was arrived at by taking last year's figure, a good question might be, "Is that a realistic figure, given the fact that postal rates have increased by 20 percent and we have added 3,000 people to our mailing list?"

Indeed, because the previous year's budget is so often the primary document from which so many estimates are made, it is easy for the budget preparers to forget to take obvious changes into consideration. Trustees should challenge the budget document, not because they doubt the ability of the staff or finance committee, but because it is they who are ultimately responsible for the fiscal health of the organization.

Step 8: Monitor and Amend

One common mistake in the budget process is to assume it has come to an end once the board approves the final document. Indeed, the very word *final* is a misnomer when talking about a budget. Few budgets can hold up over time unless they are amended and modified to accommodate new information and new conditions as the year wears on. For this reason, board and staff must set up a process by which the budget can be reviewed when necessary and changed.

Two extremes should be avoided. The board should not insist that the document they have approved "is it" and force the staff to stick to it without modification throughout the fiscal year. On the other hand, the board should not be willing to say that the budget document is only a rough approximation and give staff instructions to "come as close as possible." Rather, board-approved policies and procedures should be set up to allow staff some flexibility but give the board the final say on any significant changes in the budget figures.

For example, in a $100,000 budget, the board may tell the executive director the following (which would be documented in the minutes of the board meeting at which it was approved): "As long as you feel you can balance the budget, you may shift up to 15 percent or $2,000 (whichever is less) out of, or into, any account. However, if more significant changes are to be made, you must present a revised budget to the board for approval."

By way of example, let us say that the line item Equipment has a budgeted amount of $20,000. Using the guidelines previously listed, the director may, at his or her discretion and without board approval, move up to $2,000 to some other expenditure category or may choose to spend $2,000 more in that category. The director should not do the extra spending, however, unless he or she is relatively confident that the budget can still be balanced with additional income or by shifting the $2,000 from some other category where it is not needed. If the director anticipates that more than an additional $2,000 is necessary for equipment, then the full board must be consulted and an amended budget must be submitted and approved.

A budget can serve as a valuable measuring stick against which the growth of an organization (or project) can be evaluated. Although it is important to revise a budget to reflect special circumstances or opportunities, the original budget for a particular year can be a valuable tool when making projections for the future. Changes made during the year should be reviewed by the staff and finance committee members when making new projections so that errors made (such as underestimation of costs or overestimation of income) can be avoided when a new budget is prepared.

FRAMEWORK (OR MULTIYEAR) BUDGETS

Limiting the budgeting process to one-year projections the way many nonprofit organizations do can cause problems for medium- and large-size organizations. This is because many of these organizations have to make plans several years in advance. Frequently staff members must make commitments for major expenses months or even years before the budgeting cycle begins, as is the case for a museum planning exhibitions with a lead time of three years or a school developing a new department. The danger is that by the time the board and senior staff review and then are ready to approve the coming year's annual budget, large sums of money will have already been committed. This may significantly limit the ability of board members to react to a changing financial climate.

How can this problem be overcome? One way is through a process called *framework budget planning*, a strategy designed to provide timely long-range budget forecasts. As discussed earlier, budget planning is an integral part of any organizational planning process. The framework budget planning component furnishes a plan, particularly a long-range plan, with a crucial—and often overlooked—component: the necessary structure for board and staff to develop multiyear estimated budgets based on the specific program plans for the future.

The first stage in developing a framework budget is not unlike the beginning stage of the normal annual budgeting cycle. The staff compiles one year of historical budget figures and provides estimates of the current year's projected figures. Also included is the coming year's proposed budget once it is completed. These three sets of figures are projected in columns in such a way that all the budget categories are comparable from one year to another (see figure 6.6). Once this information has been gathered, it can be used to analyze trends and make

Figure 6.6. Framework Budget for Anyplace Community Center

	Actuals	Projected Current	Approved Budget	Conservative Version Estimated Budgets		
Income	2009	2010	2011	2012	2013	2014
Tuition/workshops	$10,223	$11,100	$13,800	$17,000	$21,000	$25,000
Corporate membership	3,250	3,350	3,750	4,300	5,100	6,100
Other contributions	2,780	2,750	2,800	3,100	3,500	4,200
Government grants	0	5,000	6,500	7,000	7,000	7,000
Total income	$16,253	$22,200	$26,850	$31,400	$36,600	$42,300
Expenses						
Staff salary	$5,500	$7,500	$8,500	$9,750	$10,500	$13,000
Professional fees	8,750	9,950	10,775	12,000	14,400	16,000
Art instruction material	1,100	1,545	1,750	2,500	3,370	4,100
Classroom rental	3,000	3,500	4,000	4,750	5,500	6,000
Contingency/reserve	0	0	1,340	1,570	1,830	2,115
Total expenses	$18,350	$22,495	$26,365	$30,570	$35,600	$41,215
Excess (or deficit) of revenues	($2,097)	($295)	$485	$830	$1,000	$1,085

Optimistic Version

	Actuals	Projected Current	Approved Budget	Estimated Budgets		
	2009	2010	2011	2012	2013	2014
Income						
Tuition/workshops	$10,223	$11,100	$13,800	$18,000	$23,000	$28,000
Corporate membership	3,250	3,350	3,750	5,000	6,200	8,100
Other contributions	2,780	2,750	2,800	3,500	4,000	4,800
Government grants	0	5,000	6,500	7,500	9,000	10,000
Total income	$16,253	$22,200	$26,850	$34,000	$42,200	$50,900
Expenses						
Staff salary	$5,500	$7,500	$8,500	$11,000	$13,500	$17,000
Professional fees	8,750	9,950	10,775	13,000	16,500	19,000
Art instruction material	1,100	1,545	1,750	2,600	3,500	4,400
Classroom rental	3,000	3,500	4,000	4,800	5,500	6,100
Contingency/reserve	0	0	1,340	1,700	2,110	2,545
Total expenses	$18,350	$22,495	$26,365	$33,100	$41,110	$49,045
Excess (or deficit) of revenues	($2,097)	($295)	$485	$900	$1,090	$1,855

Source: Compiled by the author.

projections for the future, utilizing a spreadsheet program to facilitate changes and recalculations.

Once the historical figures have been established, two separate income and expense projections for the next three or four years—called the "optimistic" and "conservative" scenarios—are developed in consultation with board members and staff. The optimistic version tends to project higher levels of earned and contributed income, while the conservative version shows easily achievable revenue targets. The expenses in each scenario may also be adjusted based on these alternative assumptions about income, or they may be kept the same in both versions, in which case the bottom line of the two scenarios will vary by the amount of the differing income assumptions.

The advantage of framework budgeting is that it allows board members to understand what the future may have in store, given different assumptions about the future, and it allows them to make plans accordingly. Sometimes, by seeing what the conservative projections look like, board members may defer certain activities. In other cases, they may adjust fund-raising goals. In either case, they will be making decisions based on better and more complete information.

By developing budgets for several years, framework budget planning provides a longer budget cycle that more accurately reflects the planning needs of many institutions. Equally important, by offering at least two alternative versions of the multiyear budgets, framework budget planning can forge a link between the budgeting and planning functions and ensure that planning decisions are based on a sound analysis of the future.

Like any good planning process, framework budgeting should not be seen as a one-time procedure but as an ongoing management tool. Each year, the board should not only review and approve a proposed budget for the coming fiscal year, but also review framework budgets for up to three subsequent years. In this way board members can see an overall five-year financial and program plan on an annual basis.

CASH FLOW

We prepared a conservative budget and thought we were in good shape. Three months into the fiscal year we found ourselves out of money. Bills were coming in faster than we received cash. The state agencies that provided tuition money for certain kids were often three to six months behind in their payments, and the federal government wouldn't allow us to keep any of its funds on hand (we could only request what we had spent). We had never heard the term cash flow *before, but we sure learned the hard way what a cash flow problem is.*

These words came from the director of a day care center. Her experience is not unusual. Like so many people who devise a sensible budget, she thought she would have no financial problems. She never thought about the fact that an annual budget only tells an organization how things should come out at the end of the year. It does not tell how much cash needs to be on hand at various points during the year. It is important to calculate the interim cash situations so that the staff knows whether it will need to make some special arrangements in order to pay the bills.

Cash flow projections are most commonly prepared on a monthly basis for the upcoming fiscal year. In the analysis, an organization's income and expenses are projected for each month. The budget is laid out on a spreadsheet with separate columns for each month. Each horizontal row lists a budget line item. In the first column is the name of the item, in the second is the annual budgeted amount for that item, and in the subsequent columns are the anticipated receipts or expenditures for that item by month. For example, if salaries for the year are $120,000, and if they do not change from month to month, the line item Salaries would appear with its annual total of $120,000 followed by the various monthly totals of $10,000 in each of the subsequent columns. The first three months would look like this:

	Total	January	February	March
Salaries	$120,000	$10,000	$10,000	$10,000

On the other hand, if all of the income from a fund-raising event is anticipated in March, the line item Fund-raising event would look like this:

	Total	January	February	March
Fund-raising event	$5,000	$0	$0	$5,000

In preparing a cash flow projection, if you are not sure when a particular expenditure is going to be due, it is best to be conservative, plan for the worst, and figure that it is going to be due on the early side; to practice the same prudence with income, you should err on the late side in predicting when cash is going to come in.

Once you have listed your estimated monthly income and expenses, you can compute your monthly net income (or loss). A monthly net income (or loss) is simply the difference between total income and total expenses during that month. If after preparing your monthly budget chart, you anticipate that your organization will take in $6,812 in July and spend $6,467, you will have a net income for July of $345. If for August you show income of $5,673 and expenses of $6,529, you will have a net loss for August of $856 (see figure 6.7).

All of this is useful to know, but it becomes even more valuable when you are able to analyze your changes in cash flow position from month to month. What you really want to see is how the ups and downs of your monthly cash balances affect a cumulative flow of cash. The way this is done is shown in the cash flow summary at the bottom of figure 6.7. To begin with, you show how much cash you will have on hand in the bank at the beginning of the month (opening cash balance). To this amount you add (or subtract) your net monthly income (or loss)—the difference between income and expense for that month. The sum of these two numbers is your ending, or cumulative, cash balance for the month. This bottom line tells you where you stand at one month's end and tells you how much you will have to start the next month with. Thus the ending cash balance for July becomes the opening cash balance for August and so on.

If you do cash flow projections early enough (four to six months before the start of the fiscal year), you are usually in a much better position to solve a potential cash shortage problem. For example, you might make a special plea to a major donor to consider an earlier than usual contribution, you might decide to do your fund-raising event earlier in the year, or you might negotiate with your printer to spread your payments over two months rather than just one. People are generally much more flexible about these requests if you give them plenty of warning. By way of contrast, if the day of reckoning comes and you have not attempted to make prior arrangements with creditors to help alleviate your cash flow problems, they will likely become impatient

Figure 6.7. Hippy Dippy Day Care Cash Flow

	July	August
Expected income		
Parent fees	$2,500	$1,810
Title XX	2,211	2,106
School lunch program	926	882
United Way	875	875
Fund raising	300	0
Other income	0	0
Total income	$6,812	$5,673
Expected expenses		
Staff salaries	$3,468	$3,468
Substitutes	280	350
Benefits	544	556
Legal and audit fees	100	100
Program development/training	50	0
Rent/mortgage	425	425
Utilities	50	40
Food	950	890
Equipment, supplies, services	200	550
Insurance	250	0
Loan repayment	150	150
Total expenditures	$6,467	$6,529
Monthly net income (or loss)*	$345	($856)
Cash flow summary		
Opening cash balance†	$200	$545
Monthly net income (or loss)	345	(856)
Ending (cumulative) cash balance	$545	($311)

Source: This example is adapted from Roger Neugebauer, "Money Management Tools—Cash Flow Analysis," *Child Care Information Exchange* 19:10.

*Equals total monthly income less total monthly expenses

†Equals amount of money in the bank at the beginning of the month (the same as the ending cumulative cash balance of the previous month)

and will tend to remember your bad planning the next time you attempt to do business with them, perhaps insisting on full payment in advance.

If all else fails and you will have a cash shortfall during the year, you have several alternatives. One is to take money from your reserve fund if you have one. For this reason, many organizations leave a substantial portion of their reserve in some liquid savings instrument so they can get at the cash quickly when they need it. If you do not have a reserve fund, you may be forced to borrow money for a short period of time. Ideally, a trustee (or several) might loan you the cash interest free. Otherwise, you will have to borrow from a bank, which can be difficult (if you do not have good credit) and/or expensive. If cash must be borrowed and interest must be paid on the loan, be sure to build the interest payment into the expenses of your budget.

This chapter began with a quote from a board member who has never taken an interest in the financial affairs of the nonprofit organization that he serves. It is hoped that he and others like him will realize that there are aspects of the financial affairs of the corporation that are, quite properly, part of their responsibilities as trustees. Although these trustees will not be expected to prepare the budget, they must at least familiarize themselves with it so they can make responsible decisions based on the information it contains. They should also understand something about cash flow and other financial matters. Leaving things completely to others is simply too risky a course.

CHECKLIST QUESTIONS FOR CHAPTER 6

1. Does the timing of your organization's fiscal year allow for meaningful financial comparisons to be made between one year's activities and the next?
2. Does your organization's chart of accounts provide sufficient detail to allow for necessary financial analysis of performance?
3. Does your organization's budgeting system allow board and staff to analyze the comparative cost of various programs and activities?
4. Has your organization developed a cash reserve fund?
5. Does the budgeting process allow for the input of board members? Is the process sufficiently conservative to prevent the incurring of unintended deficits at the end of the year?
6. Does your organization do multiyear budgeting for long-range planning purposes?
7. Does your organization do regular cash flow analyses?

SEVEN

Financial Statements and Fiscal Procedures

Samuel Snyder is the director of finance for the Creighton Home, a residential treatment center for drug addicts. His wife claims not to understand how this could be the case: "Sam's boss told me last month that he is the most meticulous person she had ever seen. He rides herd on finances—monitoring expenses and income, doing complicated final reports on grant budgets, and working with the accountants at the end of the fiscal year on the audit. But he is so casual about finances at home that I am the one who keeps our personal checkbook in balance. Last year, Sam overdrew our account three times because he forgot to enter checks in the checkbook (which I always do) or at least look at our account on line. And, as far as our taxes go, forget it. If I didn't do them, they wouldn't get done. Sam is the modern version of Dr. Jekyll and Mr. Hyde. By day, he stabilizes the financial ship at the Creighton Home. But when he leaves work, he doesn't bring his financial head home with him."

Samuel Snyder knows a very important fact. Nonprofit organizations do not enjoy the luxury afforded to individuals who can conduct their financial affairs in a relatively casual and lax manner and get away with it. Individuals can forget to enter a check that they have written or assume the bank is correct when monthly bank statements arrive and simply skip doing a reconciliation. Nonprofits, on the other hand, must maintain records carefully and should have these records reviewed periodically by an independent outside examiner who can certify that the organization is operating legally and according to *generally accepted accounting procedures*. Because nonprofit organizations enjoy numerous financially lucrative privileges and benefits (as we saw in chapter 1), they must be able to demonstrate that their fiscal houses are in order. Board members are ultimately fiscally responsible for these organizations and must be able to read financial statements and be aware of reporting requirements and fiscal systems.

It generally falls to staff people such as Sam Snyder to implement these systems.

In this chapter, we continue our discussion of finances, beginning with an explanation of accounting systems, then focusing on financial statements, and ending with a description of financial controls and reporting requirements. Again, an effort will be made to explain financial terminology and outline those areas that are critical to fulfilling the fiscal responsibilities that accrue to board members and staff.

ACCOUNTING

Accounting is the term used for financial record keeping. There are two common accounting methods. The first, *cash-basis accounting,* has the advantage of being simple and straightforward; the second, *accrual-based accounting,* is more complex but gives a more complete view of the organization's fiscal health.

Cash-basis accounting. Most people are familiar with cash-basis accounting because they do it when they maintain financial records for their checking and savings accounts. Financial transactions are recorded *only when cash changes hands.* When a person receives money and deposits it in the bank, the deposit is recorded as income and is added to the bank account balance. When cash is withdrawn from the bank (or when a check is written, which is the equivalent of a withdrawal), the transaction is recorded as an expense and subtracted from the bank account balance. The cash-basis accounting system is quite straightforward if all a person needs to know is how much money is in the account. However, what it does not reveal is the financial health of the person maintaining the account, because it tells nothing about what that individual owes and how much is owed to him or her.

Accrual-based accounting. For many individuals, credit cards have forced a kind of informal accrual-based accounting into their personal systems of financial record keeping. This system takes into account not only their actual payments and deposits but also what they owe and what is owed to them. Although few of us do formal accrual-based accounting in our personal lives, a lot of us do something very much like it when we estimate whether or not we will have enough cash to pay the mortgage or rent during the next month. If we see a nice article of clothing and try to figure out whether we can afford it by thinking about our outstanding bills and yet-to-be-received paychecks, we are engaged in informal accrual-based accounting.

Accrual-based accounting recognizes expenses not only when money changes hands but also when expenses are incurred and income is committed. If the Compton Community Center purchases office supplies for $125, an accrual-based system recognizes the $125 as a financial obligation from the moment the purchase order is written, and the amount is deducted from the organization's net worth at that time. Similarly, if the Compton Community Center receives an official notification from a funding agency of a $5,000 grant, the $5,000 is added to the net worth figure for the organization as soon as the letter is received. In the case of the $125 owed for supplies, the amount is reflected in the financial statements as a *payable* until the check is actually written. In the case of the $5,000 grant, the amount is entered on the books as a *receivable* until a check is actually deposited.

In the case just cited, if the Compton Community Center has $3,000 in the bank on the day that it charges $125 worth of office supplies and receives the grant letter for $5,000, a cash-basis accounting system ignores these transactions and only indicates the organization's bank balance of $3,000. An accrual-based accounting system, on the other hand, adds the $5,000 grant receivable and subtracts the $125 payable, showing a net figure of $7,875, which is a truer picture of the organization's net worth (see figure 7.1).

Figure 7.1. Cash Versus Accrual

	Cash	Accrual
Beginning cash in bank	$3,000	$3,000
Purchased supplies (payable)	0	–125
Grant commitment (receivable)	0	$+5,000
Ending cash in bank	$3,000	
Net worth		$7,875

Source: Compiled by the author.

Knowing the full financial condition of an organization (how much it has in hand, how much it owes, and how much is owed to it) is certainly more revealing than knowing its bank balance. Imagine that an organization with $10,000 in the bank signs a contract for $20,000 in consultant services. On a cash basis, a financial accounting would only reveal a positive cash balance of $10,000. On an accrual basis, the outstanding commitment of $20,000 would be taken into account, and the organization would show a shortfall of $10,000. From the point of view of a prospective trustee, a funder, or anyone else attempting to assess the organization's fiscal health, the second figure would give a more accurate picture.

Choosing Methods

Cash-basis accounting is much simpler than the accrual method and provides many people in a nonprofit organization with enough financial information most of the time. It keeps accurate track of income and outflow, and it tells people whether there is sufficient cash in the bank to pay the bills. Occasionally, however, the information from an accrual-based system is also necessary. For that reason, many organizations, even those with budgets in excess of a million dollars, use what is called a *modified cash basis accounting* system. According to this system, the books are kept on a cash basis except for a few accounts that are kept on accrual and usually updated only at the end of the month or at financial reporting time. Generally, these accounts include those in which regular or important outstanding obligations need to be monitored, including federal taxes payable and state taxes payable. These accounts show how much money has been withheld from employees' salaries and how much needs to be paid to federal and state taxing authorities at a later date. Accounts kept on the accrual basis may also include what are called plant fund accounts, particularly when an organization is purchasing equipment, land, or buildings over a period of years. In such cases, it is advantageous to show the amount of the annual budget committed to (or due) the plant fund for these long-term purchases. When accounts are maintained in this way, the obligated monies are factored into the accounting system so that the organization does not spend the cash on other things just because it happens to have it sitting in the bank.

In either a modified cash-basis system or a strictly cash-basis system, it is necessary, at least once a year, to convert *all* of the accounts to accrual. At the end of the fiscal year, as part of the annual audit, an accountant will take all the payables and receivables and factor them into the financial statements, thus allowing the organization to show its entire financial operation on an accrual system. It should be pointed out that this practice—presenting year-end financial statements on an accrual basis—is one of the "generally accepted accounting procedures" approved by the accounting profession. Only very small organizations with budgets of perhaps $75,000 or less should try to get by with closing statements that are not presented in this way. For organizations whose boards of trustees (or funders or regulatory agencies) may require more frequent complete accrual-based statements, the books can be converted to full accrual more often.

FUND ACCOUNTING

A small organization may have a simple budget for its entire operation—a kind of composite statement of the predicted expense and income for the entire organization. The *single fund budget* shown in figure 6.1 in the previous chapter is a good example. As organizations grow more complex, however, they may need to develop several subdivisions of this type of budget in order to gain an accurate analysis of the operation. One such method was described in the previous chapter under Project Budgeting, and an example was shown in figure 6.3.

Fund accounting is a method that allows organizations to track their financial resources according to various categories or "funds." Each fund becomes its own accounting entity, with its own categories of revenue and expense, its own assets, and its own liabilities. Some funds that are commonly established include:

- *Operating or unrestricted current fund:* any monies received, expended, held, or owed by the organization without conditions as to their use
- *Restricted current fund:* any monies received, expended, held, or owed by the organization with conditions placed either on when they may be used or for what purpose they may be used
- *Plant fund:* any monies received, expended, held, or owed by the organization in conjunction with land, buildings, and major equipment as well as the value of such items held by the organization
- *Endowment fund:* any monies received, expended, held, or owed by the organization in conjunction with an endowment
- *Cash reserve fund:* any monies received, expended, held, or owed by the organization in conjunction with a cash reserve

The total of activity in all funds becomes the total activity of the organization.[1]

Figure 7.2 shows a financial statement using fund accounting. The first column summarizes the income and expenses associated with general activities. The second column summarizes income and expenses associated with two contributions restricted for use in connection with a program for gifted and talented children. The third column summarizes income and expenses associated with improvements to the school building, and the fourth column represents the sum of the first three.

Figure 7.2. Multiple Funds of the Compton School

	Unrestricted Current	Restricted Current	Plant Fund	Total
Income				
Tuition	$41,222			$41,222
Book store sales	10,173			10,173
Foundation grant	5,496	50,000		55,496
Business scholarship	5,000			5,000
Individuals	15,621	1,000	8,000	24,621
Total	$77,512	$51,000	$8,000	$136,512
Expenses				
Salaries	$47,500	24,500		$72,000
Benefits	7,122	3,621		10,743
Honoraria	2,500	16,586		19,086
Supplies and materials	5,287			5,287
Equipment rental	3,401			3,401
Promotion	6,526			6,526
Utilities/heating	3,212			3,212
Repairs/maintenance			9,997	9,997
Contingency/reserve	711		2,900	3,611
Total	$76,259	$44,707	$12,897	$133,863

Source: Compiled by the author.

FINANCIAL STATEMENTS

Just as accounting systems are standardized, so are financial statements. When trustees and others want to assess the organization's financial health, they will look at two financial statements: the balance sheet and the income statement. A health metaphor is appropriate here, because the two statements are used as a diagnostic tool in much the same way medical reports are used. Consider, for example, a doctor wishing to diagnose a sick patient. The first thing a doctor checks is the patient's vital signs chart, which reports such things as temperature, pulse, and blood pressure *at a particular moment in time*. The second thing the doctor checks is the patient's medical history, a record of the patient's health *over the course of time*. Neither record by itself is adequate. Two patients with the exact same vital signs may be in very different states of health—the one recovering from a serious illness, the other on a decline from previously good health. Unless the doctor can assess progress over time, a vital signs chart is inadequate. Yet, the medical history is not adequate by itself either. It may be fine to know how a patient has been treated for various ailments over a period of five to ten years, but without an up-to-date reading of the patient's vital signs, there is no way to assess the patient's current state of health.

The balance sheet and the income statement serve the same function in the financial area as the vital signs chart and the medical history do in the health area. The balance sheet, like the vital signs chart, is similar to a freeze frame, a snapshot of the organization's financial condition as of a particular date (often the last day of the final month of the fiscal year). It summarizes the organization's vital financial signs—the value of what it owns, what it owes, what is owed to it, and how much is left over. The income statement, by way of contrast, is like the medical history. It summarizes financial activity over a period of time (often a month or a year). If the balance sheet tells only where the organization's finances stand as of a particular moment in time, the income statement helps the financial diagnostician determine whether the manner in which the organization arrived at that state was "healthy." Armed with the income statement, more formally referred to as the Statement of Revenue and Expenditures or Statement of Activities, it is possible to determine whether the organization had a surplus, a deficit, made any unusually large expenditures, or had any revenue windfalls.

FASB Reporting Requirements

In the mid 1990s, the Financial Accounting Standards Board (FASB) issued new guidelines and language into nonprofit accounting. The changes, described in Standards #116 and #117, were broad reaching and included altered reporting formats, new rules regarding reporting of contributions, and new classifications for assets.

The FASB standards have made the interpretation of financial statements difficult for many trustees who are not trained accountants, and while FASB standards must be used by all organizations in their annual audited statements (see section on audited statements presented later in this chapter), some organizations do not use them for their regular internal financial reporting. The following section on financial statements will focus primarily on the basic financial statements many organizations use for internal reporting. When these statements vary from those required by FASB, a reference will be made to this variation.

THE BALANCE SHEET
(STATEMENT OF FINANCIAL POSITION)

The balance sheet (see figure 7.3) is so called because each half adds up to the same total number. One half of the balance sheet (shown at the top of the statement) lists all of the organization's assets (that is, everything that the organization owns). The other half (shown on the bottom of the statement) lists both the organization's liabilities (everything that it owes) and its net assets (formerly known as fund balance). Thus the *balance* in a balance sheet is between assets on the one hand and liabilities and net assets on the other. Put in mathematical form:

Assets = Liabilities + Net Assets

Understanding this formula, we can easily see how the net assets are calculated. If we know how much we own and how much we owe, the net assets are simply the difference between the two numbers:

Net Assets = Assets − Liabilities

In a profit-making corporation, the net assets are referred to as *profit* or *owner's equity*. In a nonprofit organization where there are no owners and no profits, the net assets show the organization's financial net worth when all of its financial obligations are subtracted from all of its cash and noncash assets. The net assets also provide a link to the income statement, because the organization's financial net worth will be affected by the net income (or loss), the so-called bottom line from the income statement.[2]

Figure 7.3. Balance Sheet
(Statement of Financial Position) as of June 30

ASSETS	
Current Assets	
Cash	$2,173
Accounts receivable	8,324
Prepaid expenses	8,423
Total Current Assets	$18,920
Noncurrent Assets	
Fixed Assets (land, building)	$305,362
Grants receivable	7,885
Total Noncurrent Assets	$313,247
TOTAL ASSETS	$332,167
LIABILITIES AND NET ASSETS	
Liabilities	
Current Liabilities	
Accounts payable	$18,142
Deferred revenue	5,247
Total Current Liabilities	$23,389
Noncurrent Liabilities	
Notes payable	$18,010
Mortgage	154,840
Total Noncurrent Liabilities	$172,850
Net Assets	
Unrestricted	$115,391
Temporarily restricted	7,885
Permanently restricted	7,431
Net income (loss) YTD	5,221
Total Net Assets	$135,928
TOTAL LIABILITIES AND NET ASSETS	$332,167

Source: Compiled by the author.

Let us look more closely at a balance sheet to find out what it is really telling us. First, look at the Assets section of the statement in figure 7.3. Assets are what the organization owns: cash in the bank, land, buildings, a collection of paintings, and equipment (such as computers and copiers). In addition, because balance sheets are commonly prepared on an accrual basis, all the money owed to the organization is counted as an asset. These are called the receivables and might include things like grants on which the letter of commitment but not the check has been received or items sold and invoiced but for which the organization has not received payment.[3] There is also a line for prepaid expenses, which include such things as expenses paid for an event that is actually occurring in the next fiscal year or a final month's rent on off-site storage space.

Note that these assets are divided between current assets and noncurrent assets. Current assets are those that are cash or are expected to become cash within the next year; noncurrent assets are those that are not as liquid (including contributions or grants pledged to be paid two or more years into the future).

Moving to the other half of the balance sheet, there is a listing of all of the organization's liabilities (what it owes). On the first line under Liabilities are all of the unpaid bills (the accounts payable). Next is the revenue collected for activities that will not occur until the next fiscal year (deferred revenue).[4] Finally there are the longer-term obligations such as outstanding loans (the notes payable and mortgage).[5] As with the assets, these liabilities are classified as current (due within one year) and noncurrent (due in more than one year).

All of the liability categories are then totaled and the sum is subtracted from total assets. The resulting difference produces the net assets. These net assets are classified by standards established by FASB as follows:

- *Unrestricted net assets* are free of any donor restrictions. This includes all earned income and income from investments as well as unrestricted contributions or grants.
- *Temporarily restricted net assets* have donor-imposed limitations or conditions that will be met at some point in the future.
- *Permanently restricted net assets* have donor-imposed requirements that will never be removed. These are primarily permanent endowment funds.

What does all of this information tell us? Beginning with the net assets, we know the organization's net worth. In the case of the organization whose balance sheet is shown in figure 7.3, the net worth is $135,928. Often a large net asset line connotes a healthy organization. But not always, and this is precisely the reason why the other numbers on the balance sheet are so important. In figure 7.3, for example, the organization shows fairly sizable net assets. But on closer examination, we see that the reason for this is because it owns land and a building. Its cash position is relatively poor. It has only $2,173 in the bank and $8,324 in receivables. It owes $18,142 (exclusive of the mortgage and a loan). In one sense, the organization could be called healthy. If it was able to sell its land and building, it could pay its debts and have plenty of money left over. On the other hand, if it hangs on to the property or has trouble selling it, it will have to raise cash to pay its debts. Generally speaking, an organization that has insufficient cash and/or receivables to pay near-term debt is not considered financially healthy.

The balance sheet is an excellent tool for prospective trustees, funders, regulators, and others to decide whether the organization is a good financial risk. Prospective trustees will want to check whether the organization is saddled with debt, because this will provide a clue about whether they will spend a lot of time on the board scrambling for funds. Potential funders will want to see whether an organization has large accumulated deficits, because this often means that it will be so preoccupied with debt that it will be unable to focus on its programs and other activities. From a regulator's perspective, debt-ridden organizations are often tempted to draw on restricted funds to cover operating needs. Indeed, it is not uncommon for government auditors to check on whether restricted public funds have been properly used in financially troubled organizations.

The balance sheet can be most important to trustees and employees of an organization as a diagnostic tool if there is an understanding of how to use it. Unfortunately, many people are mystified by all the numbers. They are content to study the income statement, which is more familiar to them and easier to understand. The assumption is that it contains all the information they really need to know. But this is not the case, as we have just seen. An organization may have a surplus on the income statement (and/or a significant total of net assets) and still be in serious financial trouble. Only the balance sheet will reveal this. Consider the following case.

THE CONSERVATION TRUST

Before joining the board of a conservation organization, a prospective trustee asked what the net worth of the institution was and was told that the figure was $2 million. Content that he was joining a financially healthy organization, he agreed to serve on the board. Later, when he was shown the balance sheet, he was shocked. The organization owed over $1 million. However, its land and buildings were valued at over $3 million, hence the high net worth figure. Because the organization could not sell most of its real estate, given the terms by which it had been donated, the value of the holdings had little meaning as equity against debt. The trustee spent the next three years as a full-time fund raiser, something he had hoped he would not have to do when he joined the board.

Had the trustee in the example above studied the balance sheet *before* joining the board, he would have had a more complete picture of the organization's financial situation.

The balance sheet is one place where organizations generally do implement the FASB standards for their internal reports, although FASB requires that this statement be called the *Statement of Financial Position* and most still refer to it as a balance sheet. The category of the balance sheet now known as *net assets* was previously referred to as *fund balances*. The new FASB standards required that net assets be divided into the categories of unrestricted, temporarily restricted, and permanently restricted rather than the previously used categories of operating, plant, and endowment funds. Most organizations do use these categories on their balance sheets. However, many organizations continue their fund accounting procedures and include notes in their audited statements (or for their internal reports) about how the various categories of net assets are allocated. For example, unrestricted net assets may have a note indicating what portion of the assets is allocated to a board-designated cash reserve fund, plant fund, or other internally designated funds.

THE INCOME STATEMENT
(STATEMENT OF ACTIVITIES)

If the balance sheet tells us what we need to know about an organization's financial health at a particular moment in time, why is another financial statement necessary? The reason is simply that we not only need to know what the organization's health is today but must view the progress of that health over time. Two organizations may have identical balance sheets but one may be improving its financial condition and the other's financial health may be rapidly deteriorating. The income statement (figure 7.4) shows these financial trends over time and gives the historical perspective, which the balance sheet ignores.

Historical perspective is not the only value of an income statement. It also gives an idea of an organization's income sources and its expenditures. Revenues and expenditures are subdivided into categories that reveal such things as how much of the organization's income is earned, how dependent the organization is on certain kinds of grants, how much is spent on personnel, or how much it costs to provide program materials.

Unlike a balance sheet, in which a large number of the line item categories are predictable and similar from one organization to another and from one industry to another, the various revenue and expenditure categories on the income statement vary greatly (they usually closely parallel an organization's budgetary chart of accounts). The bottom line, net income/(loss) year to date, shows whether the organization had a surplus or deficit for the year (or whatever time period is reported on); it is calculated by subtracting total expenditures from total revenues and is carried over to the balance sheet (figure 7.3).[6]

FASB changes also had an impact on income statements. FASB requires that income statements be referred to as Statements of Activities. They also require that all expenses be reported in the three functional categories of program, management, and fund raising. The standards require that organizations report all expenses in the unrestricted category, with transfers from the temporarily restricted class of revenue when required by the nature of the expenditures. However, many organizations only comply with these requirements on their audited statements. Internal income statements have for the most part remained unchanged.

Perhaps the FASB requirement that causes most confusion in the reading of financial statements—especially the Income Statement—is

the one that insists that organizations must recognize pledged contributions as revenue at the time of the pledge, no matter when the
pledge is to be paid. Note 3 earlier in this chapter indicated that some
organizations do not do this until the time of the audited statement,
since people feel that recording pledged contributions as revenue any
earlier overstates revenue and creates a false sense of well-being on the
part of those reviewing the financial statements. But even this does
not solve the dilemma of the financial statements. In the following
year, when the second year of a pledge is paid, it is not recorded as
income because it has already been recognized in the previous year.
Board members look at the financial statements and worry that they
are not bringing in enough revenue. There is no simple remedy for
this problem except a footnote that indicates the amount of pledged
money that should be added to the year's contributions. Similar foot-
notes need to be included for any other line similarly "overstated" or
"understated" in terms of the year's actual cash position.

The income statement presented in figure 7.4 shows activity in
the operating fund of this organization. For most organizations, the
operating fund incorporates the majority of financial activities and is
most carefully analyzed and reviewed. The statement shows activity
for not only the month that was most recently completed but also all
activity thus far this year *and compares both to a monthly and annual
budget.* The annual budget is the budget approved by the board prior
to the start of the fiscal year; the monthly budget uses the monthly
allocation of revenue and expenses from the cash flow projections
described in the previous chapter.

What can we tell about this organization from looking at this
statement? To begin with, the organization is halfway through its fiscal year (the statement covers the period from July 1 through December 31). This means that one would expect that roughly 50 percent of
the budget has been met. This organization is doing well—48 percent
of its revenues have been collected, and 46 percent of its expenditures
have been made. However, there are some potential areas of concern.
For example, individual donations are well below what was projected
for the year. If we knew that the annual appeal to individuals was
scheduled for February, this would be expected. However, if the annual appeal happened in October, there would be cause for some
concern.

Figure 7.4. Income Statement (Statement of Activities) from July 1 to December 31

Revenue	Current Month			Year to Date		
	Actual	Budget	% of Budget	Actual	Annual budget	% of Budget
Earned Income						
Tuition	$2,111	$2,000	106%	$48,201	$110,500	44%
Interest	404	450	90%	2,955	5,000	59%
Other earned	2,450	1,800	136%	11,222	21,500	52%
Total Earned Income	$4,965	$4,250	117%	$62,378	$137,000	46%
Contributed Income						
Membership	$525	$1,000	53%	$14,225	$25,000	57%
Individual donations	4,230	5,000	85%	5,225	18,000	29%
Corporate gifts	2,000	1,250	160%	9,753	15,000	65%
Government grants	0	0	0%	12,655	20,000	63%
Total Contributed Income	$6,755	$7,250	93%	$41,858	$78,000	54%
Total Revenue	$11,720	$11,500	102%	$104,236	$215,000	48%
Expenses						
Salaries and benefits	$9,374	$10,750	87%	$56,244	$129,000	44%
Professional fees/contractual	2,500	1,200	208%	15,400	15,000	103%
Office supplies/telephone	333	500	67%	2,987	6,000	50%
Travel and subsistence	400	0	400%	5,531	7,500	74%
Printing and promotion	723	1,000	72%	2,423	10,000	24%
Educational materials	3,655	2,500	146%	4,091	18,500	22%
Utilities and insurance	562	425	132%	2,755	5,000	55%
Mortgage interest	295	295	100%	1,750	3,500	50%
Grounds maintenance	245	500	49%	4,000	10,000	40%
Other	1,150	875	131%	3,834	10,500	37%
Total Expenses	$19,237	$18,045	107%	$99,015	$215,000	46%
Net income (loss) YTD	($7,517)	($6,545)	115%	$5,221	$0	

Source: Compiled by the author.

Similarly, there are some potential problem areas with expenses. Professional fees are over budget already—and there is still half the year ahead! On the other hand, a number of expense categories are at less than half of what was budgeted, which indicates careful planning. A trustee of this organization might be concerned, however, that only 22 percent of projected expenditures for educational materials had been made. Does this reflect a planned delay, or are programmatic materials not receiving the attention they should?

Clearly, there is much information to be gained from examining the financial statements of an organization. The intimidating columns of figures can actually be quite revealing if the reader has a sense of where the most important information lies. Responsible board members will take the time to familiarize themselves with at least the highlights of each statement in an effort to be as informed as possible about the organization they are overseeing. A narrative report accompanying the statements can draw attention to the more significant numbers and is highly recommended.

CONTROLS

One of the major responsibilities of board members is to establish fiscal policies that protect the organization from either intentional or unintentional misuse of funds. They must decide how money will be handled internally to ensure that it will be safely received, recorded, deposited, and expended in a manner that meets time-tested standards. These policies are called *controls* and there are guidelines that they should follow. Any responsible accountant can advise them on generally accepted and appropriate procedures. For example, many controls are based on the notion that two people are less likely to make a mistake, either intentionally or accidentally, than one. So one category of financial control is ensuring that more than one person is involved in transactions involving the receipt of cash, the preparation of financial statements, the expenditure of funds, and other financial matters. Other controls are discussed below.

Budget Monitoring and Amending Procedures

Budget monitoring and amending procedures were discussed in the previous chapter where it was suggested that trustees should be consulted on any significant change in the budget. However, a suggestion that trustees be consulted is not deemed sufficient control. It does not assure the trustees that such consultation will take place. Nor does it assure a funder that the board is in a position to monitor carefully the staff's spending of its dollars. To establish a reliable procedure, the board generally requires that two people should be involved in processing all payments. One person who is familiar with the budget, the organization's operation, and the appropriateness of specific expenditures should be responsible for approving payments. That person is sometimes the director of the organization or, in larger organizations, his or her designate. Another person should write the checks and monitor the expenditures for the trustees. If the limits established by the budget, or the limits beyond the budget set by the board, are adhered to, a check can be written. If payments that exceed these limits are requested, the matter must be referred to the treasurer, the finance committee, or the full board for approval or for an amended budget.

There is a simple method for documenting the processing of payments. The organization invests in a stamp with the following designations:

Date Received:
Date Paid:
Account:
Check Number:
Approved:

Every invoice, before it is paid, gets stamped. When no invoice exists for a particular item, a dummy invoice is prepared by the staff and stamped. The executive director, or the person responsible for approving invoices, fills out the first, third, and bottom lines. The first line indicates the date the invoice was received, the third indicates the account or line item that the expense gets charged to, and the final line allows the director (or designate) to indicate his or her approval of the payment with a signature. The person responsible for writing the checks fills out the second and fourth lines after making sure that there is enough money remaining in the budget account to pay the bill. After the completion of the transaction, the invoice is placed in a file so that an auditor can review the paper trail backing up the particular payment. For organizations with a fairly heavy volume of transactions, it is recommended that there be a separate file for each account or for each month.[7]

Other Controls on Check Writing

It is generally not recommended that the person who writes checks have the power to issue a check to himself or herself without at least a countersignature on the check. Another control is that of requiring two signatures on all checks over a certain amount ($5,000, for example). While banks probably will not monitor these, the policies can be recorded in the minutes of a board meeting and a person can be held in violation of a fiscal policy if the rule is not followed. To further monitor expenditures, use of checks made out to "cash" should be forbidden or severely restricted.

It is a great deal easier to monitor check writing and other financial activity if organizations do not maintain a large number of bank accounts. Ideally an organization should have only two cash accounts: checking and savings (money market). To the extent that it is feasible, all checks and deposits should be to one account (the checking account), with the second account serving solely to hold cash reserves or unexpended restricted funds. Some may argue that more accounts are is necessary to be sure that restricted funds are not used for other than their intended purpose (a very few funders may require that their funds be held in a separate bank account for this very reason). But proper accounting methods can accomplish the same goal. Furthermore, maintaining separate bank accounts can be time consuming and wasteful if smaller amounts of cash that could earn interest if held in aggregate are held in several non-interest-earning accounts or if service charges are accruing on several accounts. From the point of view of controls, more accounts require more monitoring by an accountant when the books are audited.

Controls on Incoming Monies

Again, the assumption is that two people are less likely to err than one. Where incoming monies are involved, the person who opens the mail should record all incoming checks and cash and keep a list. Checks and cash should then be forwarded to the financial officer who prepares the deposit slip and keeps a record. Periodically, someone other than these two people (authorized by the board treasurer or the executive director) should check to see that the two sets of records agree. In addition, all incoming money, whether cash or check, should be deposited promptly in the organization's bank account before it is used to pay a bill.

Bonding

Bonding is a form of insurance that protects an organization from financial losses stemming from either intentional or unintentional irregularities in the handling of money. Generally, those people who handle money and sign checks are listed in the bonding document. Like any form of insurance, a limit is placed on the amount an organization can collect in the case of a loss. The greater the limit, the greater the annual premium. As a general rule of thumb, an organization should not use total annual expenses as the bonding limit figure even though at first glance this would seem to be prudent. The total budgeted dollars are rarely available to spend at any one time, and so it is unlikely that any loss would be so great. The organization should determine the maximum amount of money it anticipates having available at any one time, increase the figure by 20 percent, and use that number as the bonding limit. Some funding sources require evidence of bonding before they will contribute dollars to a nonprofit organization. Whether or not they do, it should be a comfort both to funders and trustees to know that such insurance against loss is in place.

Physical Controls and Security Measures

Physical controls such as fireproof filing cabinets or safes and offsite (or online) storage of computer backup tapes or drives provide additional protection for a responsible fiscal system. If appropriate (in the case of gift shops and other retail outlets), the use of electrical or mechanical equipment in the recording and execution of transactions can reduce the likelihood of errors or irregularities.

REPORTING REQUIREMENTS

Nonprofit corporations may not have to file income tax forms, but there are other forms that must be filed each year for an organization to maintain its nonprofit status. Although generally the forms are prepared by staff or by the independent auditor who reviews the books each year, it is important for board members to be aware of the reports that must be filed in order to ascertain that it is done in a timely manner. Because requirements vary from state to state, board members should check their own state regulations to determine what specific state forms should be filed. Generally state requirements include filing an annual report in addition to some kind of tax return (which may require an attached copy of whatever version of Form 990 the organization is filing). The State Office of the Attorney General often provides information on filing requirements for nonprofit organizations in that state. The following is a general overview of federal forms required:

- *Annual return.* Most nonprofit organizations must file an annual information return with the IRS called Form 990.[8] This form provides information on the ongoing activities of the organization in support of its tax-exempt status and includes statements regarding all income and expenditures for the year. The returns are due on the fifteenth day of the fifth month following the fiscal year end. Failure to file can result in civil and criminal penalties as well as loss of nonprofit status.

- *Unrelated business income tax.* In recent years, nonprofit organizations have come under increasing scrutiny as more inventive and atypical methods of raising money have been implemented. Tax must be paid on "unrelated" business income, which is income produced by regular activities that are not substantially related to the exempt purpose of the organization (excluding income from passive investments such as money market interest and stock dividends). This income (if it exceeds $1,000) must be reported on Form 990-T, due with Form 990. As it is sometimes complicated to determine whether or not income is considered unrelated, it is best to consult with the independent outside examiner who prepares the Form 990 or conducts the annual audit as to whether this additional form is required.

- *Employment taxes.* All organizations with employees are required to withhold income taxes, social security, and Medicare from salaries and to pay and report amounts withheld to the IRS. Nonprofit organizations other than 501(c)(3) organizations must also pay federal unemployment taxes (FUTA) on salaries paid. Income taxes and social security are reported on Form 941, which is due one month after the end of each calendar quarter. FUTA is reported on Form 940, which is due by January 31 of each year. In addition, all employers must prepare Form W-2, which is the annual wage and tax statement for each employee. This form must be mailed to the employee by January 31 of each year, and copies must be filed with the IRS by February 28 of each year with Form W-3. Details on payment of withholding and FUTA are available from the IRS through the publication (Circular E), Employer's Tax Guide.

- *Other information returns.* Form 1099-MISC must be used to report on an annual basis any nonemployee compensation paid in amounts exceeding $600. This form must be mailed to the recipient by January 31 of each year and should be filed with Form 1096 with the IRS by February 28. Form 8282, Donee Information Return, must be filed with the IRS if a donee organization sells, exchanges, or otherwise disposes of gifts of property other than money or publicly traded securities within three years of the gift. This form is not required if the gift was valued at less than $500.

AUDITED STATEMENTS, REVIEWS, AND COMPILATIONS

Many nonprofit organizations are required to provide an annual audited statement of their financial activities to their state, a funder, or others. This audit provides a formal statement in a standardized format about an organization's financial status, activities, and history (an audited statement generally compares the current year's activities with those of the previous year). Whether or not this statement is required varies from organization to organization and state to state. However, generally organizations with budgets of $500,000 or more must have audited statements prepared.

An audited statement is prepared by an independent certified public accountant (CPA) who prepares a formal report that includes a Statement of Financial Position (balance sheet), Statement of Activities (income statement), and Statement of Cash Flows (a report on how the organization's cash position changed during the year). These reports must comply with all the FASB requirements. An audit also includes notes that provide details on various items presented in the various reports. It may also include a Statement of Changes in Net Assets, Supplemental Schedules (details on various revenue or expense breakouts), and a Statement of Functional Expenses (allocation of line item expenses into program, administration, and fund-raising categories). The audit also includes an opening letter from the CPA as to the reliability of the reports. These letters most often state that the reports are considered reliable by the CPA and that they reflect generally accepted accounting principles. However, sometimes the CPA will also issue a separate comments and recommendations report (called a Management Letter) that makes suggestions about improvements to the existing financial systems.

Because the audit can be such an important document for an organization, selection of the appropriate CPA is an important process. An organization generally works with the same auditor for a number of years, so it is important to select someone that staff and board members trust and respect. If possible, a CPA should be selected who is familiar with the operations of nonprofits in the organization's field of activity, whether human services, health, religion, the arts, education, or some other area. It is also important to meet with potential auditors in person, both to get a sense of the people who will be working with staff and board and to ascertain their level of knowledge about the field.

Evaluation of proposed cost is another important step. Pro bono (or donated) audits are sometimes available, but be careful that this does not mean a lower priority for project completion, less qualified personnel assigned to perform the work, or an audit and report that is of lesser quality. Once a CPA has been selected, it is important to sign a letter of agreement that specifies the services to be performed and the cost.

There are two lower-cost options for organizations not required to provide audited statements. The first of these is a review, which is a more limited examination of financial statements by a CPA. A review provides limited assurances that the financial statements are accurate. Some states require organizations with smaller budgets to submit a review rather than an audit. A compilation, also prepared by a CPA, presents an organization's financial information in standard financial reporting formats but makes no statement about accuracy and involves no review of supporting documents. A compilation is the least expensive option.

OTHER REPORTING/POLICY REQUIREMENTS

While not directly under the purview of financial staff, there are some other requirements of nonprofit organizations that are important to maintaining nonprofit status.

- All nonprofit organizations are required to provide written receipts if they receive a contribution of $250 or more. This receipt should include information on whether or not any goods or services were provided in return for the gift. (If yes, then a description and value for the goods and services must also be provided.) Many organizations opt to provide written receipts for gifts of any size, but it must occur for all larger gifts.
- Nonprofit 501(c)(3) organizations may not attempt to influence legislation as a substantial part of their activities, and they may not participate in any campaign activity for or against political candidates. Form 990EZ and Form 990 ask direct questions about these types of activities, and information must be reported about any lobbying-related expenditures.
- Form 990 asks a number of questions about the existence of various governance/management policies. While there is no requirement yet for nonprofit organizations to have such documents in place, it is recommended that the board consider such policies as they are important tools to ensure healthy operations. These documents include:
  - Conflict of interest policy
  - Whistleblower policy
  - Document retention and destruction policy

  Samples of policies are readily available online[9] and can be adapted to meet the needs of each organization.

COMPUTER SAFETY

It is a rare nonprofit organization today that does not rely on computers in all areas of operations. They are particularly essential in recording financial data and preparing financial reports. Even relatively small organizations with single-fund statements kept on a cash basis will benefit from a standard off-the-shelf accounting package to maintain ledgers and create financial reports. There are also customized accounting packages for nonprofit organizations that provide some specific adaptations of standard accounting procedures, terminology, report design, and links to membership and fund-raising packages. Computer spreadsheets are invaluable tools for budgeting and cash flow analyses, simplifying projections and recalculations and reducing the possibility of errors.

Use of a computer for financial record keeping requires additional control procedures to ensure a responsible fiscal system. These may include control of access to records and data entry through use of passwords, regular review of output and reconciliation to assets on hand (especially cash) by a second staff person, specific requirements on systems backup, and clear documentation of data entry and report generation procedures.

In addition to in-house computer systems, many organizations hand all of their payroll record keeping over to a specialized computer payroll accounting service. This service may include the preparation of paychecks, the maintenance of tax and benefit information, the issuing of W-2 and 1099 forms, and other payroll-related tasks. For organizations with frequently changing payrolls (hourly staff) and numerous contracted services, these services are often less expensive and more accurate than having comparable tasks done by staff, because they are fully computerized and are performed by those specializing in payroll services.

This chapter has explained accounting procedures, financial statements, and financial controls and has reviewed reporting requirements that nonprofits need to meet to maintain their special tax status. Too many nonprofit organizations have failed because of lack of attention to these areas. Staff members may have been lax in the maintenance of financial records, or trustees may not have bothered to analyze the financial statements or put controls in place. Although the plethora of procedures and reports described in this chapter may seem overwhelming, no nonprofit organization can afford to be casual about its financial affairs if it wants to protect its nonprofit status and ensure its continued survival. No board member can afford to be casual about these matters either, if he or she is to meet the responsibilities of public trust, which are part of the conditions of trusteeship.

CHECKLIST QUESTIONS FOR CHAPTER 7

1. Has your organization determined which method of accounting is most appropriate for its needs (i.e., cash basis, modified cash basis, or accrual)?

2. Does your organization have a properly prepared balance sheet (statement of financial position) and income statement (statement of activities) that together accurately report the organization's net worth and fiscal year's financial activity?

3. Has your board developed a regular procedure for monitoring income and expenditures and amending the annual budget?

4. Are there proper controls over check writing, dealing with incoming money, and handling cash in your organization? Is the organization properly protected through bonding against financial loss?

5. Are your organization's computerized financial records adequately protected and backed up?

6. Does your organization file required financial forms in a timely manner (including IRS Form 990, Form 990-T, Form 940, Form 941, Form W-3, Form 1099-MISC, and Form 1096)? Does your organization provide the necessary forms to employees and independent contractors in a timely manner (including IRS Form W-2 and Form 1099)?

7. Does your organization meet all the filing requirements for your state (including annual reports and tax returns)?

EIGHT

Fund Raising

Josephine Tierney is an affluent seventy-two-year-old widow who is still an active volunteer in Compton. Over the years she has supported many causes. She has donated time and money to more organizations than she can count. She is greatly beloved by her community. She is also a fund-raising target for a large number of nonprofit organizations.

Josephine Tierney is opening her mail a week before Christmas. Of the seventy-two pieces of mail before her, there are twenty-two Christmas cards and the same number of requests for money. This is not an unusual day for her. In fact, during the month of December alone, she will be receiving more than five hundred letters asking her to support some charity or other. Many of these requests will go straight into the wastebasket unopened, but others will receive at least a cursory review. Mrs. Tierney will take the time to open some of the envelopes, scanning the contents of the packet. Of this material, most will also be thrown away. But some of the packets she does save. If a letter is from one of her particularly favorite charities—an organization that she is planning to contribute to anyway—she will put the letter and enclosed material on what she calls the yes pile on her desk. With the remaining letters, if her eye happens to pick up something that makes her hesitate, she will put the letter on another pile, her maybe pile.

What keeps letters out of the wastebasket? To quote Mrs. Tierney, "I certainly do have favorite charities, and their requests are always attended to. Many times, I have given to them before I receive their request. But with the others, I take the letter in my hand, and as my arm is moving toward the wastebasket, I am scanning the material, checking to see whether there is any personalized message from someone I know. If not, and now my hand is very close to the trash, I check to see if I recognize any of the names of people on the board—this list is usually printed on the letterhead or is somewhere in the material. Finally,

I may be struck by the kind of activity the organization is engaged in—the big organizations for cancer or world hunger can't personalize their messages, but I support them anyway. In the case of the others, it is the personal aspect of the request that gets my attention. Mind you, a personalized approach doesn't mean I am going to make a contribution. It just means I will consider it."

Mrs. Tierney's daughter Roberta Sims is a corporate contributions officer. This month her company will receive more than fourteen hundred requests for money. The requests will come from colleges and universities, from hospitals, from social service agencies, from cultural organizations, and from other kinds of nonprofit organizations. Roberta Sims is not an expert in any of these fields. Her background is in corporate finance, and she was assigned to her position with no special training or expertise in philanthropy. She has a staff of two people. Her assistant organizes the material with a summary cover page for each proposal that always includes anything relevant to the company like any employees connected to the specific requesting organization. He also helps maintain Roberta's calendar and tries to protect her as much as possible from people who call on the phone. The second employee, an office administrator, attempts to stay on top of the incoming mail and email (most of the requests are sent in electronically), answers the phone, proofs outgoing letters, and deals with organizing files on the computer. She also serves as a receptionist and timekeeper for meetings. None of these three individuals has a lot of time to spare.

Twice a year Roberta Sims is expected to make recommendations to the contributions committee, keeping track as she does so of the various executives' favorite charities. Her strategy, as she has often admitted to herself, is to make order out of chaos. She identifies for the company the obvious blue-chip organizations that it should be supporting—for example, the United Way, the university teaching hospital, and the orchestra—and for the balance of the giving program she tries to put together a package that is consistent with the goals of the company's contributions program. She wants to get the most for the company's charitable dollar, to be able to have the company look good to its customers, its employees, and the community. Just as important, she wants to avoid all contributions that have any potential for becoming an embarrassment for the company.

Roberta Sims smiles as she divides the proposals she receives into three categories. It is just as her mother does. One is for those organizations she knows the corporation will fund. A second group is like her mother's wastebasket category—it includes those proposals that are clearly not fundable. The organizations are too small or badly managed, the projects will not serve her company in any visible way, or the projects involve too much risk. Then there is a third group, which Roberta Sims intends to check out more carefully, her mother's "maybe" pile.

In another city, Roberta Sims's brother, Charles Tierney, is a psychologist affiliated with the local university. Periodically he is invited to serve as an outside reviewer for a government funding agency. Although his regular teaching job and his research are very demanding and represent more than a full-time commitment, he always responds enthusiastically when called on to lend his expertise to the review of grant applications. He knows that this is important for his career and for his own search for funds, as it provides a wonderful opportunity to network with colleagues. Twice a year, the federal agency expects him to read proposals and then go to Washington and make recommendations about funding. Three weeks before the Washington meeting, he is forwarded a large number of proposals, organized as 312 summaries and fifteen complete proposals. He is instructed to read through all the summaries and review the fifteen proposals, together with backup material, in depth. He is to rate the proposals according to scoring criteria that are included in the cover email. He will be responsible for reporting on these fifteen proposals at the Washington meeting. Altogether, there are over one thousand pages he is expected to read.

Says Charles Tierney: "The first time I received the material, I wondered whether the federal agency was really aware that I had another job; I spent every night for three weeks reviewing it. Conservatively, I would say I spent twenty hours and still did not finish to my satisfaction. When I arrived in Washington, I found most of my fellow panel members much less prepared than I. My hunch is that some looked at the material the night before or on the airplane on their way to Washington. It was very revealing and quite shocking. To say our review of the proposals was superficial is an understatement. As a result, the predictable occurred. It was another version of what my mother and sister do—the proposals ended up in three categories. The key organizations in our field received most of the funding without a lot of discussion; organizations that didn't have their act together weren't even given the time of day; and we spent the bulk of our time fighting like cats and dogs about who would get the rest of the money. What the experience taught me is that a great fund raiser is not someone who can raise money for an established organization. It is someone who can be successful for an organization on the next rung of the funding ladder where the competition is really fierce."

Finally, there is Roberta Sims's daughter Agnes who is a senior in college. Her parents had felt strongly that their children should understand the importance of giving to others. So when Agnes became a freshman, they offered to match any money she put aside for charity up to $1,000. "Wow, what a deal," she recalls. "It was a huge incentive. There were so many things I wanted to support. Of course, I thought my parents and grandmother were old-fashioned and I knew better."

Agnes laughs when she remembers her grandmother's mail piles. "Who has time to look at mail? I do everything on the web—I've never read a fund-raising snail-mail letter in my life, and I never use the mail to send money (who can bother with stamps?). But I suppose my grandmother and I have something in common. We both have our favorite causes, and we know we are going to support them—some I feel so strongly about, I have set up automatic monthly deductions from my checking account. Then there are those—most of the unsolicited email requests I receive—that I just trash. But there are some that might interest me or that are forwarded to me by friends. I check them out, often going to a philanthropy website and doing whatever research I can. Some of these become my regulars."

These four family members all are involved in philanthropy in different ways, but they share common dilemmas. They know they cannot say yes to most of the requests they receive. They have limited money, and they also have limited time. But pressures make it difficult to say no to certain requesters. At the same time, these are strong-minded individuals who have definite ideas about what they want to support. Like most people who have become experienced in giving money, they have developed a technique for very quickly dividing requests into those that should be funded, those they will not fund, and all the rest. In fund raising, this is what some people call the three-pile phenomenon. There is a yes pile, a no pile, and a maybe pile.

Many nonprofit organizations that are responsibly managed and provide a service to their communities are placed in this third category—the maybe pile—much of the time when they request funds. Those that are successful manage to accomplish two difficult tasks. First, they beat out the competition on a fairly regular basis. Second, they manage to get themselves placed in more and more funders' yes piles. The techniques for accomplishing both of these feats are the subject of this chapter. But it is essential to keep in mind that even those who have accomplished them are accustomed to failure much of the time. The successful fund raiser, like a talented Major League Baseball batter, will be unsuccessful more often than successful. In baseball, a 30 percent success rate in hitting (or a .300 batting average) is considered very good. In fund raising the odds are even tougher. Good fund raisers do not expect to be successful all the time and quickly learn that the secret of success is in improving their averages every year.

THE ROLE OF THE BOARD IN FUND RAISING

Chapter 2 dealt with the need for board members to contribute to an organization and assist in the general fund-raising effort. Many funders will be interested in answers to three questions:

1. What percentage of trustees is contributing to the organization? (The answer should be 100 percent.)
2. How much, in total, does the organization receive in board contributions? (The answer should be a substantial proportion of the total individual contributions—perhaps 20 to 30 percent.)
3. How active is the board in soliciting funds? (The answer should be very active.)

As one contributor put it, "Trustees are the bellwether. They provide the leadership. If they are not giving generously themselves, if they are not out there asking for money, the organization is going to have some problems."

Mrs. Tierney, whose funding approach was described at the outset of the chapter, is always interested in who is on a board and how much they are giving. "It helps me to know whether to give and how to scale my gift," she says. Similarly, Roberta Sims claims that her corporation does not contribute to organizations unless there is strong board involvement—not only in giving money but in raising it. "And if a member of our corporation serves on the board, so much the better. We talk around here about the three Gs for trustees—Give, Get, or Get off. While not all trustees will feel comfortable asking for money, they still can involve themselves in the general fund-raising effort. For those not comfortable with direct solicitation, there are other activities. These include working on a fund-raising event, updating the database, analyzing donor records, writing or typing personalized fund-raising letters, researching funding sources (like corporate and foundation donors), and hosting fund-raising lunches or breakfasts. There are plenty of jobs for everyone."

The most important reason why trustees have to be active in fund raising is that people give to people, but most especially, peers give to peers. To the extent that the trustees are active in the community, are givers themselves, and are not afraid to ask for money, the organization will be more successful in the fund-raising effort. Furthermore, the fiscal health of the organization depends on the extent to which the trustees feel that the income gap (the difference between what is earned and what is expended) is their responsibility. Board members can be extremely helpful in direct solicitation and in arranging fund-raising calls for the staff. Their involvement is one way that the funding community takes the measure of the organization's vitality and health.

UNRESTRICTED GIFTS AND INDIVIDUAL CONTRIBUTORS

All money raised by nonprofit organizations is not of equal value to their operations. Certain gifts are most useful because they can be used for any purpose that is consistent with the organization's mission, including basic administrative costs. These gifts are called unrestricted because the donor has not attached any strings to them. The other category of gifts, the restricted ones, can only be used for a specific purpose, or at a specific time, or both. Organizations that rely entirely on restricted gifts often find it difficult to cover basic operating expenses. Furthermore, restricted gifts can occasionally get an organization into serious trouble, because a single gift may partially fund an expensive new project that requires substantial additional money. Instead of getting the organization ahead financially, the gift forces it to set even higher fund-raising goals.

Clearly, the most valuable money is that which is unrestricted, because it can be directed in so many ways. It can be used to pay for staff salaries, occupancy costs, utility bills, telephone, and other office costs. For many nonprofit organizations, finding adequate unrestricted income is a constant worry. Funders often want to pay for projects and programs but are less enthusiastic about making a general gift. For that reason, fund-raising planning must concern itself with identifying, first and foremost, the sources of ongoing unrestricted support.

By far the greatest source of unrestricted income comes from individuals. Healthy nonprofit organizations generally work hard to build relationships with individual donors that continue year after year. Indeed, the underpinning of most sound fund-raising programs rests on a base of *many small to medium-size ongoing, individual, unrestricted gifts*. While many individual donations may seem modest and some hardly worth the effort to acquire, the total take can be very large. If a single individual gives $100 each year for ten years, and if the funds are unrestricted, this person represents an important asset to the organization (especially if the gift is multiplied by one hundred other people doing the same). If half of those individuals end up doubling their gifts in time, another $50,000 gets added to the coffers of the organization. For this reason, many fund raisers tend to work on building loyalty among their individual contributors and raise more from them each year. This involves two efforts:

- Increasing the number of donors giving unrestricted funds on an annual basis
- Upgrading the amounts that these individual donors give from year to year

It is desirable to identify several donors who will contribute substantial sums—board members should figure prominently in this category. Often 90 percent of the dollars come from as few as 10 percent of the donors. But it should be kept in mind that these individuals generally require a great deal of attention, and as many of them make larger and larger contributions, their willingness to keep these gifts completely unrestricted may diminish.

Individuals can be solicited in a number of ways—in person, by mail, over the internet, by phone, through fund-raising events, even through the media. Whatever technique is used, *the more personalized the approach, the greater likelihood of success.* Many organizations have fund-raising committees (also called development committees), volunteers, or paid callers charged with in-person solicitations. Whether it is part of a program of carefully orchestrated face-to-face meetings or simply part of a door-to-door community campaign, the success rate for person-to-person solicitation is far greater than that for any other kind of fund raising. However, because this approach can be time consuming, other approaches need to be part of the mix. Schools and colleges have found great success with telethons in which alumni, parents, and students solicit funds from individuals who have had some kind of connection with the institution and are likely prospects for support. But keep in mind that phone solicitation has become far less popular in recent years as prospects feel strongly about their privacy. The web has replaced the phone as an effective tool, and direct mail continues to be a tried-and-true approach for many organizations.

The Annual Fund and Direct Mail

Most organizations have an "annual fund," the basic fund-raising category for ongoing unrestricted gifts, generally from individuals. One of the primary ways to raise money for the annual fund is by mail. In the age of the internet, direct mail may seem almost quaint as a fund-raising tool. But it continues to be a predominant vehicle for raising money, allowing for great efficiency in time spent and people reached. Because it is so universal, however, it is often unsuccessful unless carefully tailored to give the impression of a personal approach. The "Dear Friend" fund-raising letter of yesteryear, printed by the thousand and sent out bulk rate in envelopes with mailing labels affixed to them, most often ends up unopened in wastebaskets. It is true that large nonprofit organizations that mail hundreds of thousands of pieces of mail must resort to impersonal approaches, but these organizations usually have the advantage of universal name recognition, broad appeal, and media coverage, which helps spread their message. For smaller local groups that are less well known and that appeal to a more specialized group, a personal approach in direct mail is an absolute must.

How can direct mail be personalized? The most obvious way is for individualized letters to be written to known supporters or constituents by board members, other volunteers, and even staff. Though this is time consuming, it results in a much higher rate of return than preprinted letters. The letter can be personalized, of course, either through computer programming or by the addition of handwritten messages on the letter itself or short individual notes written on personal stationery tucked into the envelope.

Other pieces of the direct-mail packet can be made to appear more personal. For example, a good direct-mail packet will consist of the following pieces:

The External Envelope. The purpose of the external envelope is to get the packet opened. Toward this end, a hand-addressed envelope can be effective. Envelopes with mailing labels affixed are least effective, because they look the most impersonal (or as many donors claim, like junk mail). Envelopes with stamps—preferably large colorful ones—are more effective than those with preprinted or metered postage. An eye-catching photograph can also be used on an envelope to attract attention and encourage the recipient to investigate further.

The Letter. Most letters will not be read in detail. They should be short—one page for most organizations. If detailed information needs to be conveyed, it can be included in a separate flyer. The easiest way to compose a good fund-raising letter is to ask board members and volunteers to save good examples of such letters from other organizations. They provide a wealth of ideas about style, flow, content, even choice of words, and it is often easy to compose an entirely original letter by combining ideas from several other organizations' letters.

One of the more important things to remember about a general appeal letter for unrestricted funds is that the wording must *not* specify that the funds will be used for a particular project or purpose. For example, if the letter asks for funds to support a scholarship fund, it becomes a request for restricted funds, and the money that comes in can only be used for the scholarship fund. Some organizations that wish to be more specific in their appeals for general support use a clever strategy of listing several specific areas where the funds may be applied (e.g., the scholarship program, the seniors program, the inner-city program), but they end the list with the short phrase "and other activities." This allows the contributions, when they come in, to be considered unrestricted.

In general, all letters to previous donors should thank them for their most recent gifts, provide the amount, and ask for an increase. For example, "Your last gift of $250 was so helpful to us. We do hope you will consider an increase as our program has grown." Some organizations also include the date of the gift in the paragraph. All of this information can be easily programmed to insert into the letter from the fund-raising database so that it does not require human customization.

Another effective device is providing for a matching "challenge," which promises that for each dollar contributed another matching dollar (or two) will be provided by another donor or donors. Finding the major donors to provide such a challenge may be easier than it would first appear. People like the idea of a challenge—those providing the incentive and those responding to it. In many cases, a donor or group of donors who are planning to give anyway can be asked to put their contributions on a matching basis. There is some risk involved that the dollars may not be forthcoming to elicit all of the match, though this risk can be eliminated if the challenge donors agree to provide the balance of their unmatched gifts to the organization later. In the meanwhile, the fund-raising letter that offers a second $1 for each one contributed is a way to distinguish your message from so many others.

The Return Envelope. The return envelope has the organization's name and address preprinted on it for the convenience of the donor. There is some debate about whether or not it should also have prepaid postage. Some organizations include preprinted return postage that they only have to pay if the envelope is used; others forego this expense and simply include a printed note in the upper right hand corner that says, "Your stamp helps our efforts. Thanks."

However, there is one group of donors for whom it is useful not only to include prepaid-postage on the return envelope but also an actual stamp on the piece itself. This group comprises the organization's lapsed donors, the LYBUNTs, donors who gave *Last Year But Not This.* There is an extremely strong likelihood that an organization will get a contribution from these individuals if it keeps at the effort, and because these donors tend to be the kind of people who put a first request aside and forget about it, sending a second packet with an actual postage stamp on a return envelope commands a bit more attention and often elicits a quicker response.

The Return Device. The return device is sometimes a separate card but often is simply printed on the back of the return envelope with a wide flap that covers the printed material when folded and sealed. The device should include the categories (or amounts) of donations as well as lines where the donor can indicate name, address, phone (as well as opt-out options for anonymous gifts). It should also include a space for an email address (with permission to use it for communication). Most organizations will include credit card payment options on the return device, and these will require a signature line. Occasionally, the return device will ask about matching programs, planned giving, and/or include a space where the donor can write a message (e.g., information for the alumni bulletin in the case of a school or college, or indications of program preferences in the case of a musical organization).

A sample return device is shown in figure 8.1.

There are several features of the card shown in figure 8.1 that are important. First, the categories of giving are listed with the highest categories first. This makes it less easy for the donor simply to check off the lowest category. Second, the smallest listed amount ($100) is larger than the smallest anticipated gifts (which may be $25 dollars or less). This encourages those who give smaller donations who are uncertain precisely how much to give to gravitate to a higher level of giving. Third, donors are asked to show how they want their names listed—and it is very important that their instructions are honored. There is an opportunity for donors to keep their gifts anonymous, to indicate interest in planned giving, and to provide matching gift information. Finally, it is important to reinforce both the tax deductibility of gifts and your organization's appreciation.

Figure 8.1. Sample Return Device

NAME OF ORGANIZATION

Yes! I want to contribute as follows (check one):

____ Regency: ($10,000 or more)   ____ Patron: ($500–$999)
____ Director's Circle: ($5,000–$9,999) ____ Sponsor: ($250–$499)
____ Grantor: ($2,500–$4,999)   ____ Contributor: ($100)
____ Benefactor: ($1,000–$2,499)   ____ Friend: ($ ____)

Does your employer have a matching gift program? ____ Yes   ____ No
(If yes, enclose necessary information, if available, or we will contact you.)

You will be acknowledged as a donor on our organization's material unless you request otherwise. Please check here if you do not wish to be listed. ____

Please contact me about bequests and planned giving opportunities.
____ Yes   ____ No

Name(s) _____
                As you wish it to appear in our material
Address _____
City _____ State ____ Zip _____

Yes, I want to receive notices and special offers by email. My email address is:
_____

____ Check enclosed
OR Charge my contribution to ____ Mastercard   ____ VISA
Card number _____ Exp. Date _____
Signature _____

CONTRIBUTIONS ARE TAX DEDUCTIBLE.
THANKS FOR YOUR SUPPORT.

Informational Flyer (optional). Some organizations like to include another piece in the direct-mail packet that gives facts and figures about the organization. Where complex information has to be conveyed, or where detailed financial information is important, such a flyer or brochure can be inserted in a mailed device, although it does add to the cost of producing the direct-mail package and, occasionally, to the cost of mailing. Obviously, if the material is going out by email, an attached file of material costs no more to distribute as will be discussed below.

Testing. Organizations that do a fair amount of direct mail—especially to large numbers of people—will be wise to test mail packages with a small group before they go out in huge numbers. If more multiple content packages are tested, return envelopes can be coded on the inside slot to match the packets that go out. Testing can range from simple (what is the rate of return? what is the cost per dollar raised?) to sophisticated (which zip codes respond best to certain messages? do different return devices elicit different size gifts?).

Thanking for the Gift. While more will be said later in the chapter about thank you notes, some people believe this is the most important aspect of successful direct mail, since, done effectively, it can set up the next gift. Contributions need to be acknowledged immediately, but to the extent that the acknowledgement can be personalized to make the donor feel special, it can go a long way toward realizing the most important strategy of all—making someone a regular donor.

FUND RAISING USING THE INTERNET

When the previous edition of this book was published in 1999, fund raising via the internet was a relatively new phenomenon and did not seem a prominent enough feature of most organizations' fund-raising arsenal to include it. By the time this edition was being discussed just over a decade later, internet fund raising was so ubiquitous that some organizations were relying on it almost exclusively. As in other things, the internet has revolutionized many aspects of fund raising, from donor research to solicitation to donor communication. But just as the past decade saw huge changes brought about by computers and the world wide web, many of the techniques discussed today may seem archaic a decade hence. The challenge is to identify those that seem here to stay.

At the same time, it is important to identify those techniques of fund raising that remain unchanged in the age of the internet. First, it is still true that organizations must be responsibly managed and must provide an important service to their constituents if they expect to receive support. Second, short and pithy messages are essential to get the attention of donors quickly, and that is probably truer over the internet than in conventional mail devices. Third, relationship building is still the name of the game, and the more personal you can make it, the more effective the pitch. Finally, thanks are important once a gift is received.

Email. One device for internet-based fund raising is certainly email. The advantages are obvious. It is cheap and quick, messages can be tailored easily with specific messages customized for different categories of donors who have been coded in a database, and donors can be given the option of making a gift electronically with the click of a button. There are disadvantages too. Unlike regular mail, where addresses are readily available through many sources, email addresses are more difficult to acquire. Also unlike regular mail that will be delivered (for the most part whether the individual wants it or not), there are many ways that email gets screened. In some cases, it will be screened electronically and never reach the intended recipient's inbox. And, if the recipient is feeling the slightest bit reluctant to receive emails, he or she can opt out of all future emailing from the organization and there is no way to recapture the opportunity to use email unless specific permission is granted.

The first part of the process is securing email addresses, and organizations must use every imaginable opportunity to do so. Most have some kind of regular e-newsletter or message that goes out, and if the content is interesting (a key strategy) and substantive values are available through it, more and more people will sign up. Whenever the organization sells anything—memberships, tickets, or merchandise—email addresses should be requested (together with permission to use the email for "special offers and updates"). The organization's reception desk should have email sign-up forms, and its website should have a sign-up form on its template so that the form appears on every page. Social media sites should be utilized, and the organization can sponsor a free raffle or an offer that makes clear that those signing up will receive a free copy of some sort of e-news from the organization. When people receive these materials, they should be encouraged to forward them to friends who might be interested.

When it comes time to use the email lists for solicitation, the challenge is similar to regular mail—you want the prospect to open the email. Here the subject line is critical—it can ask a provocative question; it can make a statement that provokes curiosity, expresses something urgent, or provides what looks like a very special opportunity. The email itself should have great content, be visually arresting (several images are often better than one), and provide a clear and easy way to click through to where a contribution can be made. Monitoring responses to these devices, including the number that bounce back, the number that are received, the open rate, the number who click through, and the response rate, is as important with email as it is with conventional mail. Fortunately, because the process is electronic, analysis can be done quickly and accurately.

Using the Organization's Website. Giving to a nonprofit organization via the web needs to be simple, straightforward, and quick and should involve as few clicks of the mouse as possible. For those going to the website specifically to give, there should be a clear option right on the home page that says "Donate" or "Giving." The subsequent page should include immediate choices for how much to give and the payment options if there is more than one (e.g., credit cards, electronic checks, PayPal). It might also include categories of gifts (e.g., a general gift, a memorial gift, or an "honor" gift such as birthday, wedding, or anniversary) and categories of giving (e.g., general fund, research, or scholarships). This page might also include the organization's security policies to assure the donor that providing personal financial information is safe. Finally, there should be something to click to get the donor to the next page where personal data and financial information is provided.

Some organizations include a second option on the home page for those people who have not yet decided to make a gift. It might be something at the bottom such as "Give back" where a click takes someone to a page prior to a donate page that provides a short, pithy message about why donations are important, what they support, and other ways of supporting the organization that can be explored (e.g., volunteering, participating in a walkathon, advocacy, or sending an e-card to your friends, promoting various activities of the organization and/or encouraging them to donate).

Social Media. Social media has transformed the way we think about friendship and the way we are able to communicate quickly and effortlessly with many people. It also has introduced the idea of viral messaging—the exponential multiplication of people who send and receive the same messages. It has been credited with mobilizing hundreds of thousands of people to topple governments by the instantaneous power of wide communication, and much of that power can be used effectively in fund raising. Of all the aspects of technology that have been added to the fund raiser's arsenal, this one may have the greatest power to be a game changer as more and more young people come of age to become donors.[1]

Because social media provide vehicles for people to talk about themselves and engage in conversation, the approach to developing a message is a bit different. The direct-mail letter or the message on the website is static—that is, it offers a single approach to the donor via an unchanging message. With social media, many can enter a dynamic conversation, one that can pique interest, result in contributions, and, most important, encourage others to spread the message in their own ways.

Another dynamic aspect of fund raising via social media is its ability to draw people into a team effort to realize a goal. For example, let us say that an organization wants to fund a new initiative and needs $12,000. Word spreads via social media about how one can pledge to the project (the vehicle for doing so is often a secure website). But people are told that their pledges will not be redeemed unless the full $12,000 is raised, and they are encouraged to find other friends who will donate (often as little as $5) to the cause. Regular updates are sent out so that as the goal seems within sight, the encouragement to find others to contribute becomes an even greater incentive.

Once donors are found via social media, the networks created provide a vehicle for continued conversation. Unlike organizational email, which, when abused, results in large numbers of "unsubscribe" requests, people can continually send new stories about their favorite charities and why they like them, what they are doing, and how others can join up. Once again, those who give want to be acknowledged and thanked, and it is up to the nonprofit to ensure that those donors become committed friends who feel special.

Phone Solicitation

One of the most popular fund-raising tools in the late twentieth century was the telephone, but its popularity has waned somewhat. Today increasing numbers of donors no longer have landlines, and unless they have provided it, their cell phone numbers are hard to determine. Others who do have landlines complain that telephone solicitation invades their privacy. Yet the phone continues to be an effective device for some organizations' fund-raising efforts. Some organizations will do telephone solicitation to find new donors. This is particularly true for the larger organizations whose image is already well established. They hire callers who read from scripts and are paid on commission. It is these calls that many donors find invasive. Smaller organizations may prefer to limit their calling to individuals with a known history of interest in the organization and who might respond well to a volunteer or staff member who can "bring them up to date." In particular, those people with a history of giving are the best prospects, and the telephone is an ideal way to get them to upgrade their gifts.

Generally donors will feel far more comfortable with calls from volunteers, particularly those who identify themselves as such on the phone. What they may lack in polish and experience, they gain in credibility. If volunteers are used, they must be trained and they must be scripted. Training can be done by combining a meeting explaining the process with an actual series of phone calls in a group session. During their first evening of a telethon, first-time volunteers can be paired with those who have more experience. This helps overcome the initial fear of the process.

Scripting the Volunteers. It is essential that the volunteers be provided with a script from which they can work. In the beginning, the script may be followed verbatim; later, as the volunteers acquire more confidence, they may (and probably should) vary what they say and improvise conversations based on the responses of the person at the other end. However, even the most seasoned caller will sound more knowledgeable and be more secure with a script.

In addition to a script, organizations should also provide callers with a prospect information card for each individual who is to be called. The cards give the caller the necessary background information to customize and personalize the script. In addition to giving a prospect's name and address, the card might tell what the prospect has donated over the last few years as well as other pertinent information (e.g., for a college, the card might typically give the year of graduation, the departmental major of the prospect, and whether he or she played on any athletic teams). If the caller is asking the prospect for an increased gift, the amount sought will usually be listed.

In the following example, a parent/volunteer for Abbott Academy, the small private school described in chapter 5, was given the prospect card shown in figure 8.2 for a telethon.

Figure 8.2. Prospect Card

PROSPECT: Benjamin Smith

SALUTATION: Ben

ADDRESS: 112 Holden Street, Compton, Massachusetts 02438

PHONE: 617-294-4111

YEAR OF GRADUATION: 1998

COLLEGE: Swarthmore College (BA)
          Harvard Graduate School of Education (EdM, EdD)

OCCUPATION: College instructor of music

WIFE: Denise (not Abbott Academy graduate)

CHILDREN: Sally (age 5), Joshua (age 2)

2010 GIFT: $150

2011 GIFT: $150

OTHER INFORMATION:

1. Smith is a musician; while at the school he played flute in the orchestra, sang in the choir, and won the music prize in his senior year; be sure to tell him about this year's choir trip to Europe.
2. Smith has given every year since graduation; be sure to thank for this.
3. Be sure to address Smith as "Dr." not "Mr."; use "Ben" if you feel comfortable doing so.

The conversation that resulted from the prospect card (together with the script and outline provided by the school) offers a glimpse of a well-executed call. The parent/volunteer who made the call was Sam Evans, whose son was a senior at the school. Evans himself did not attend Abbott Academy, so he could not rely on the "fellow alumnus, remember our great years at the old alma mater" approach. Nevertheless, by taking the basic script and then improvising, he created a special approach to the prospect.

Phone rings.

SMITH: Hello.

EVANS: Is this Dr. Smith?

SMITH: Yes.

EVANS: This is Sam Evans, a parent/volunteer calling on behalf of Abbott Academy. Do you have a few minutes?

SMITH: Yes.

EVANS: I am calling for the alumni fund drive, and though I am not an alumnus myself, I think the reason I was selected to call you, Dr. Smith, is that my son is also a flutist, and his ambition is to win the music prize as you did when you were a senior. I gather you have continued with your music since then.

SMITH: Well, yes, actually I have. I continue to play a few concerts now and then, though my teaching keeps me quite busy. I have always been grateful to Abbott Academy for giving me so much encouragement.

EVANS: Yes, that is one of the reasons my wife and I are so enthusiastic about the school. The choir is going to Europe to perform this coming summer, and our son will get to go on the trip.

SMITH: That's wonderful. He is a lucky kid just as I was.

EVANS: Well, we're lucky to have graduates like you, Dr. Smith, and actually that is one of the purposes of this call. On behalf of the school, I want to thank you. You are among that special group of alumni that has given every year since you graduated. That is terrific, and we all appreciate it.

SMITH: It's the least I could have done. I often feel greater loyalty to my high school than I do to the college and university I attended afterward.

EVANS: Well, I know the school is grateful. But we are also concerned about the future. There are so many new plans, and we really need special help from alumni like you who understand what we are doing and who can make a difference. This call is important because we want you to consider a substantially increased gift this year to the alumni fund.

SMITH: I see.

EVANS: Yes, we wonder if you would consider a gift of $500.

Pause.

SMITH: That's an awfully large increase.

EVANS: Would $300 be more comfortable?

SMITH: Yes, it would.

EVANS: Well, I know the school will appreciate a gift of $300. In fact,

I personally want to thank you. This kind of gift will make it possible for the school to move ahead and continue to do the things that both you and I feel are so important. May I send you a pledge card tomorrow for the $300 amount?

SMITH: Okay.

EVANS: Now let me confirm the information. (*Evans checks Smith's name, address, and amount of gift.*) Many, many thanks for your support. I know the committee will be thrilled with your generosity.

SMITH: You're welcome.

EVANS: Good night.

After the phone call, Evans sent Smith the pledge card with a personal note of thanks. After Smith sent in his contribution, another personal letter came from the headmaster of the school, thanking him for his increased gift.

As it turned out, this call not only resulted in a gift that represented an increase of $150 over the previous contribution, but the following year the donor, without a special call, decided to continue giving at the $300 level. Thus by using a personal approach to request the initial upgrade and by making the donor feel good about himself and his gift, a permanently higher level of giving was achieved.

Mobile Phones. Mobile phones have changed the rules for fund raising and many of those who relied on donor landlines with listed numbers believe that the era of phone solicitation is fast declining. But new technologies spawn new techniques. For example, some nonprofits have advertised the availability of a designated fund-raising number to which donors can send a text message. In the case of larger nonprofits, technology enables them to automate much of the follow-up. In smaller organizations, texts are forwarded to staff who do the follow-up. Texts can also go the other way. Where nonprofit organizations have access to mobile numbers, they can send periodic "updates" via text, with some including a fund-raising message.

Unrestricted Income through Events

A proven way to generate unrestricted income is through fund-raising events. There are several advantages to such events:

- Fund-raising events widen an organization's donor pool by attracting people whose interest may be in the event rather than the organization.
- Fund-raising events can generate good public relations and exposure for an organization.
- Fund-raising events allow an organization to raise additional money from people who are already making contributions; if someone buys a ticket to a dinner dance, purchases items at a silent auction, or pays to attend a benefit concert, that person may still make a general gift.
- Fund-raising events provide a vehicle by which boards and volunteers without any particular fund-raising experience can assist in bringing in contributed money.

The disadvantage of events is that they often involve a great deal of planning and effort and can overtax the organization's volunteer pool. For organizations with a seemingly inexhaustible supply of volunteers (schools with a great number of parents, for example, and colleges with a large number of alumni), numerous events may turn out to be practical. But when organizations do not have such a large supply of volunteers and have to rely either on their paid staffs or on their already overworked volunteers, even one event a year may be a stretch.

In planning events, there are certain rules that are important to follow:

- *Set a dollar goal early in the planning process and stick to it.* Many event planners get off course by confusing public relations functions with fund raising. The logic seems to be that if the organization does not make a lot of money, at least everyone who comes will have a good time and there will be good coverage in the local paper. A dollar goal reminds volunteers that the primary purpose of the event is to make money, and it gives them a criterion by which success can be judged.
- *Remember, the secret of success is net income, not gross income.* What counts is how much the organization has left over after all the expenses for the event have been paid. Budgeting for an event must be done carefully and realistically, always with an eye

toward the bottom line. Don't let last-minute enthusiasm for little extras bloat the expense line.

- *Plan an event that people will enjoy.* It is easier to get people to participate if the event itself is a drawing card as well as the organization sponsoring it. Avoid events that are esoteric and will not have wide appeal.

- *Establish a committee with a strong chairperson (or two) to work on the event.* The chair (or cochairs) often determines the success of an event. Hard-working, well-organized, personable individuals are preferred. Keep in mind that those who serve on the committee may themselves represent part of the draw for others to attend. For that reason, it is always good to include several very prominent people on the committee as honorary officers (e.g., elected officials, their spouses, corporate leaders, big donors, or media personalities).

- *Exaggerate the number of volunteers and dollars you will need in order to make the event a success.* Like budgeting, planning for a fund-raising event usually requires overstating needs at the beginning of the planning process.

- *Allow plenty of planning time.* Things always seem to take longer than expected, and there should be plenty of margin for error in a timeline for a fund-raising event.

- *Build in plenty of ancillary ways to pick up money in conjunction with the event.* An auction can include a preauction cocktail party (with an income-producing cash bar), a potluck dinner (for which people have to buy tickets), a raffle for some high-priced items, a souvenir table, a game room for youngsters, and so on.

- *Involve local merchants.* While local businesspeople may be reluctant to make a cash contribution to a nonprofit organization, many are more than willing to donate goods and services for an event. Keep in mind that when merchants are willing to give an organization things "at cost," the recipient may be saving 40 to 60 percent off the retail price. When the gift is made outright, it is a lot less expensive for the merchants than if they were to give cash. It is also a way for them to get a little free advertising for their wares.

- *Attempt to find a type of event that works for the organization and stick to it for several years.* As knowledge of the event spreads, people will begin to plan for it, building it into their calendars and their budgets. It is always best if the event can happen at a predictable time each year (like the first Saturday of a particular month) so that people do not have to wait for an announcement to save the date.

The variety of fund-raising events is almost endless. Dances, special dinners, fairs, auctions, theater or concert benefits, art shows and sales, raffles (except where prohibited by law), garden and house tours, wine tastings, and trips to exotic or interesting places represent only a beginning list. Other ideas include showcase houses (where decorators and contractors each participate in the renovation of a house that is then toured by participants), food festivals (in which local restaurateurs and caterers compete for prizes), and fund-raising "nonevents" (in which participants pay for the privilege of not attending a fund-raising event). The creativity surrounding the event theme and the image that this projects will often determine the event's draw for participants.

Saying Thank You

Once funds are received from individuals, the organization must acknowledge the gifts immediately. For small gifts, a standard thank you letter expressing appreciation for the gift together with the date and amount is generally sufficient though it is often desirable to have the person signing the letter personalize it with a few words at the bottom. For larger gifts, the letter should be more personal, and an additional letter of thanks (often sent separately by a board member or the executive director) can make the donor feel special. As mentioned earlier in chapter 7, the IRS requires that a formal acknowledgement be sent for any gift of $250 or more. But the personal note is just that—a personal expression of how much the gift means to the organization and to the individual sending the note.

Whatever combination of thank you pieces is ultimately sent, for cash gifts the donor must receive something (either in the letter or on a separate form) that specifies: "Your contribution of $ _____ to XYZ organization has been received and is gratefully acknowledged. For your records, this confirms that you received no goods or services that would reduce the tax-deductible amount of your donation." In the event that goods or services were provided, an estimate of their value would be included in lieu of the final sentence. For example, a gala dinner ticket that cost the donor $500 would not be fully tax deductible because the dinner that the donor received had a certain value. In that case, an estimated value of the dinner would be included in the acknowledgements.

In some organizations, larger gifts elicit a phone call or email of thanks from the director or board chair in addition to the mailed thank you pieces. Others hold thank you parties and receptions for donors who contribute over a certain sum—these donors can be part of a giving group that receives a name like the Landmark Society or the Conductor's Circle. Most organizations recognize their contributors in printed material such as annual reports, program booklets, and even newspaper articles. It is important to think carefully about how to say thank you. Done properly, it can create a positive feeling on the part of the donor that will make next year's request for funds even easier.

Local Business Giving

Properly cultivated, local businesses can provide another source of ongoing unrestricted income. Any particular business's contribution—often coming in the form of a membership or an in-kind gift—will probably be small, but if there are enough of them, they can provide an important source of revenue. In some cases, the contributions are in forms other than cash. The local supermarket may contribute food toward a fund-raising event, a law office may contribute free legal help, or the bank may contribute its advertising space in the newspaper to help promote an event. All of these contributions should be encouraged no matter in what form they come. The idea is to be as inclusive as possible in soliciting from local businesses—and the more contributors an organization has, the easier it is to get more.

In attempting to make local businesses ongoing donors to your organization, there are certain rules to follow:

- Always have a suggested dollar range for unrestricted contributions from local businesses. The minimum should never be less than $100, and the maximum should not be too high (perhaps between $500 and $2,500). Remember, the idea is to get ongoing gifts from the same sources year after year, and this is only possible if the amounts requested are modest.

- If a new building or special project is planned, fund raising for this can be done separately, and larger amounts can be requested. Such one-time requests for special items should not interfere with the regular annual campaign.

- Make it more convenient for existing donors to give again than to drop out of the annual-giving program. You might send a letter at the beginning of your campaign asking them to let you know if they do not wish to be listed as a donor again in your program booklet. Once the booklet is printed, send them a copy, underscore the firm's name, and suggest that this would be a good time to send the check.

- Figure out a way to thank businesses publicly. They are contributing to the organization in order to be good community citizens, and they generally want everyone to know that they have done their part. In addition to printed acknowledgments in publicity and press materials, a thank you party or other gesture of gratitude is important.

- First-time solicitation of businesses for the campaign should be done by peers. It is desirable to have a special committee, chaired by a local businessperson who is responsible for this campaign. This person should find others in the business community to assist with solicitation. If there are not enough businesspeople available, board members and volunteers who are good customers of particular business concerns can also be used.

- Use service clubs such as the chamber of commerce or the Rotary Club to let the business community know of the organization's activities. No one wants to contribute to an organization that is not well known in the community.

- Do not confuse program advertising from local businesses with contributions. An advertisement may be an important first step in winning the support of a business firm, but the ultimate goal should be to get that same business to make a contribution as well.

Some larger local businesses will have the capacity to make larger gifts, and they should be treated separately. Many have organized giving programs and staffs with whom you should meet and discuss the business's giving goals and your ability to assist in meeting them. The business may be able to make a major cash or in-kind gift in exchange for a named sponsorship of a program or an event—a media outlet providing a certain amount of free advertising or printing, a hotel chain offering free or subsidized housing for visiting artists. In most cases, there should be a search for a clear quid pro quo. Indeed, if both sides benefit, the relationship is more likely to endure.

In general, local business support is important both for the revenue it brings in and for what it tells other funders—especially large corporate donors, foundations, public agencies, and even some wealthy individuals—about community support. Similarly, while funders are generally quite understanding of a nonprofit organization with little support from large corporations, they look askance if there is no support from the local business community. It tells them something about the kind of profile the organization enjoys at home.

PREPARING TO RAISE LARGER GIFTS[2]

Asking for a larger gift will often produce restricted funds—that is, the money will be given for a particular project, activity, or capital need. For that reason, much work needs to be done before a specific request is made. Potential donors (individuals, corporations, foundations, and government agencies) need to be identified, researched, and rated (a rating determines a dollar range for a potential gift). Matches have to be established between specific programs and projects of the organization and donors' own philanthropic interests. Promotional literature must be assembled. Prospect cards must be prepared (these are similar in format to the prospect card shown in figure 8.2, but they contain additional information such as how much will be asked for, what the money will be used for, and so on).

The Case for Support

In preparing to solicit larger gifts, an organization must develop a convincing case for support. The case for support is a series of statements that can be used in oral presentations in meetings with prospective donors and can also be incorporated into written proposals and grant applications, as will be discussed later in this chapter.

For nonprofit organizations, there are three steps to developing a creditable case for support:

1. Identify the important problems or needs that the organization intends to address with the help of the larger contributions.
2. Demonstrate the organization's capability to address these needs.
3. Match the proposed areas of organizational activity with the funder's own philanthropic interests.

Problem (or Needs) Statements. Nonprofit organizations are established for the purpose of solving societal problems and addressing the needs of particular constituencies. Fund raisers who wish to solicit larger gifts must develop short, tightly written problem (or needs) statements that clarify precisely what these needs are and what constituencies they serve. To the extent possible, these statements should be expressed in quantitative terms. For example, an organization offering financial aid to college-bound students in Compton might state, "In the town of Compton, two out of three graduating seniors cannot afford to attend college without some form of financial assistance." A social service organization might state, "In the past three years, requests for free meals at the Compton facility have increased by 37 percent." An organization that can prepare a varied list of these statements is developing a "menu" of giving opportunities that can suit a number of potential donors with different philanthropic agendas.

Capability Statements. In developing the case for support, an organization must also be prepared to answer an implied series of questions from the funder: "Why you? What makes your organization so special? Why shouldn't I give my money to some other organization that serves the same constituency?" The way these questions are answered is through capability statements. The big four capability statements that every organization must be able to express clearly are as follows:

- The program and activities of the organization are of high quality.
- The organization provides service to a broad constituency.
- The organization is well managed and has fiscal accountability.
- The organization provides service cost-effectively.

In arguing that the programs and activities of the organization are of high quality, it is desirable to use either outsider opinions or specific quantitative measures. Favorable press statements about an organization's service to the community or documented statistics on client usage will always be more effective than flowery self-assessments.

Funders are concerned that nonprofit organizations serve a broad public because *level of service to the public* is one criterion that many use to determine whether or not an organization is deserving of funding. If an organization serves a multicultural clientele, low-income people, the disabled, senior citizens, students, or other special constituencies, that fact should be documented and stressed. In rural areas, geographic reach is important (e.g., "We serve young people in forty-one towns in seven counties."). Organizations should be able to point to the number of people they are serving by type and show a broad mix.

Finally, capability can be argued on the basis of organizational efficiency, prudent financial management, and cost-effectiveness. Other organizations may be able to solve the same problems and may be able to show the same program quality and service to the public. But can they provide the same level of service with the same assurance of financial stability, a quality board, and an experienced staff? Can they provide the same level of service at the same price? If not, they are at a strategic disadvantage in fund raising. Funders, like the rest of us, like to get more quality for less money.

Strategic Fit. No funder can afford to be interested in everything, and donors develop their special interests, particular reasons for giving, and unique philanthropic predilections. Organizations that are successful in garnering funds are those that take the time to learn all about donor preferences and idiosyncrasies.

How is this information gathered? In the case of public agencies, there are usually published guidelines that make clear what the agency will support, and there is almost always a staff person to clarify any ambiguities in these guidelines. Some corporations and foundations also have printed guidelines; others will have annual reports that show the patterns of past grants. In the past the national network of cooperating collections of the Foundation Center in New York was the main resource for the large databases of information about foundation and corporate donors. Today much of that information is available with the click of a button via the internet.

With individual donors, determining strategic fit may be a less predictable process. Some organizations have large development committees that assemble information on potential donors through what one skilled fund raiser calls "systematic gossip." Other organizations collect annual reports and other published donor information from several nonprofits in town, cross-referencing donor lists and trying to establish the capability and interests of particular individual donors. Finally, analyzing an organization's own donor history records is a good way to review the giving pattern of individual contributors over time. Again, the internet has made what used to be an onerous process a little less so.

It is important to add a cautionary note here. There is sometimes a temptation to respond to a donor's enthusiasms by developing a special program to meet his or her interests. Although this can sometimes produce more cash in the short run, it can also produce financial problems down the road. What happens if the donor does not fully fund the new program? What happens when he or she loses interest and stops funding it after a year or two? In either case, the contribution can force an organization to increase its fund-raising goals while diverting staff time to a program that is not critical to the organization's mission or long-range plans.

A good example of this problem was described by the director of a touring opera company several years ago. "We undertook a tour of the opera *Carmen* against our better judgment because a large national foundation was willing to contribute several hundred thousand dollars but only for that project. In retrospect, that grant almost bankrupted us. We had never toured such a large production. We ended the tour with a near million dollar shortfall. I learned that a contribution can often get you further behind financially than you were before you started."

Accountability. In the first decade of the twenty-first century, many events contributed to a new focus on accountability. Corporate scandals, economic upheavals, and the terrorist attacks at the beginning of the decade all contributed to changing a somewhat laissez-faire attitude on the part of funders. Organizations needed to demonstrate that they were well governed and well managed, that they could withstand uncertain economic times, and that they had the strength and sense of responsibility to focus outward and deliver programs and services rather than inward, simply trying to survive.

For funders, it was a time of reassessment too. "If I give the money, will the organization deliver on its claims? How will I know?" For established organizations with a substantial track record, the funders' concerns can be at least partially addressed on the basis of past performance. But all organizations need to provide systems of ongoing monitoring and evaluation at the very least during the period of the project. Funders will want to know that these methods of evaluation not only will provide them with a report card at the end of the project period, but will offer opportunities for program adjustment during the project itself.

CORPORATE SUPPORT

One source of larger contributions is corporations.[3] In trying to understand what will motivate a corporation to give money, it is important to remember that the business of a profit-making company is to make money, not to give it away, and its decision to act in a philanthropic way is usually related to some business interest. Generally, one of three factors motivates a corporation to give:

- The gift will influence public opinion about the corporation.
- The gift will benefit employees.
- The gift will assist in marketing efforts.

Influencing public opinion. There are many companies that have generous philanthropic programs, because they wish to impress upon the public that they care about their communities, the environment, the needy, or some special cause. Oil companies, cigarette companies, big banks, and companies that manufacture war machinery are just four kinds of corporations that have historically used corporate giving as a means to counteract a specific public image problem. Other companies maintain an edge over their competitors by projecting an image of strength, generosity, and power through charity.

Employee benefits. Some companies use philanthropy as a way to enhance loyalty and positive feelings among employees. Sometimes the benefits for employees can be very direct such as company-supported day care centers or cash-matching programs for employee giving.

Sometimes they are indirect—such as gifts to major nonprofit organizations in cities and towns where their employees live. Another aspect of this form of giving is enhancing the status of senior executives by the credibility that such gifts bestow.

Marketing. When a company comes out with a new product, it is sometimes advantageous to give free samples as a marketing device. When the recipients of these freebies happen to be nonprofit organizations, the company gets credit for a charitable contribution as well. Another kind of marketing uses philanthropy more subtly to get customers to participate jointly in a philanthropic effort by buying a company's product. Typically, in this form of *cause-related marketing*, the company agrees to contribute to a particular nonprofit organization a share of the profit from each product sold.

Given these sorts of motivating factors, it is extremely important to find out precisely what is behind a corporation's contributions policy before a proposal is submitted. What kinds of contributions has it made? Which kinds of organizations have benefited? Where have they been located? How much, on average, have they received?

There are several ways to find out this information, and there is a logical sequence of steps to follow:

1. Do some basic research about the corporation. There are several initial things to determine. Is philanthropy handled by a corporate-giving department (or some variant such as community relations), or is it handled by an independent corporate foundation? In the case of the former, the level of money to be given will be closely related to company profits in the previous year; in the case of the latter, giving levels will be more predictable from year to year because the corporate foundation's assets are less tied to annual profit figures. It is also important to find out who might be a key person to talk to in the corporation. Sometimes there are several departments involved with nonprofits, such as employee relations, marketing, and contributions—a nonprofit group might eventually want to talk to representatives from each of them. Get whatever material you can (such as the company's annual report or other material about corporate giving that will be available online), and see whether you can get any clues about what kinds of activities were supported in the past.

2. Spend a considerable amount of time trying to find someone from the company who will get involved with your organization as a volunteer or who will at least visit. Later, that person may help you get an appointment with a decision maker in the company or at least put in a plug for your proposal. Alternatively, see if you can find someone outside the company (e.g., another corporate funder or a friend of an officer) who can introduce you either by phone or email to the funder. At the very least, find someone who agrees to allow you to use his or her name as an introduction.

3. If your contact has called or written on your behalf requesting that the company representative talk to you for a few minutes, call and ask to speak to that person, telling the person answering the phone that your contact told you to call.

4. If you are introducing yourself, you can either send an email or letter ten days ahead, saying that you will call in about a week, or you can attempt to get through using your contact's name without a letter.

5. Be polite but firm with the person answering the phone. Reiterate that your contact told you it was important to speak to the company representative directly. If pressed, say you are seeking advice.

6. If and when you finally get through (it may take several calls), explain to the person at the other end of the line that your contact said that he or she could be helpful to you as you plan your fund-raising efforts and that you would like to take fifteen or twenty minutes to discuss your plans. If the person appears negative about your getting money from the company, explain that you really want general advice on your strategy, on other contacts, and on your program and that a short conversation would be very valuable in any case.

7. When you get your interview, keep several things in mind:
   • The most important purpose of your visit is to find out as much as you can about the company's approach to contributions (the best way to find this out is to get the company representative to feel comfortable and talk freely; start the conversation with something informal such as asking about the family photograph on the desk).

- The second most important purpose is to get the names of other business representatives you should be talking to (ideally, you would like this person to make other introductions for you by phone; more often than not, however, the best you can hope for is being able to use his or her name when you make the calls—but this is a good deal); try to get five names before you leave.

- You do want to say something about your organization (remember, though, the person you are talking to is not an expert in your field and will be bored by details); keep the description of your organization short, and practice at home making a cogent three-minute presentation that emphasizes how your organization's projects can be helpful to the corporation.

- Be sure to confirm the best time to submit a proposal, what the range of actual grant amounts have been in the past year, and if possible, what kind of project your organization might undertake that would most likely be funded; do not beat around the bush; you are there to get this information, and the person you are talking to expects to be asked these questions. Be aware, though, that much of this information is probably on the corporation's website, so you should not be wasting time with asking for information that is readily available.

- *Know when to leave;* plan on staying no longer than twenty-five minutes, and watch carefully to be sure the person you are talking to is not getting bored (don't mistake politeness for enthusiasm; if you are unsure about whether you should continue, test the waters with a comment such as, "I know you must be awfully busy and I do not want to take too much of your time"; this gives the person a chance to move you out comfortably or to keep you around a little longer).

- Send a thank you note within a day of the visit summarizing the advice you were given; this will provide good background material when your proposal actually comes into the corporation (if you do not send a proposal within three months, keep in contact with regular letters informing the person of your activities; you have broken the ice and you must keep the contact alive).

An important piece of information that should be garnered from the interview is the proper form for a written proposal. Some corporations just want a one-page letter with a budget. Others want a more formal proposal. Some want it in paper form, others via email. Unless specifically told to do so, nonprofit groups should not submit anything longer than four pages. Ideally, it should have a short introduction that summarizes the project and its financial need (preferably this should be in larger type), a detailed description, and a budget page. Additional supporting material, such as the organization's tax determination letter, financial statements from the last completed fiscal year (preferably audited), a board list, and promotional material, may also be requested.

In most cases, support from a corporation will be for a restricted purpose, and it will be only for a short period of time. Organizations that receive substantial unrestricted gifts from corporations on an ongoing basis are rare. This is why nonprofit organizations must assess very carefully whether it is worth spending the time and effort in approaching a lot of corporations. They must ask themselves whether they have a program to offer that will give a specific company the kind of exposure or benefits it seeks, whether they have the staff resources to research and cultivate corporate relationships, and whether they want to invest so much time and effort raising money for specific short-term projects.

WRITING PROPOSALS FOR FOUNDATIONS AND PUBLIC AGENCIES

Foundations and government agencies are other important sources of larger restricted grants. In general, research identifying which prospects might be potential funders is quite different for foundations on the one hand and government agencies on the other. In the case of foundations, for those who have the time, the best place for a nonprofit organization to begin is at one of the Foundation Center's regional collections. These reference centers—located throughout the United States—vary in the amount of material they contain, but most have extensive libraries of books, periodicals, and online information, and many include foundation annual reports, newsletters, and, in some cases, foundation tax returns. Some offer user services, and the beginning grant seeker may need this kind of help in learning to use such sources as the Foundation Grants Index, the Foundation Directory, sourcebook profiles, state and regional directories, the *National Data Book,* IRS Form 990s, and other materials. They often publish their own information on state and regional grantmakers. For those who do not have the time to actually visit a collection, the Foundation Center maintains a very comprehensive online service to which nonprofit organizations can subscribe. For those skilled in knowing what they are looking for, the internet has become the essential place to begin (and for some, it is all they require).

In the case of government funding, the search for funders is more challenging. It is true that the *Catalogue of Federal Domestic Assistance* contains information on every federal funding program with program objectives, types of assistance, uses, and restrictions. But the sheer volume of material in the catalog reduces its effectiveness in locating potential sources of grants. Furthermore, it provides no information on grants that may be available from city, county, and state sources. There is also www.grants.gov, which again is so comprehensive that many find it overwhelming (similar websites exist for state grant opportunities). On the other hand, these publications can help identify the specific agencies that provide the grants, and then it is easier to follow up agency by agency and get more specific information on grant opportunities and eligibility requirements. A more effective way to proceed might be to talk to representatives from other nonprofits in the field to find out where they traditionally apply for money. If the field has a national service organization, this too is an excellent source of information. Finally, public officials and civil servants will often not only be helpful in providing information on where dollars may be available, but they may also help in securing the funds. Elected officials especially like to see money coming to the areas they represent, and they like to help voters who might help to elect them in the future. They should not be overlooked in seeking government support.

Some foundation and government funders will have detailed forms to fill out, which make the application process easier because the expectations of the funders are clear. In every case, it is important to read the accompanying instructions carefully and give exactly the information that is asked for. Whenever possible, the person filling out the forms for the applicant organization should have a conversation with a representative of the foundation or the agency to clarify precisely what is wanted and how the forms are to be filled out. In certain cases, it may even be possible to find out the kinds of emphases the funder might wish to see in the responses to particular questions.

Where forms are not provided, foundations in particular will often simply request a proposal, without specifying in detail what it should consist of. Again, it is best to seek as much clarification as possible before writing a proposal in order to customize each proposal to the specific funder who will receive it. One may want a very short proposal with an emphasis on the personnel who will be carrying out the activities. Another may wish to know a great deal about how the activities will be evaluated. In every case, it is important to find out how many pages, on average, successful proposals have run and to make sure the proposal that is produced conforms closely to this model. Sometimes a foundation or agency staff person may be willing to send a sample successful proposal (always ask to see one), and at other times staff may be willing to review and comment on a proposal before it is submitted.

While proposals vary in length and content, there are certain standard formats that funders expect to see. A typical proposal outline might have the following sections.

- *Introduction/abstract.* Typically the proposal begins with an introduction that contains all the pertinent and critical information. It might start with the following words:

  The [name of applicant] seeks [amount requested] from [name of funder] for [purpose of grant]. Funds are sought for the period beginning on [begin date] and ending on [end date]. The total cost of the project is [amount], and matching funds will be provided by [give either the names of specific funders if you know them or give anticipated categories of matching support such as earned income, individual contributions, government grants, and so on]. This project follows the successful completion of [a board planning retreat, a feasibility study, a pilot program, six years of successful programming, or something else that makes it appear logical in the organization's development].

- *Problem/needs statement.* Some description of the problem and needs that the applicant organization will be addressing and the constituencies being served needs to be in the proposal. It is often appropriate to follow the introduction with this section.

- *Goals and objectives.* The proposal should go on to describe what is to be accomplished in general terms as well as the specific quantitative objectives and targets to be achieved by the proposed project. For example:

  The goal of the project is drug prevention, and it will be accomplished through educational programs for junior high schoolers. Specifically, in the course of one year, five certified drug counselors will meet with thirty-two junior-high classrooms in the greater Compton area for at least four forty-five-minute sessions.

In drafting the specific time-bound quantitative objectives, it is important to remember that evaluation of the project (assuming the proposal is funded and the project goes forward) will involve assessing whether these targets were met.

- *Program description.* This section of the proposal addresses the basic logistical questions of how the program will be carried out and by whom. Timelines and program details are appropriate for this section as is a description of the qualifications and backgrounds of the individuals who will have primary responsibility for the project. (In some cases, the résumé of the project head may be included as an appendix to the proposal.)
- *Capability statement.* Capability statements were discussed earlier in this chapter. They provide a rationale for why the applicant deserves to be funded. Some proposal writers like to put capability statements near the beginning of a proposal (after the abstract); others like to place them later (after the project description). Either format is acceptable.
- *Evaluation.* As mentioned earlier, accountability is extremely important to funders, and they want to know that the applicant organization intends to evaluate the success of the activity in which they are being asked to invest. At the very least, the proposal should specify how the applicant organization intends to measure whether the objectives and targets were met and how the funder will be informed. On larger-scale projects, outside professional program evaluation may be appropriate.
- *Budget.* The budget should show that project expenses will be

met by income from all sources (including the requested amount from the funder). On the income side, it is understood that not all contributions and grants will have been firmed up, so anticipated amounts can be used. On the expense side, most funders do not like to see high overhead figures; program-related expenses, which may include the salaries of program personnel, should not fall below 80 percent of the total. Some grant seekers like to build in-kind contributions into their budgets. The preferred method of presenting a budget is to include only cash income and expense in the budget itself and to list the value of in-kind contributions separately.

PLANNED GIVING

In most organizations, individuals provide a substantial number of the large gifts, and in many instances, innovative ways are found to extend the advantages of giving to this very important segment of donors. Planned (or deferred) giving offers many contribution vehicles that can provide substantial benefits to a number of different kinds of donors.

Planned gifts involve arrangements by which a donor makes a commitment of funds but defers the actual transfer of cash, securities, or tangible assets for a period of time. On the surface, it would appear that deferred gifts would be discouraged by nonprofit organizations, especially those that have a need for immediate cash. However, these deferred gifts can be so advantageous for donors that these individuals may make much more substantial contributions under such arrangements. Ultimately, nonprofit organizations can benefit handsomely, and many build endowments almost entirely through gifts of this type.

What are some situations in which a planned gift might be appropriate?

- An individual would like to make a substantial contribution to a nonprofit organization but feels that he cannot give up the security of the income that these funds provide him and his wife during their lifetimes.
- Another donor would like to establish a scholarship fund in honor of her husband but feels that she must hold on to her

assets while her aged parents are still living in case they incur large medical bills.

- A businessperson who has just sold his company wishes to receive a large charitable income tax deduction in a particular year but does not have enough cash to make a gift that would be sizable enough to realize such a large deduction.

- A fifty-year-old woman has just been named president of a company and wants to defer income during her peak earning years; she wants to enjoy this income later when she is in a lower tax bracket.

- A forty-year-old man wants to set up an endowment to honor his father but does not have enough cash for an outright gift; he wants to find some way to make annual payments toward the endowment, but he wants the fund guaranteed should he die before all the money has been provided.

- A woman has inherited stock that has appreciated tremendously in value but that pays no dividend; she does not want to incur substantial capital gains taxes by selling the stock but would like to figure out some way she could derive income from it.

- A fifty-year-old individual has already put aside enough money to retire as long as his health stays strong, but he wants to work another twenty years if he can. He wants to find a way to shelter some of his income from taxes, handle the investments, and have a lump sum to give to the charity when he retires so long as he does not need the money for health-related issues.

For each of these individuals—and for many others—there are a variety of deferred-giving instruments that allow them to accomplish their goals and help a nonprofit organization at the same time. A few of the most important are discussed below.

Bequests

A bequest is a gift that is made through a donor's will. The advantages to the donor are as follows:

- By deferring the gift until after a donor's death, the individual has the use of the assets during his or her lifetime.

- A bequest usually provides a tax savings because the gift is deductible from the adjusted gross estate.
- A bequest can be changed during the donor's lifetime; it is not an irrevocable gift until the donor dies.

From the nonprofit organization's point of view, a bequest can be welcome, but its revocable nature is problematic. Whereas a donor may feel positively toward an organization today, he or she may feel less so at a later date and may change the will. A second disadvantage of a bequest is that there is no guarantee that there will be adequate money in an estate to provide the specified funds. Indeed, in some cases, such as a residuary bequest (in which a nonprofit is named to receive the *remainder* of an estate after specific legacies have been fulfilled), the assets of the estate may be inadequate to provide any funds. Nevertheless, bequests have provided the major portion of endowment funds held by nonprofit organizations, and their importance in fund raising from individuals should not be underestimated.

Gifts of Life Insurance

Gifts of whole life insurance policies, those that buy protection for a lifetime rather than for a limited time period (as is the case with term insurance), are another important type of deferred gift. Commonly an individual will purchase a policy with a certain face value (the amount the company will pay when the individual dies) and a schedule of premium payments. The individual who wishes to make a gift of life insurance must assign ownership of the policy to a nonprofit organization, making it the beneficiary of the policy as well. In order to secure a tax deduction, the individual will make a contribution of the premium payments to the nonprofit organization, which in turn pays the insurance company.

A gift of life insurance offers the following advantages to donors:

- As soon as the policy is purchased, the gift is secured; thus even if the individual dies immediately after making the first premium payment, the organization is assured of the gift in full.
- The donor enjoys the pleasure of planning the uses of the gift during his or her lifetime.
- In the case of younger donors (those under forty-five years of

age), a sizable fund can be created with a rather modest investment (for example, a nonsmoking forty-year-old man created a $225,000 gift by purchasing a policy that required contributions of $4,000 a year for seven years).

Life insurance gifts also offer benefits to the nonprofit organization. The *cash value* of the life insurance policy can be listed as an asset on the organization's balance sheet even during the donor's lifetime, and this can be used as equity against loans. A life insurance gift can be an excellent way to develop an ongoing relationship and other cultivation opportunities with a donor. The most substantial disadvantage is that the donor can choose to stop paying premiums before the policy is paid up. Under these circumstances, the nonprofit organization itself can choose to pay the premiums or it can cash in the policy for whatever its cash value is at the time.

Charitable Trusts
There are several types of charitable trusts that are used as deferred gifts.

Charitable Remainder Trust. The most important is the *charitable remainder trust,* which allows a donor to make a substantial gift but to receive income based on the value of that gift for a period of time—either a fixed number of years or the balance of a lifetime (or lifetimes). The donor creates a formal trust and provides a certain sum (usually a minimum of $100,000, which is often given in the form of securities, although it can be cash or even real estate). The asset is transferred to the trustee who is responsible for managing the funds during the specified time period of the trust. When the specified period is over, the asset passes to the nonprofit organization. Depending on the type of vehicle, the trust can:

- Pay a fixed percentage of the fair market value of the original investment to the beneficiaries (the donor, a spouse, or anyone else named in the trust agreement) for the time period specified in the trust; such is the arrangement with a *charitable remainder unitrust*
- Pay the actual amount of income earned by the trust to the beneficiaries, as is the case with an *income only unitrust*

- Pay a specified fixed amount annually to the beneficiaries, as is the case with a *charitable remainder annuity trust*

It should be noted that a variety of other special payout arrangements can be designed to meet the needs of specific donors.

There are several advantages to donors:

- The most obvious advantage is that the donors need not give up potential income by making a large gift; an income stream can be directed to designated beneficiaries for a specified amount of time, thus reducing the risks involved in giving up capital.
- Donors get an immediate tax deduction based on what the U.S. Treasury estimates will be the remainder of the original asset after all income has been paid out (for example, a fifty-five-year-old female sets up a trust with a $100,000 contribution that is to pay her $6,000 annually during her lifetime; her tax deduction in the year of the gift is approximately $50,000).
- In the case of gifts of securities that have appreciated in value while held by the donor, the trust can sell and reinvest these securities without any capital gains taxes (this is particularly helpful in cases where the original securities were paying no dividends and the donor wishes to get income from them).
- Donors are relieved of the responsibility of managing an investment portfolio.
- Donors derive the considerable satisfaction of making a major gift during their lifetimes.

The advantages to the nonprofit organization are also considerable:

- The gift is irrevocable, which means that even if the donor becomes disenchanted with the organization, it will still receive the funds at the end of the income payout period.
- Often the donor will make a larger gift because he or she is not giving up income that would be lost if the gift were made outright.
- Because the organization has not had to wait for the donor's death to get a significant commitment, there is time for further cultivation for additional gifts.

Charitable Lead Trust. It should be pointed out in passing that there is one other type of charitable trust that allows donors to retain not the income derived from the gift made to the nonprofit but the principal. In a charitable lead trust, the donor transfers income-producing assets to a trust for a period of time. During that period, the income from the trust is paid to one or more nonprofit organizations. At the end of the period, the asset—securities, real estate, or cash—returns to the donor.

One of the main advantages to donors of certain types of charitable lead trusts is that their tax deductions on the gift can be accelerated into the first year of the gift (as is the case with trusts established for periods of less than ten years). Thus for someone who wants to offset a particularly high-income year with a substantial tax deduction, a charitable lead trust may be an answer. However, because the donor is the owner of the trust, all income earned by the trust will be taxable (this is one reason why such trusts are often created with tax-exempt securities).

For nonprofit organizations, charitable lead trusts produce predictable flows of funds—this is one reason why they are often used to pay off multiyear pledges for capital campaigns (short-term fund-raising drives for new buildings, endowments, or other uses). However, because the asset portion of the trust passes back to the donor, they are often considered a lower priority in the nonprofit organization's fund-raising portfolio.

Pooled-Income Funds

A pooled-income fund operates much like a mutual fund. It is set up by a nonprofit organization to attract donors. A donor makes a gift by buying shares (or units) in the pooled-income fund. These are invested by the fund's manager (either the nonprofit organization itself or a designated trustee) in a large diversified portfolio. The donor receives income based on the proportionate value of his or her investment. On the death of a specified beneficiary or beneficiaries (e.g., the donor, a spouse, a friend), the original investment passes out of the pooled-income fund as a direct contribution to the nonprofit organization.

Many of the advantages to the donor of a pooled-income fund are similar to those offered by charitable remainder trusts:

- The donor need not give up income associated with contributed funds.
- The donor can get higher yields on capital-appreciated stock in his or her portfolio (the pooled-income fund manager simply sells these and reinvests the proceeds without any negative capital gains tax consequences for the donor).
- Donors are relieved of the responsibility of managing an investment portfolio.

In addition, there are some other benefits offered by pooled-income funds:

- Unlike with charitable remainder trusts, individuals can participate for a relatively small investment—some nonprofit organizations price a unit (or minimum gift) as low as $2,500.
- Unlike a charitable remainder trust, a pooled-income fund allows donors to add to their initial contribution as often as they wish.

For nonprofit organizations, pooled-income funds offer the same advantages as charitable remainder trusts in that the gifts made to them are irrevocable, and they often encourage larger and more frequent gifts from major contributors. However, there are some disadvantages. Perhaps the most serious one is the requirement that the organization must either manage the pooled-income fund or find a trustee to do so. Unless a pooled-income fund is sizable and will end up paying a large return to the institution, it may not be worth the effort and responsibility associated with its management. In this connection, some charities place a sizable portion of their endowment with community foundations that are willing to provide the management services associated with pooled income funds as well as trusts. They charge a fee for the service, but their investment expertise often results in higher yields that will offset much of the cost. Generally, however, the foundation requires that the assets are transferred to them, which has the disadvantage that the nonprofit's balance sheet is reduced by that amount. Exploration of relationships with community foundations and other endowment management entities is something that smaller nonprofits wishing to be involved in deferred giving should certainly explore.

Planned giving represents one of the most important sources of long-term, substantial gifts to nonprofit organizations over the next few decades (one estimate puts the number at $1 trillion in gifts as substantial numbers of baby boomer parents leave estates). Although planned giving is technical in nature, few nonprofits can afford to ignore this source of funding, especially in the area of endowment building and finding funds for substantial facilities and projects.

VENTURE PHILANTHROPY

At the end of the twentieth century, several people noted a new trend in philanthropy led by young successful entrepreneurs who were impatient with old-style charitable giving. While the examples of this change were diverse, they had enough in common that the new kind of giving was given a name—venture philanthropy. The theory behind venture philanthropy was that strategic long-term investments in nonprofit organizations, together with hands-on management assistance, could provide greater impact than old-fashioned patronage—characterized by the passive writing of checks to organizations that donors liked.

Venture philanthropy borrowed many elements from the concepts behind venture capital through which many of America's most successful companies were built. Find a good idea, infuse it with cash and management expertise, set parameters for measurable results, grow the company, and then get out. With venture capital, of course, the exit strategy involved getting a handsome return on investment. With venture philanthropy, the result was leveraging much more public service delivered in a more efficient way.

Many elements of venture philanthropy are beginning to enter the mainstream. Donors increasingly want to see quicker results, they want outcomes to be clear and results to be measurable, they want frequent reports on progress, they seek organizations that meet precise readiness criteria before investing, and they want to see good ideas "brought to scale"—not only serving more people but serving them more effectively. Perhaps most significant, the traditional hands-off philosophy in charitable giving—that funders maintain an arm's length relationship with the organizations they support rather than set policy, guide programs, and design budgets—is also beginning to evolve.

As with any new concept, there have been problems with some of the examples of venture philanthropy. As Peter Hero, the former President and CEO of the Community Foundation Silicon Valley, wrote: "The most important accomplishments of nonprofits are not easily bottom line quantifiable. Often the outcomes that can be most easily measured are least important. Meanwhile the processes of non-profits (consensus-building, opportunity for volunteer leadership, the creation of civic engagement) sustain the very fabric of civil society. But this can be just an annoyance to ROI (return on investment)-obsessed donors. Also, where is the major 'take-out investor,' essential to execute VP's exit strategy in this era of shrinking government intervention?"[4]

The esoterica of the debates about venture philanthropy aside, there is a new generation of major donors that looks very different from previous generations. Old-fashioned patronage is evolving, and non-profit organizations must adapt to the changing ideas if they wish to capitalize on this new money.

THE TEN COMMANDMENTS OF FUND RAISING

Volumes and volumes have been written on the subject of fund raising, with far more advice than can fit into this chapter. Nevertheless, a few more tips follow. These tips, the so-called ten commandments, represent a distillation and condensation of many ideas that, together with good old common sense, make ordinary people into skilled fund raisers.

Commandment 1: Remember, Only Prospectors Find Gold

A good fund-raising team spends far more time assembling lists of prospects and researching funding sources than it does actually asking for money. Knowing whom to ask is more important than knowing how to ask.

Commandment 2: Be Sure That Courtship Precedes the Proposal

You would never dream of asking someone to marry you before you had a chance to get acquainted and find out whether you were compatible. In the same way, it is far preferable to ask for money after you have had a chance to get to know someone and to find out areas of compatibility between your organization's activities and his or her approach to philanthropy.

Commandment 3: Personalize the Pitch[5]

Every request for money should be tailored, to the extent possible, to the predilections of the giver. Obviously, it is not always practical to customize every request, nor will you get in front of every donor (though you should try with as many as possible). Nevertheless, every different type of giver deserves some thought about what approach will be best, and the largest prospective donor deserves specially tailored requests that take into consideration everything you know about his or her likes and dislikes. Blanket fund raising is rarely as successful as targeted requests.

Commandment 4: If You Want Bread, You Need Dough

What is true for the baker is equally true for the fund raiser. Money rarely materializes without something to prime the pump. People who give money are conservative, and they are more likely to contribute to an operation that already has a long list of donors associated with it. Public agencies will require matching funds; corporations may wish to see substantial earned income. But in almost all cases, donors will want to see that you have other sources of cash before they join in.

Commandment 5: When Asking for Money, Assume Consent

Do you remember the last time someone tried to sell you life insurance? He or she never used the words "if you buy this policy" but rather "when you buy this policy." He or she avoided being tentative and did not give you many opportunities to say no without actually being rude. A good fund raiser should use the same approach, always assuming in all communication that the prospective donor will ultimately be making a contribution.

Commandment 6: In Written Requests, If You Can't Scan It, Can It

Most fund-raising letters and proposals are not read carefully, they are scanned. All other things being equal, those that receive the most thorough review are the ones that are most legible and easy to read at a glance. Emails should have enticing subject fields. Fund-raising letters should be short with ample margins; proposals should have plenty of headings, bulleted lists, underlinings, and other scanning devices. Also, of course, brevity is the greatest of all virtues. As one funder says, "The success of proposals being funded is in inverse relation to their length and weight."

Commandment 7: In Designing Budgets, Use Traditional Math

Those lucky souls trained in what was once called the "new" math have a sophisticated understanding of mathematical concepts even though they may be a bit rusty on their multiplication tables. When asking for money, however, these individuals better get hold of a calculator and make sure their figures add up correctly. Nothing makes a poorer impression than a budget that is incorrect. It gives funders little faith in the organization's ability to handle money if the numbers do not even look right on paper.

Commandment 8: When in Doubt, Communicate in English

Why is it that fund raisers think that jargon impresses? There is nothing as nice as a clear, short sentence, composed of words of one syllable or less. (Obviously, there is no such thing as a word of less than one syllable, but funders wish there were.) Nouns and verbs, especially when they are very specific, are the meat and potatoes of a good proposal or letter. A large number of adjectives and adverbs is usually the mark of a weak request. When you claim that your organization is wonderful, the funder is unimpressed—after all, what else are you going to say? If you want to include such value judgments, at least have the good taste to quote someone else.

Commandment 9: Don't Take a No Personally

Fund raising is hard on people who are sensitive and do not like rejection, because even good fund raisers hear the word *no* more often than they hear the word *yes*. But after a time, the experienced fund raiser looks on a no answer to a request as a challenge—it may be no this year, but it will be yes the next time around. The good fund raiser should insert an internal translator in his or her brain that converts the word *no* to the words *come back*. Persistence, after all, usually pays, especially in fund raising.

Commandment 10: No Matter How Many Times You Said Thank You, Say It Again

The secret of fund raising is not in getting the donor's first contribution, it is in getting the second and third. Developing an ongoing group of loyal supporters is essential and can only be done if just as much attention is paid to donors after they give as before. For those contributors who give large amounts of money, there should be regular correspondence updating them on the progress of the organization's activities. For smaller donors, an occasional newsletter may be much appreciated. Mention of contributors in press materials or a special thank you party is another way of showing your gratitude. Never take your contributors for granted and never miss an opportunity to say thanks.

CHECKLIST QUESTIONS FOR CHAPTER 8

1. Has your organization developed strategies to increase the number and amount of ongoing, individual, unrestricted gifts?

2. Does your organization do at least one fund-raising event annually? Are volunteers utilized effectively? Does income from events increase each year as it should?

3. Is your direct mail attractive, and is it properly targeted and personalized? Are messages compelling and short? Is there follow-up to those who do not respond?

4. Are contributions via the internet growing in number and percent of total gifts? Have you maximized the ways to grow your email list and keep people on it? Does your website make it easy to give? Are you effectively using social media in your fund-raising strategy?

5. Does your organization raise funds by phone? Are callers properly trained and scripted? Is adequate research done on each prospect and his or her giving history before a call is made?

6. Does your organization raise funds from a wide variety of local businesses? Is solicitation done by peers (other local business people) and/or customers? Is there a convenient way for businesses to renew their gifts each year without responding to a special request for funds?

7. Does your organization do extensive research on corporate prospects and visit them before submitting proposals? Do proposals to foundations and public agencies reflect the guidelines and priorities of the funder?

8. Has your organization explored bequests, gifts of life insurance, charitable trusts, and pooled-income funds? Does the organization educate donors about the advantages of these and other deferred-giving vehicles?

NINE
Planning

Some years ago, in an imaginary part of the United States, two mousetrap companies enjoyed halcyon days. Business was good—sales were strong, profit margins were large, employees were happy. While the two companies vied for the title of number one in the mousetrap manufacturing business, demand for the product was so strong that the competition was friendly. The two companies manufactured quality mousetraps that were hardly distinguishable from each other except for the company labels: the traps had a wooden base, and the spring-action mechanism connected to it was of high-grade copper wire. Indeed, the very names of the two companies—Better Mousetraps, Inc. and the Superior Trap Company—gave an accurate indication to consumers that the products being manufactured were top of the line.

Although the products manufactured by these companies were similar, their respective styles of management were very different. Better Mousetraps, Inc. (BMI) was a fourth-generation family business. Its president prided himself on running the company the way his father, grandfather, and great-grandfather had. "We make the same product the same way we always have," he used to boast, "and I have no doubt that four generations of our customers have used our product with complete satisfaction." The president of the Superior Trap Company (STC), a relative newcomer to the industry, was a business-school graduate who was constantly involved in product and market research as well as in strategic planning. While BMI's president took larger and larger profits out of his company, STC's president used some of his company's earnings to fund a planning division that experimented with alternative materials in the manufacture of traps, considered other uses for its products, and assessed possible changes in consumer demand.

At about the same time, both companies experienced some serious reversals brought on by greatly increased costs for materials and a decreased demand for mousetraps. The price of copper doubled in a period of less than eighteen months, and there was a mysterious, gradual, and unexpected drop in consumer demand. Mousetraps simply were not selling as well as they once had in spite of the increase in the general population. This seemingly unexplainable shift in demand turned out to be the result of an oil crisis. Because the price of oil had shot up so rapidly and gasoline was in short supply, many people were traveling less and staying home more. The increased hours at home were so lonely that a large number of these people decided to keep pets. The majority of the pets were cats, and because cats perform the same services in the mouse-elimination business as traps do, the need for mousetraps decreased.

For BMI, the double reversal of increased cost and decreased demand spelled disaster. The president, who had done everything the way three generations of his family had done it, was convinced that bad times would pass and that persistence, hard work, and tradition would pay off. He was wrong. BMI ultimately had to declare bankruptcy. For STC, the situation was quite different. When the price of copper increased, the company substituted a scented shiny steel wire, claiming, as it did so, that ten years of product research had proven that this new, less expensive trap was 22 percent more effective than the old models. For the next five years, STC captured a larger and larger share of the trap market, thereby further exacerbating BMI's problems. But STC's president knew that this was only a temporary solution and that, indeed, the trap business was doomed by changes in consumer habits and living patterns.

As a result, STC created a wholly owned subsidiary, SuTraComp. The high-tech-sounding name stood for Superior Trap/Computer, which was appropriate given the product for which the company became best known. That product was a high-quality computer printout clip—a clip that looked remarkably like the mousetrap the parent company was manufacturing except that its wooden base was decorated not with the head of a mouse but with a pictorial rendition of a computer terminal and printer spewing forth reams of paper that were gathered up in a comp clip (as the product was called). STC spent the next three years marketing the compclip. Ten years of research and planning had indicated that the compclip would be a tremendous seller and, thanks to the company's patent, would be without serious competition.

In the same year that BMI declared bankruptcy, STC discontinued its manufacture of mousetraps. Or perhaps it would be more accurate to say that STC discontinued calling its product a mousetrap. The compclip was now selling so well that STC's president bought up the remnants of the BMI business and hired the former employees to manufacture the "deluxe compclip," as the copper-wire mousetrap was now called. That same year, STC went public and gained a listing on the American Stock Exchange; its president turned down the top job at ailing General Motors. That was also the year that he managed to pay back all of his outstanding loans to his business school. Though he chose early retirement with his well-deserved new wealth, his legacy continued at STC. The company developed a number of new products in the early twenty-first century as it anticipated the advent of electronic file storage and saw the market gradually reducing its reliance on computer printouts requiring compclips. Everyone had learned the importance of being in front of market changes.

The preceding apocryphal story illustrates the importance of planning. Two companies, both with identical products and markets, ended up at very different points principally because one was willing to allocate resources to planning and the other was not. The successful company (STC) was willing to forego some of its profits in order to underwrite the cost of a planning team; the less successful company (BMI) was not. STC's planners evaluated the company's current operations, charted long-range trends in the marketplace, and considered the ramifications of a variety of alternative scenarios; BMI did none of these things. Although BMI appeared to be more profitable than STC at one point in its history, the failure to allocate some of its resources to planning proved very costly in the end. The company's president learned too late that planning is not a luxury; it is a necessity.

PLANNING FOR NONPROFIT ORGANIZATIONS

In the environment of the profit sector, planning is fairly straightforward. This is because the mission of profit-making companies is clear: they are supposed to make money. In the nonprofit world, where the missions of organizations revolve around the more nebulous concept of public service, planning is less straightforward. Whereas profit is an easy thing to measure, public service is not. In a profit-making company, a planner can devise and evaluate a number of strategies for making more money and can measure the relative effectiveness of each through quantitative tests. But when the same planner looks to the future in a nonprofit organization, he or she may discover that the governing group does not even agree on the central mission of the organization. While all may agree that the organization is supposed to serve the public, the form of this service may be a bit different in each person's mind. For example, a hospital may define its central mission as providing quality health care to the public, but each member of the board and staff may interpret that mission a little differently. One person may believe that the emphasis should be on quality care (top-flight doctors, up-to-date equipment, and a university affiliation), while another may believe that service to the public mandates health care for a very broad group of clients, including the indigent and others who cannot or will not pay.

If the lack of agreement over mission is one problem in planning for nonprofit organizations, disagreements about strategies to accomplish the mission is another. Supposing that the board and staff can reach a consensus about an organization's mission, they must then debate the best strategy for carrying out that mission. Should a senior citizen service organization emphasize information and referrals to its clients, or should it run programs such as Meals On Wheels or recreational activities? Should a multiracial, multiethnic day care center support itself through government contracts or by sliding-scale tuition? Should a food co-op fulfill its mandate of political activism by developing position papers for political candidates or by boycotting the purchase of produce harvested by nonunion workers? Because the missions of the respective nonprofit organizations are general at best and ambiguous at worst, the strategies for accomplishing them are not clear-cut.

Finally, as if the problems over mission and strategies were not enough, there is an additional problem in determining success criteria and evaluation strategies in nonprofit organizations. How does a nonprofit know whether it is doing a good job in carrying out its mission and accomplishing its goals? For the profit-making company, the measurement of success is relatively simple. It is accomplished through an examination of the financial balance sheet. A series of numbers shows whether the company is succeeding and compares its current performance with performance in other years. Unfortunately, in the nonprofit world, success is not only more difficult to measure but it is even difficult to define. One trustee of a community theater might argue that the cost-effectiveness of the organization's inner-city program is an appropriate measure of its success; another may feel that the proper criterion is the number of clients served; still another may argue that success should be judged by the critical response to the program.

With so much disagreement over mission, strategies, and success criteria, it is no wonder that many nonprofit organizations find planning challenging. The reasons for not planning are varied. Typically, nonprofit organizations will argue that:

- Planning takes too much time and effort—staff and board are already overworked (a variant of this argument is that this is simply not the right time for planning because there is too much work or too many crises to deal with).
- Planning is too expensive—there is no extra money in the budget for consultants, the costs of meetings, and other expenses.
- Planning saps organizational initiative—a long-range plan does not allow an organization to remain open and responsive to constituents.

Not one of these arguments is justified. To argue that staff and board do not have enough time to do planning is a bit like arguing that the financial officer does not have time to prepare a budget and the treasurer does not have time to review it. Because these tasks are a part of their job responsibilities, they must make time. To argue that there is no money in the budget to pay for planning is like saying that there is nothing in the budget for rent and utilities. If the money is not there, it should be put there. To argue that an organization should be responsive to its constituency is an argument *for* planning, not against it, because planning involves an analysis of the needs of the constituency both in the present and in the future.

There is only one justifiable argument against planning. When planning is done badly, it is not only a waste of time but also saps the energies and the spirit of an organization's board, staff, and sometimes even its constituency. Long, laborious, expensive planning processes that result in voluminous documents that no one reads are an argument against planning. Yet planning is so important, and its absence leaves an organization so vulnerable, that it is worthwhile to attempt to find a planning process that can work, which is the subject of the balance of this chapter.

WHAT IS A PLANNING PROCESS?

Planning is an ongoing process involving several steps that are listed below.

Step 1: Set parameters and boundaries.
Step 2: Identify limiting conditions.
Step 3: Change limiting conditions where possible.
Step 4: Design a plan of action.
Step 5: Carry out the action plan.
Step 6: Evaluate what you have done.
Step 7: Repeat what you have done.

Planning a Garden

In order to gain a better understanding of what each step involves, imagine that you are a gardener and have been given the task of taking a plot of land, turning it into a garden, and maintaining that garden year after year. If you went through the seven steps, you would do the following things.

Set Parameters and Boundaries. First, you would determine the boundaries of your garden, taking into account your property lines, the general contour of the land, how much you wanted to produce in the garden, and how hard you were willing to work. You would make your decisions with care, thinking about the long-term future of this garden. After all, once you decided on the boundaries, prepared the ground, built fences, and put in the surrounding trees and lawn, you would be reluctant to go through the time, expense, and stress that would be required to make a change.

Identify Limiting Conditions. Second, you would identify conditions that determined what you could plant in your garden. Climate would be the first limiting factor: When does the ground freeze and thaw? How much rainfall is there, and how long are the dry periods? How many hours of daylight and how much direct sun will different parts of the garden receive? A second factor would be soil conditions: Is the soil acidic or alkaline? sandy or clay? Does it have adequate organic nutrients? A third constraint would involve your budget: How much money are you willing to spend on the garden? How much help are you likely to get (both in manpower and dollars) to stretch the resources that you have?

Change Limiting Conditions Where Possible. Third, you would now see if there were ways to change some of the limiting conditions you identified in the previous step. For example, if you determined that the ground stayed frozen until late March, yet you knew you wanted to start some of your vegetables well before that time, you might consider investing in a greenhouse or a cold frame, or you might decide to buy seedlings instead of seeds. If you discovered that an oak tree shaded half of the garden for three hours in the afternoon, you might decide to cut it down or at least remove some of its limbs. If you found out that your soil was poor, you would seriously consider adding fertilizer. But how much money would you be willing to spend in preparing the soil and making some of these other changes? Remember, your limited budget has to cover these modifications plus the cost of the garden itself. Or does it? Is your budget really inelastic, or is this another limitation that you may be able to modify?

Design a Plan of Action. Fourth, you are now ready to plan the specific actions you will take. In essence, you are ready to lay out the garden. You will decide how to prepare the ground, what seeds and plants to buy, whether to do some preplanting in a greenhouse or cold frame, when you need outside help, when to harvest the produce, what you must do to winterize the garden and protect certain plants from harsh weather after the first growing season, and on and on. Unfortunately, there are many gardeners (even experienced ones) who initiate the planning process at this point, without completing the essential preparatory steps. While they may have excellent gardens, the gardens themselves tend to look the same year after year. The boundaries have been established years before, and there has never been any thought about changing them. The gardeners have learned, often by trial and error, what grows and what does not, so they tend to plant the same thing in the same place year in and year out. But despite the fact that their gardens look nice, these gardeners are creatures of habit. This can be a problem if changes occur over which they have little or no control (a sudden shrinking of budget, climate change, a need to expand the boundaries of the garden). These gardeners have few strategies for responding to such change.

Carry Out the Action Plan. Fifth, you are now ready to carry out the plan for the garden. If you have done all the preceding steps correctly, your garden should end up growing well. There will be some surprises and some disappointments, but for the most part your garden should look quite acceptable. If it does not, chances are you skimped on your planning because you were so excited about actually starting right in on planting. This, unfortunately, is the plight of most inexperienced gardeners. They actually begin by planting their gardens, and the results are often unfortunate. Because they have done virtually no planning, they do not know what grows best or what they can do to improve the conditions for growth. They go to a nursery and buy lovely healthy plants only to see these plants wither in the ground two weeks later. They complain that they do not have the proverbial green thumb, not realizing that green thumbs are not inherited but are earned by good planning and hard work.

Evaluate What You Have Done. Sixth, if your garden is growing well, you are probably more worried about weeds, rodents, and insects than you are about next year's garden. But as you plant, cultivate, and weed, and as you pick your flowers and harvest your vegetables, you must carefully observe your successes and your failures with an eye toward next year's garden. Evaluation is an essential component of good planning because it allows you, the gardener, to test your hypotheses and adjust them in the future based on actual events.

Repeat What You Have Done. Seventh, it is time to repeat the process for next year. Actually, the process is a bit different the second time around. As you were planning your first garden, you spent a great deal of time on Step 1—determining the shape, contours, and boundaries of the garden. During the second year, it is unlikely that you will spend nearly as much time thinking about this. However, you will find it important periodically to review Step 1. As your resources increase, you may become more ambitious and want to add a rock garden where you originally thought gardening was out of the question; as you grow older, you may want to shrink the boundaries of your garden so that you can still manage things without too much strain. Whatever you decide, you want to do it with adequate thought and deliberation, not just on impulse.

There are a couple of other observations to make about your garden planning. First, although a sequence of steps has been given, it is quite possible that a skilled gardener may be working on several steps at the same time and may be planning for several different years at once. For example, a gardener may be thinking now about changing the boundaries of his garden five years hence. At the same time, he or she may be planning the ramifications this will have on budget, soil preparation, and cold frame construction over the next three years while planning the specific layout of this year's garden. A skilled planner knows that planning is an ongoing process in which many things interact simultaneously.

Second, as even experienced gardeners will tell you, they benefit from expert advice. Hiring professionals may cost money, but it might save more by avoiding costly mistakes. A professional can also make suggestions that never occurred to the person whose vision was limited by experience and preferences. Finally, if many people are involved in planning the garden and there is a range of opinions, a professional can help resolve differences and find compromises that please everyone.

Planning in a Nonprofit Organization

In a nonprofit organization, each of the steps just described must take place in a planning process.

Set Parameters and Boundaries. When the organization is first set up, the broad parameters of its activities must be established. They are generally documented in a mission statement. Periodically, this mission statement should be reviewed so that trustees can make sure the organization is still operating within the established boundaries. If it is appropriate, the mission statement should be amended to set new boundaries for organizational activities. Indeed, an organizational planning process should always involve a careful review (and, if necessary, a reworking) of the mission statement. Together with this review is a discussion of the organization's values (what it believes in) and its vision for the future (what the world would look like if the organization was successful in carrying out its mission).

Identify Limiting Conditions. Planners for a nonprofit organization must also look at those factors that constrain its activities—budgetary considerations, government regulations, the wishes of its constituency and membership, societal trends, increased competition, and a negative public image—to understand what limitations must be taken into account in planning.

Change Limiting Conditions Where Possible. The planners must then decide which of those constraints can be modified or changed and which are worth changing. For example, additional fund raising might eliminate some budget constraints, a public relations or education campaign might reverse a negative public image, and political activism and advocacy might lead to changes in certain government regulations.

Design a Plan of Action. After changing what limiting conditions they can, the nonprofit organization's planners must map out a specific action plan for the immediate future. The plan should include goals, objectives, action steps, and a budget (which makes priorities clear).

Carry Out the Action Plan. The specific activities described in the action plan must then be implemented.

Evaluate What You Have Done. The activities must be evaluated to help future planning.

Repeat What You Have Done.

LEVELS OF PLANNING

One way to think about planning is to view it sequentially as a series of steps as we have just done. This can be somewhat misleading, because a group of planners will probably not wait for one step to be completed before beginning on another. In fact, several planning steps may be taking place at the same time. For that reason, it is probably more useful to talk about levels of planning as follows:

- The level of purpose or mission
- The level of goals
- The level of objectives
- The level of strategies (timeline, action plan, budget)
- The level of actions
- The level of evaluation

Planning levels relate closely (but not precisely) to the planning steps described in the previous section. Let us look at this more carefully. A planning process is a road map to help an organization make a journey from one place (here and now) to another (some point in the future).

- Level one, *purpose or mission*, reveals why the organization is making the journey.
- Level two, *goals*, provides the general direction in which it is heading.
- Level three, *objectives and targets*, reveals the destination.
- Level four, *strategies*, tells specifically how the organization will get there.
- Level five, *actions*, is the trip itself.
- Level six, *evaluation*, determines whether you have arrived.

How can these levels be translated into a planning process for a nonprofit organization? The question can be answered by looking at planning within a specific nonprofit organization.

THE COMPTON MEMORIAL HOSPITAL

The purpose or mission of the hospital was set out at its inception, is reviewed periodically, and occasionally is even amended. A mission statement tells the world why the organization exists and the general categories of activities within its purview. The mission of the Compton Memorial Hospital is "to provide high-quality health care to the residents of Compton." At first glance, it would appear that such a mission statement would never have to be revised. After all, providing high-quality health care is what a hospital is all about. Yet, it is quite possible that fifty years hence a new, more modern hospital may be established in Compton. At that point, Compton Memorial must decide whether it wants to compete (with its outdated plant and equipment), wants to go out of business, or wants to change its mission (it might become an out-patient facility or a facility for seniors). At that point, its governing group must examine the mission statement and determine the nature and scope of changes that need to be made.

Two other related areas are part of mission-level discussion—the vision and values for the institution:

- The vision for Compton Memorial Hospital is a healthy community in which citizens partner with the hospital to ensure good physical and emotional well-being.
- The values of the hospital are:
  - Safe care
  - Cost-effective care
  - A positive patient experience
  - Communication and teamwork among all staff and constituencies
  - Leadership in the community

Each of these statements set out the larger frame that defines the hospital and should guide the planning process.

At the second planning level, the level of goals, a more specific series of statements must be developed setting the direction of the organization's activities for the shorter term. Thus, while the Compton Memorial Hospital's mission is "to provide high-quality health care to the residents of Compton," its specific goals for the next five years might be:

- To ensure quality improvement to increase patient safety

- To establish out-patient services
- To upgrade administrative practices
- To pursue collaborative planning of health-care delivery with surrounding hospitals
- To establish greater financial stability through increased fund raising

Although goal statements are more specific than a mission statement in setting a direction for the organization, they do not state exactly what the organization is going to do, how it is going to do it, and what the criteria will be to determine success. What goal statements do provide is the framework for deciding these more specific questions.

It is at the third planning level, the level of objectives and targets, that the goals are interpreted, made more specific, and quantified. An objective is a destination statement. It describes very specifically where an organization wishes to go. Every objective carries with it either a stated or an implied target, a measurable benchmark that determines whether the organization achieved the objective. Thus, goals give a general indication of direction, objectives indicate the destination, and targets offer criteria for judging whether the destination was reached.

For example, one of the hospital's goals is "to upgrade administrative practices." The problem with that statement by itself is that it is too general. No one knows specifically what things need to be achieved in order to carry out the goal successfully. Therefore, an objective and a target must be developed, such as computerizing medical records within five years. Another goal of the hospital is to establish greater financial stability through increased fund raising. A related objective and target might be to increase private donations by 10 percent a year for three years.

At this point in the planning process, great care must be taken to set realistic targets, because the targets will determine the success criteria by which performance will be evaluated. In the case of the computerized billing system, staff members should not agree to an unrealistic timetable; in the case of the increased fund-raising target, board members should be confident that they have the time and are willing to make the commitment that such an optimistic target suggests. In the end, success is judged not by the optimism of the original objective but by whether the target was achieved.

The fourth level of planning involves strategies and actions for carrying out the objectives and reaching the targets. Strategies are also called action plans. If objectives tell us where we want to get, strategies and action plans tell us how we are going to get there and how much it will cost. (A complete action plan includes a detailed budget.) Because action plans assign specific costs to particular objectives, they are generally worked up by staff and fully discussed by the board before a set of objectives and targets is approved. For example, the board of the Compton Memorial Hospital did not agree to increase private donations by 10 percent a year for three years until the staff had come up with an action plan to show how this could be accomplished and how much it would cost. The action plan budgeted for a fund-raising consultant during the first year of the campaign, called for additional volunteers (to be recruited by a board committee) to work on an annual auction, mandated another board committee to explore internet fund raising beginning in the second year, and suggested the need for a senior-level staff person (with clerical assistance) to coordinate the campaign. These strategies represented only a small part of the staff's total action plan for this objective.

The fifth level of planning is the implementation of the action plan itself (actions). Very little actual planning goes on at this level as this is more of a doing phase. However, careful monitoring must take place to be sure that the implementation is proceeding on schedule. For example, the Compton Memorial Hospital assigned two board members to develop a volunteer list for the fund-raising auction. After two months, nothing had been done (one board member had had a death in the family, and the other was simply overwhelmed by the task). For that reason, modifications were made in the action plan—four board members were asked to find volunteers, and a staff person was assigned to assist this group on a half-day-a-week basis.

The sixth and final level of planning is evaluation. Evaluation asks the questions: Did we achieve our targets? Why or why not? How can we do better next time? Evaluation is an extremely important planning tool, because it provides concrete information on the organization's performance potential based on past experience. As a result, it makes future planning easier and more realistic. For example, when the board of the Compton Memorial Hospital examined the performance of its fundraising drive after three years, it found that private donations had not increased significantly for the first eighteen months of the campaign but thereafter increased 25 percent in a twelve-month period. The conclusion was that it takes several months to set up a good fund-raising campaign and that the board should not have expected concrete results immediately. This fact was extremely useful to the board as it planned its fund-raising target for the next three years. The target called for a 30 percent increase over a three-year period with the increases phased in annually at 5 percent, 10 percent, and 15 percent.

Planning Level Responsibilities

One of the advantages of looking at planning in terms of levels is that it can be a more useful framework for determining who is responsible for what in the planning process itself. For example:

- The board of directors, with the assistance of the chief executive, bears primary responsibility for the mission statement.
- The board, with the assistance of senior staff, is responsible for setting goals.
- Board and staff are jointly responsible for setting objectives and targets.
- Staff, with some assistance from the board, is responsible for determining strategies and actions.
- Staff is responsible for implementing the action plan.

- Board and staff are responsible for approving an evaluation plan in which some of the evaluation may be done by an objective outsider.

Although planning level responsibilities are allocated between board and staff, it is important to keep in mind that others may also participate in the process. These include:

- Constituents, funders, and other important community representatives whose opinions might be sought in the process of planning
- Organizational volunteers, who can be used strategically in gathering information and participating in planning discussions
- A community resource person (or several), unconnected with the organization, who might be invited to become part of the core planning group to provide an objective view of issues
- A paid consultant who might assist with setting up a planning process and schedule, might lead discussions, do research, write reports, and assist the staff with logistics

PLANNING MODELS

There are numerous approaches to planning in nonprofit organizations. It is probably not very important for administrators and board members of nonprofit organizations to become familiar with each and every one of them. What is important is to understand the two underlying approaches to planning—linear planning and integrated planning—which ultimately dictate what planning approach is chosen. Each of these approaches has its own particular advantages and disadvantages. Once these are fully understood, the governing group of a nonprofit organization, together with its senior staff, can develop a specific model of planning that seems appropriate both for the organization and the particular planning situation.

Linear Planning

Most of the planning that has been described in the chapter so far is linear in nature. It begins with a general discussion about mission and ends with a formal document laying out goals, objectives, strategies, and so on. The approach assumes that planning is initiated periodically at particular periods in an organization's history and that such a planning "intervention" will have a beginning point and an end point. The linear model is usually quite comprehensive and can be undertaken for several reasons:

- To create new organizations
- To develop and approve an organization's mission, goals, objectives, and action plans for some interval (e.g., every five years)
- To develop plans that may be required by a funder as a condition of receiving grant support
- To develop a clear vision of the future, as when organizations take on major new programs, build a facility, undertake a capital campaign, or consider a change in direction
- To demonstrate wide involvement of the general public in the planning process or to draft a plan that will become a public document open to review and comment by friends and foes alike

Figure 9.1. Linear Planning

TIME

Mission Statements

Goal Formulation

Objectives

Strategies

Action
Plans

Action

Evaluation

Linear planning proceeds by a process of condensation and distillation following the steps outlined earlier in the chapter. It considers a whole range of options at each level of planning (mission, goals, objectives, and strategies), and in each case eliminates all but the very few that appear most reasonable and sensible. The triangle in figure 9.1 serves as a visual metaphor for linear planning over time, revealing two special characteristics of this approach to planning. First, it shows how linear planning always proceeds from broad mission and goal formulation to the more narrow and specific writing of action plans. Second, it shows how linear planning tends to slough off many options and narrow down to a very few.

Linear planning has advantages and disadvantages. The principal advantage is its comprehensiveness. When a nonprofit organization wants to look at itself in a systematic way, evaluating and speculating about its future in a wide variety of areas, the linear approach works well. Similarly, when the organization undertakes a controversial, risky, or expensive new project, or significantly changes its mission, it can prove to the world at large that the new direction has not been undertaken lightly, that many people have been consulted, and that many options have been considered. Another advantage is that a linear planning process often generates a formal public document that provides the framework for actions and protects the organization from pressures to consider other approaches.

Unfortunately, the very comprehensiveness of linear planning is one of its major disadvantages. It is often a slow and frustrating process. Many organizations spend months drafting mission statements, begin to tackle goals, and simply give up in exhaustion without a plan and without a willingness to continue planning in the future. Inflexibility is a second disadvantage. Once a plan has been drafted and approved, it can be very difficult to change. Should conditions change—if opportunities arise, if the plan itself does not seem to be on track—the plan is not easy to modify. Additionally, such a lengthy process often places an organization in a holding pattern that restricts the implementation of new initiatives. A good way to see how a linear planning process might work is to review how one organization managed the task.

THE CRAFT SOCIETY

The Craft Society is a thirty-year-old nonprofit whose activities have included the exhibition and sale of contemporary crafts, the establishment of a permanent craft collection, and an educational program. The group decided to undertake a planning process after a major funder stated that a five-year plan would be required if the organization wished to apply for a major challenge grant to develop an endowment.

The first step in the process was to lay out a schedule and budget for the planning process itself. This was done by a planning committee of the board, which included the executive director as an ex officio member. The schedule and budget for the planning process were reviewed by both the staff and the full board. After making some changes based on suggestions from these two groups, the board approved the schedule for planning. A budget range was also approved and an effort was made by some of the trustees to secure outside funding. In the end, a $30,000 grant was secured toward a $75,000 planning budget. Funds were to be used for consultant assistance ($50,000), temporary assistance to ensure sufficient staff release time ($20,000), and miscellaneous travel and office expenses ($5,000).

The next step was to identify potential consultants who could assist with the planning process. Through phone calls to similar organizations around the country, six consultants were identified. Five expressed interest and sent material about themselves and their firms, but one of these was far too expensive to be considered by the Society, and two did not seem to have the right mix of experience. The remaining two were interviewed by the executive director and members of the planning committee. A consultant was ultimately selected whose expertise, approach, and personality seemed best suited to the Craft Society's needs.

The kickoff for the planning process itself was a two-day retreat planned and led by the consultant. The retreat was designed to give the board and the staff an opportunity to review the mission statement and then to evaluate each of the Society's major areas of program activity (exhibition, collection, education, and

sales) and organizational areas (governance, staffing, fund raising, and general administration). Participants were also asked to
develop a list of the most important activities the society should
engage in over the next decade, put them in priority order, and
then identify the organizational changes that would be required
to accomplish these things.

After the retreat, the planning process continued. Committees
were appointed by the president of the board to focus on the various programs, activities, and functions of the Society identified
and discussed at the retreat. These committees were composed of
board members, staff, and some community people not formally
associated with the organization (it was felt that this latter group
could contribute a great deal to the discussion). For the next
six months, the committees met to flesh out the priorities for
the areas assigned to them. To accomplish this task, additional
research was needed in certain cases. Staff members and the consultant were used to investigate the feasibility of certain activities,
conduct market and best practice research in the field, and interview key committee leaders, funders, and media representatives.

At the end of the six months, each committee had a short
written document representing the group's consensus. It began
with a statement that outlined the importance of the area in the
overall functioning of the Society. It also included:

- A *list of the goals* to be accomplished by the program during
  the time period covered by the plan (including *specific and
  measurable objectives* for each goal)
- A preliminary description of budget and staff implications
  of the goals
- An outline of the necessary fund-raising, marketing, and
  other activities needed to accomplish the goals

The material from each committee was collated and summarized
by a staff person and sent to all participants. A second board retreat was organized to review all of the material presented, to
set priorities, and to begin to assemble and approve the goals

and objectives of the long-range plan. Senior staff was invited to participate in this retreat and provide a reality check on whether the directions, targets, and activities being considered by the board were reasonable and achievable.

The next step involved completing the action plan for a five-year period. The consultant wrote a report consisting of:

- A summary of the goals and objectives already approved by the board
- A five-year timeline, broken down into six-month units, showing when particular activities would occur
- A narrative description of what would be taking place in each of the activity areas
- A discussion of staffing issues including staff additions and reorganization
- Two versions of a five-year budget—one based on conservative assumptions about revenues (and activity levels and expenses), the other based on more optimistic assumptions (this product was similar to the framework budgets described in chapter 6)
- A five-year fund-raising plan
- An evaluation plan

The planning document was circulated to the full board a month before the final planning meeting. This allowed adequate time for board members to read the report carefully. At the meeting, which was led by the consultant, the board asked questions, raised concerns, made modifications, and ultimately approved a somewhat revised version of the plan. The consultant then made the revisions in the planning document and produced a PowerPoint distillation of the plan for broad distribution.

In designing this process, the Society ran into some problems that required special solutions:

- *The makeup of the working committees.* Ideally, the committees were to be composed of board members and other individuals, including senior staff and community resource people. However, in some cases, there were limitations both on the time board members were willing to commit to the process and the availability of others outside the organization. Thus, the Society used two other approaches to prepare the initial planning papers. First, the board itself served as a planning group for some areas, making sure that efforts were made to gather ideas and opinions from a larger body of interested individuals. Second, a consultant was used to research other areas and make written recommendations. In particular, his expertise was sought in evaluating and making recommendations about the internal operations of the Society because it was decided that no one on the board or staff had sufficient objectivity to conduct this assessment. Furthermore, a group of the staff was assigned some areas and prepared position papers that were submitted to the planning committee for review and comment.

- *Oversight of the planning process.* It was clear that such a complex process, involving so many volunteers, would require a kind of project management group to be sure that deadlines were met and to reassign work that wasn't getting completed on schedule. The planning committee was responsible for this oversight function. In order to be sure that there was a proper liaison between board and staff, the executive director served on the planning committee.

- *The role of the staff.* It was agreed that staff members had to be involved in the planning process if the plan was to be effective and realistic. But the planning committee felt that it was equally important that the staff not dominate the process of planning. Staff members were therefore asked to serve as "resources" to the committees with at least one staff member assigned to each committee. Staff also tended to logistical details, making sure that meetings were scheduled and materials were prepared and sent out. Finally, staff reviewed and commented on all materials and helped the consultant prepare documents for the final board meeting.

Integrated Planning

There are other approaches to planning that rely less on a predictable sequence of steps and emphasize instead an ongoing process, one that is integrated into the regular operation of the organization. Such integrated planning models do not have predictable beginning and end points, nor do they assume that one step in the planning process determines subsequent steps. Rather, this approach utilizes the concept of strategic fit, suggesting that the various components of planning must fit together to make a coherent whole. To accomplish such a fit, every detail in the planning process must be capable of influencing every other. As a result, all components of planning—mission statements, goal formulation, the development of objectives and targets, action plans, implementation, and evaluation—must take place constantly so that as information is generated from one area, it can influence decisions and choices made in another.

In linear planning, information flow tends to be in one direction. Thus information about mission determines goal formulation but not the other way around. Goals determine objectives, objectives determine strategies, and so on. In integrated planning, information flows in several directions because every planning component is interdependent and can affect and be affected by any other. An organization's mission is tied inextricably to its actions, to the evaluation of those actions, to available resources that often determine strategies, to the needs of the constituency as defined in many of the goals, and so on. As a result, integrated planning must be informed by various kinds of ongoing information gathering. It is not sufficient to collect information for a particular phase of planning only once. Information must be collected continually as other phases of the planning process redefine the original questions asked.

An integrated planning model is best represented visually by a circle that resembles a wheel with spokes (figure 9.2). The planning coordinator or coordinating group sits at the center of the wheel, collecting information from, and communicating it to, the wheel's perimeter via the spokes. At the perimeter, various people are working on specific tasks. These tasks are already familiar to us—one group may be evaluating current activities, another might be reviewing statements of purpose, a third might be surveying the organization's membership to formulate new goals for the future, a fourth might be talking to potential funders, a fifth might be working on budgets relating to specific action plans, and so forth. (In some cases, one group or even one individual might take on several of these tasks.) In order for the wheel to turn—representing the organization's forward progress in planning—the planning coordination process must take place at the center. This involves three types of activity: collecting information from the planning groups at the wheel's perimeter, communicating relevant information back to these groups, and ultimately fitting all the pieces of information into a coherent plan.

Figure 9.2. Integrated Planning

Integrated planning is by its very nature an ongoing process. Like the wheel that serves as the visual metaphor for the process, it has no beginning point and no end point and is continually moving. For this reason, integrated planning tends to emphasize the *process* of planning. This is one of its advantages over linear planning. Unlike linear planning, an integrated process enables an organization to be immediately responsive to change, opportunity, and setbacks. It does not have to begin the process of planning all over again in order to respond to a sudden change in the funding environment, political reversals, or in staffing and governance that could lead to new opportunities and activities. Rather, when changes occur, goals can be reformulated and action plans can be drafted all at the same time. It is the role of the planning coordinator (or planning committee) to see that all of these tasks are completed, that there is adequate communication flow, and that the results of the various components of planning dovetail to make a coherent whole.

A second advantage of integrated planning is that it encourages the board, staff, and constituency to remain involved in the process in an ongoing way. In linear planning, people often have only one or two opportunities in each decade to take a fundamental look at mission and goals. They tend to spend a lot of time being careful to "get it right," and then the discussion is dropped. In integrated planning, the process drives itself forward continually, and the discussion of mission, goals, objectives, and strategies is repeatedly revisited. Furthermore, a discussion of strategies does not wait for the discussion of mission to be completed, because there is no such thing as closure on that discussion. What does happen is that a continually evolving plan is drafted and updated. Because the plan can always be revised as the planning process moves forward, and because the various planning components fit together, no air of finality hangs over the draft passed along. It is true that the planning document rarely gets printed up into a pretty brochure as is possible in linear planning, because some of its parameters may soon change. However, there are working policies adopted by the board periodically, goal statements (reviewed at least annually), as well as objectives, strategies, and specific activity schedules to guide the actions of the staff.

A third advantage of integrated planning is that it tends to move more quickly toward action. Linear planning models, as we have seen, are slow because they assume that distillation is the essence of planning and that in any planning decision, every reasonable alternative should be considered. Although this does lead to informed choices, those choices may be a long time in coming. Integrated planning cannot claim to be as comprehensive. What it gives up in comprehensiveness, it gains in time.

The very advantages of integrated planning suggest the disadvantages. Its lack of comprehensiveness can lead to uninformed decisions that result in rash actions; its flexibility can have a negative effect on people's confidence in the organization's long-term plans; and the emphasis on process usually means that a carefully organized, well-documented, written plan is a secondary priority, one that is often not addressed. What does an integrated planning process look like? The following example may be helpful.

THE COMMUNITY FOUNDATION

The Community Foundation, a broad-based, grant-giving non-profit organization in a Midwestern city, has used integrated planning for a number of years. The trustees decided on this approach for several reasons:

- Donors were establishing restricted funds at the foundation, and additional monies were being added to the endowment at unpredictable times; thus it was extremely important to be able to review the foundation's philosophy, goals, and programs regularly in light of available resources.
- Community needs appeared to change rapidly; issues such as the economic dislocation engendered by a major plant closing or a sudden change in the demographic composition of the community required quick and decisive responses, and the board was not comfortable in reviewing its priorities only every five years as would have been the case with linear planning.
- The board wished to discipline itself about looking toward the future. They found in the past that linear planning allowed them to relax in years when a structured planning process was not moving forward, but they preferred to force themselves to debate future needs and activities every time the group came together.

To do effective integrated planning, the foundation established a planning committee composed of some trustees, staff members, and, occasionally by special invitation, resource people from outside the organization. The role of the planning committee was to collect and organize material that could be presented to the full board for discussion and action according to a predictable annual schedule. In addition, the planning commit-tee developed a built-in liaison with other committees so that it could coordinate the planning of each group and organize all of the specific plans into a coherent whole.

The foundation's planning committee decided that it was necessary always to be considering three time frames as it went about its work: the immediate future, the medium-range future, and the long-term future. At each meeting, different emphases were placed on each of these time frames depending on where the group found itself in the annual planning cycle. For example, at one meeting held in 2012, the planning committee spent almost the entire time talking about a single long-term planning issue—education after the year 2025—and did not discuss anything relative to the foundation's activity in the decade to come. At its next meeting, the discussion focused on a three-year strategy for dealing with the homeless. The determining factor for the agenda in each case was the needs of the full board. If it was necessary for the trustees to have specific action items relating to the immediate future, the planning committee had to have all the information ready with preliminary recommendations well in advance of that meeting. Thus the committee's work was completely coordinated with the decision cycle of the board itself.

Several features of the foundation's approach to planning should be highlighted:

- The foundation's planning committee was under constant pressure to produce material for the full board to discuss and act on. It could not sit back and have general philosophical discussions leading nowhere. Rather, it needed to come to closure and complete very specific assigned tasks. As a result, the meetings of this group were highly structured and very efficient. Every member of the committee was given an assignment, and reports were prepared in advance of meetings for everyone to read and discuss.
- The foundation's planning committee relied on others to do much of its basic research and work. It called on special ad

hoc groups (or sometimes paid consultants) to bring recommendations on specific activity areas such as education, the homeless, cultural activity, economic empowerment, drugs, and so on. It also depended on information provided by the finance committee on short- and long-term budget trends. From time to time, consultants or staff members provided additional information at the request of the committee.

- In many organizations, the work—which in this case was done by the foundation's planning committee—is carried out by the executive committee. The foundation's board decided not to use the executive committee in this fashion inasmuch as nonexecutive committee members might have felt a sense of disenfranchisement from the important issues and decisions the organization faced. By setting up a separate planning committee, many more board members became involved in critical issues. Nevertheless, all of the planning committee's work was reviewed by the executive committee before being circulated to the full board. It was the executive committee that was responsible for placing this material in the context of the full agenda for board meetings.

WHICH MODEL TO CHOOSE?

The extensive discussions in the second half of this chapter about linear and integrated planning—and the two case studies of the Craft Society and the Community Foundation—have demonstrated that each approach offers advantages and disadvantages for particular kinds of organizations in particular situations. For this reason, *a single organization may end up utilizing both linear and integrated planning at different times in its development.*

Most organizations should attempt to complete a linear planning process at least once every decade (many of the best-run organizations carry out such plans at five-year intervals). If an organization is moving in new directions or undertaking a controversial activity or an activity that will require broad-based support, the *comprehensiveness* of a linear approach is also probably appropriate. If the emphasis of planning is the written product (to satisfy the board, the community, funders, or others), the linear approach will again make good sense.

On the other hand, an integrated approach to planning is certainly better for deliberations about the future that allow the board and staff to have an *ongoing* structured planning process as well as a continual focus on planning issues. Integrated planning is also useful for organizations that find they must often respond quickly to change.

This is one reason why a new organization often does well with integrated planning. Until the organization stabilizes, it is essential that the board and staff monitor events, take advantage of opportunities, and respond to threats in a timely manner. For older organizations, too, especially those experiencing crises and reversals, the responsive nature of the integrated approach is beneficial. Finally, integrated planning establishes a kind of discipline on the part of board and staff members, forcing them to look continually at the future and chart the course of the organization in a responsible manner.

It is also true that each kind of planning can be adapted somewhat, encompassing elements of the other. For example, many organizations do a five-year linear planning process every five years but conduct a detailed review annually that incorporates elements of integrated planning. These organizations hold annual planning retreats in which elements of their linear plans are modified and updated, sometimes with the addition of a subsequent out-year. In this way, by adding the additional year annually, the organizations are always dealing with a five-year time horizon even though the formal linear planning process may only happen twice in a decade.

In the end, every organization should decide on a planning approach that seems right for the time, the situation, the people involved (both within and outside the organization), and the organization itself.

FINANCIAL PLANNING

No organization can undertake a planning process without making sure that there is a strong budgeting component. What are the most important things that people need to know?

- What has been the financial pattern in the past? How much revenue and expense has there been, and from what sources?

- Are there financial trends that could have an impact on the organization in the future that should be taken into account?
- What are the financial ramifications of proposed new activities and structures? What are the costs, and where might the income be found?
- What are the most optimistic and pessimistic financial scenarios that can be imagined for different courses of action? On what basis are these projected estimates being made?

Chapter 6 suggested that the technique of framework budgeting is an important tool in carrying out a planning process. By projecting more than one financial scenario, the decision-making group can more accurately assess risk and opportunity. By basing projections at least in part on actual performance, the group can feel more confident that the numbers are rooted in reality.

There is one more reason why careful budgeting is so important in planning. Increasingly, funders want to see the results of a planning process before committing significant funds to an organization. They have a particular interest in the financial aspects, wanting to know that if they invest in the organization, it has a good chance of succeeding. The more complete and reasonable the financial projections, the more likely a funder will gain confidence in the organization's ability to project for the future.

MAKING DECISIONS

One of the greatest hurdles in a planning process is getting from the phase of generating ideas and recommendations to the stage of making choices and final decisions. Achieving closure on the process of planning and effecting the transition from planning to action requires discipline. But it also requires a system that encourages swift movement on items about which there is general agreement.

One of the best systems yet devised is the consent calendar, which is extensively used in decision-making meetings of public bodies but can be easily adapted for private nonprofit organizations. The procedure associated with consent calendars involves several steps:

1. A planning report should be written, and proposed actions should be condensed into a series of recommendations. Each

recommendation should be followed by a brief justification and explanation. This work can be done by the planning committee, a consultant, a staff member working with the planning group, or anyone else designated by the board.

2. The planning report should be sent to members of the decision-making group (generally the board) with a response sheet. On the response sheet, each recommendation is written out in full and followed by three words: *Agree, Disagree, Discuss*. Board members are asked to circle their choice for each of the recommendations and return the sheet by a certain date.

3. By prior agreement, a predetermined percentage of *Agree* responses will be sufficient to put a particular question on the consent calendar. Once a recommendation is on the consent calendar, it is removed from the agenda for discussion, and all such recommendations are simply voted on as a block at the meeting in which the plan is to be approved. A 60 percent *Agree* rate should be a minimum for inclusion on the consent calendar, though 75 percent is preferable. Some organizations might wish to see the figure as high as 90 percent. It is important not only to have a majority of people approving some action but to have higher percentages fully understanding it and feeling relatively comfortable with it.

4. At the meeting at which planning decisions are to be made, all recommendations other than those on the consent calendar are placed on the agenda for discussion. They can either be taken in the order in which they appear in the report, or if there is overwhelming consensus on recommendations that should *not* be approved, these can be taken first.

The consent-calendar system has many advantages. It streamlines the decision-making process by eliminating discussion where there is no controversy. It points out those areas where there may be confusion or disagreement at a point in time when corrective measures may be possible. Because the response sheet requires people to make their opinions public before the meeting, there is usually sufficient time to discuss specific points with individuals whose opinions might be swayed or even changed. Finally, the consent calendar prevents one or two people from filibustering, prolonging discussion, and preventing approval of actions that the majority believes are appropriate.

For any organization setting up a planning process, the following comments may be especially useful to keep in mind:

- The simpler the planning process, the more likely it is to succeed.
- There is no one right way to plan; the best planning processes are those custom designed to fit the needs of an organization and the working styles of board and staff.
- The primary benefit of planning is often the process itself; planning is a structured way of involving a number of people in thinking about the future, and this is often its chief value.
- Planning is not necessarily a synonym for growth; scaling down activities (or eliminating them) may often be an appropriate planning decision.
- Planning produces conflict and anxiety; no one can completely control the outcome of a planning process, and this can cause tensions among board and staff (this feeling is often augmented by frustration over the amount of time required in planning).
- The desire for consensus almost always impedes the planning process; it is important to hear everyone's views, but it is not advantageous to incorporate every minority opinion into a plan.
- To be successful, a planning process must have the strong support of top-level staff, key trustees, and others of influence in the organization.
- Planning should not be left completely to professional planning consultants; staff and board must be involved so that the decisions reached are their own.
- Perhaps most important, there must be a climate of enthusiasm within the organization toward planning; without it, a planning process has little chance of success.

CHECKLIST QUESTIONS FOR CHAPTER 9

1. Do planning activities in your organization include a review of the mission, vision, and values, the development of goals and objectives, the formulation of an action plan, the development of a timeline, and the preparation of appropriate budgets for purposes of analysis?

2. Is some kind of evaluation scheme built into the planning process so that the plan can be adjusted if things do not work out as predicted?

3. Are both board and staff involved in planning activities? Have appropriate ways been found to involve volunteers, constituents, funders, and other important community representatives?

4. Are consultants being used by your organization in planning? Are their responsibilities clearly defined?

5. Does your organization have a fully documented process for planning with clear deadlines? Is it well understood by all participants?

6. What is the mechanism for preparing alternative budget scenarios? Are they in a form that will be useful to the people who must make big decisions about the future?

7. What is the strategy for garnering support for long-range planning in your organization? Is there an effort to develop a climate of enthusiasm around the process of planning?

TEN

Sustainability and Leadership

Fred Coolidge is the longtime executive director of the Compton Community Foundation. Nearing retirement, he can look back over forty years of accomplishment since joining the foundation as an assistant grants officer in 1977. Among the many things he can point to with pride is the foundation's growth. In the late 1970s, its assets were around $8 million. As he was preparing to step down, the portfolio stood at over $175 million, providing almost $10 million each year in grant funding.

Coolidge can also claim major credit for the growth and expansion of the nonprofit sector in Compton. From a handful of nonprofit organizations in 1970, Compton saw the birth of scores by the end of the decade and hundreds by century's end. Fred Coolidge has been honored numerous times by these organizations for his own personal efforts on their behalf. He cannot count the celebrations and accolades he has received. He is clearly regarded as one of the people who transformed Compton in positive ways.

Under the circumstances, one would expect Fred Coolidge to be a completely contented man. He has made things better in the community, and people recognize him for his work. But as he faces his retirement, he is uneasy. He cannot quite put his finger on what troubles him, but he worries that the nonprofit sector is not as healthy as he had once thought a decade ago. For one thing, he does not see the kind of sustained board leadership and volunteer involvement that he took for granted in earlier years. It seems that everyone is so busy. Forty years ago, a small group of people in town could be relied on to chair boards, volunteer their time, and look to the long-term future and health of the community.

Coolidge knows he should be cheered by the fact that Compton's nonprofit boards of trustees have become less clubby, and he applauds the growing diversity on local boards. Certainly, more people are involved in nonprofit organizations than ever before. But their level of commitment does not seem as intense. He is concerned about the inexperience of many trustees and the lack of continuity and follow-through among the volunteers.

Part of this, he realizes, can be explained by a change in the way people conduct their lives as well as major shifts in the larger society. In earlier times, the wealthiest members of Compton society took their places on the boards of nonprofit organizations as a matter of course. In those days, there were business leaders who were born and died in Compton, and they often took the board seats of their fathers before them. Today, a significant number of wealthy people do not serve on boards at all, and there are many younger business executives who come to Compton for a short time and then are transferred by their companies to other communities, not giving them time to establish roots. More women work, so the volunteer groups that used to be composed entirely of women cannot get the same number of hours from those who are willing to volunteer their time. Indeed, no one has as much free time—even teenagers have jobs outside of school.

Coolidge remembers back to the time when he had a "kitchen cabinet." He used to be able to pick up the phone and speak confidentially with a few leaders about repairing some damage to one or another of the local nonprofit organizations. His loose collection of associates could take care of things quietly and without a fuss. But the people he used to call have died or are no longer active, and the younger leaders barely have enough time to return his phone calls. He doesn't blame them. Their work lives are so demanding.

Coolidge is also worried by the failures of several nonprofit organizations in recent years. He used to pride himself on the fact that no nonprofit organization had gone bankrupt in Compton on his watch as foundation director. But within the last three years alone, five organizations have closed their doors. In one case, a local nonprofit hospital closed, unable to cope with the competition from the profit-making chain that had bought up the other two nonprofit hospitals in town. The foundation board had struggled with the dilemma but had decided in the end that it simply would be too expensive to modernize the hospital and make it competitive. And this was only one of the organizational failures. Many smaller organizations—formed during the heady days of his early tenure—have gone out of business or become moribund. In a couple of cases, there was simply no one around to go through the formal process of closing down the organization, and the corporate shells simply languished, with no programs, no volunteers, and no staffs.

But perhaps the thing that troubles Coolidge most is the lack of sustained staff leadership in local nonprofit organizations. After all, he muses, visionary leaders are what have always made the difference in forging strong, vital organizations. The leaders today do not stay as long, and they do not have time to make their marks. None of the executive directors Fred Coolidge remembers from the time he took over as executive director of the foundation are still in their jobs. In some cases, specific organizations have gone through three or four executive directors in that period. Sometimes, these competent individuals have been recruited by organizations in other cities; some have burned out. In several cases, financial necessities have forced them to seek employment elsewhere. And when an individual has left the organization (and, often, the field), the pool of leaders from which to draw for a replacement has seemed meager.

On the occasion of his fortieth anniversary as director, Coolidge shared his concerns with a good friend. "You're getting old, Fred," the friend said to him. "We always look back and think the grass was greener in the old days. This is a sure sign that you are ready for retirement." Coolidge mused about his friend's comment for several weeks and finally was prepared to agree. But then he went to a national conference of community foundation executives and he found that others—many others—shared his concerns.

At the conference, sessions that only a decade before had been devoted to techniques for fostering the development of start-up nonprofit organizations had been replaced with sessions that had titles such as "Stress and Time Management," "Crisis-Oriented Grant Making," "Bail Out or Get Out: When to Let Nonprofit Organizations Die," and "Motivating Younger Trustees." There were sessions on leadership development, sustainability, and the role of community foundations in a world where the pace of change escalates every year. Coolidge noticed that these sessions were being attended by some of his old friends in the foundation world. But surprisingly, it was his younger colleagues who were most in evidence. And they seemed most worried.

SUSTAINABILITY AND ADAPTABILITY
IN THE TWENTY-FIRST CENTURY

Today, many knowledgeable people are concerned about nonprofit organizations and the special difficulties they face. Largely unanticipated a quarter century ago, the underlying conditions and causes of these difficulties had years to incubate and ultimately wreak havoc. When the problems of nonprofit organizations could no longer be ignored, many executives and trustees predicted they would go away as naturally as they appeared, and this also undermined the health of many organizations. Now the widespread consensus is that the trends that Fred Coolidge worries about mark a permanent change in the operating realities for the nonprofit sector, and they add significantly to the complications and challenges in managing organizations.

The issues are many and complex, but taken together, they might be characterized by two superordinate and related challenges—*sustainability* and *the ability to adapt to a rapidly changing world.* Nonprofit organizations must cope with increased competition, more diversity among constituents, higher expectations from the public and from funders, increasing costs, declining support, rapidly changing technology, and substantially different ways of conducting business. Surviving in such an environment (sustainability) depends upon the ability to adapt.

Why did so few anticipate that nonprofit organizations would have to worry about survival issues back in the second half of the twentieth century, and how can a similar myopia be avoided in the future? The answer is simple: change must always be anticipated—things will never stay the same. Because the earlier time was a period of unprecedented growth and optimism, few thought that nonprofit organizations would ever truly be at risk. There was an increase in the number, size, and professionalism of nonprofit organizations; it was a time when the nonprofit sector as a whole grew at an astonishing rate. The consensus of government officials and private-sector leaders seemed to be that more money and more organizations could go a long way toward solving society's problems. It was so vibrant a time that most people assumed that the growth curve would continue upward indefinitely.

But then a reassessment period set in resulting in retrenchment. It was a wrenching time for many organizations, especially those that continued to assume that the change was only temporary. Costs continued to rise, but income in many organizations started to shrink for the first time. A generation of leaders—many of whom were founder/directors working for less than acceptable wages—retired, resigned, or were asked to step down. Replacing them was often arduous. Recruiting board members was also becoming more difficult as the demands of work and family took their toll.

Why did it happen? Why did the bubble burst? The answer to this question can help people understand the dynamics of change that will be so important to nonprofit organizations in the first decades of the twenty-first century. Some say it was a natural correction—a pendulum reaching the end of its directional cycle of growth, swinging in the other direction toward retrenchment. But it was probably more than that.

The federal budget deficit was in large part to blame. Government, which had been raising its funding to nonprofit organizations for decades, began to question its underlying assumptions. Nonprofit organizations were chartered to solve society's problems, but the problems themselves seemed to be getting worse. The simple explanation was that nonprofit organizations were not doing the job effectively. Furthermore, occasional periods of inflation and rises in energy costs as well as America's shrinking prestige abroad added to Americans' general unease about the status quo. There was a growing crisis in confidence that more nonprofit organizations and more public money was clearly not the answer to society's problems.

Over the years, influential private-sector funders joined the growing segment of leaders who felt that the nonprofit sector had gotten too large and ineffective. Most refused to allow their grants to make up for government cuts in funding, and many began cutting back on their level of operating and program support, a level of support that had led to the proliferation of nonprofit organizations in the first place. They asked difficult questions that revolved around five basic issues:

- *Constituency and Community.* Were nonprofit organizations' claims that they were truly serving a broad public totally justified? What about the apparent large segments of underserved and truly needy that were not being reached by their programs?

Might the problems of society in general and the communities that nonprofits serve be addressed more effectively by organizations that were more effectively serving people in need? Shouldn't the boards of nonprofit organizations be more reflective of these communities?

- *Effectiveness.* Were nonprofit organizations run efficiently, taking advantage of pragmatic and proven business practices? Were they delivering the products and services they claimed to deliver? Were staffs too large? Was there too much waste? Was there sufficient expertise on the boards and staffs to be truly effective?

- *Accountability.* Were nonprofit organizations and their boards and staffs truly accountable for their performance? How did they substantiate their claims of service delivery? How could an outsider, such as a funder, evaluate their performance or their overall effectiveness? Was there sufficient oversight of the finances both internally and externally? How could donors be assured that their money was going to be used properly?

- *Leadership.* Who was in charge? Did that person (or those people) display true leadership qualities? Could they motivate people within and outside the organization? Did they inspire confidence?

- *Sustainability.* Had nonprofits come up with sustainability strategies that did not constantly require larger and larger handouts and operating grants? Had they built proper reserves and endowments? Were they being supported locally by a broad mix of individuals who were willing to support them year after year because these organizations had demonstrated a proven ability to address need?

A key theme of the critics was that nonprofit organizations were unable to adapt to a rapidly changing world. Many organizations came of age half a century ago, at the peak of one of the most sustained economic booms in history. As the realities of the world and this country's economics changed, they continued to operate as if conditions were the same. Their programs hadn't changed very much. They served the same clientele. Their boards were composed of the same sorts of people. Their operating models had not evolved. Indeed, as long as the money continued to come in, there was little incentive to do things differently.

But the money did not come in as easily as it once had, and this led to the concern about sustainability. Sustainability, in this context, was not simply the ability to keep a nonprofit organization afloat and in business. It suggested more—building capacity by developing a vital organization, one that could be described as relevant to the needs of its constituents, financially healthy, well managed, and accountable.

As this idea of sustainability was explored, it cycled back to the original concern about adaptability. Building the capacity of a non-profit organization could not be achieved through a one-time process of growth or increased funding. It had to be seen as an *ongoing* process requiring constant adaptation to a changing world. Thus were the two concepts of sustainability and adaptability seen as inextricably inter-linked.

THE USE AND LIMITS OF ENDOWMENTS IN SUSTAINABILITY

When the experienced foundation director Fred Coolidge listened to conference sessions for funders about what people were calling "the crisis" and the themes of sustainability and adaptation to a changing world, he realized that his own thinking, like that of so many of his contemporaries, was out of date. For years, he had thought that if one could only nurture an organization to the point where it was large enough, building its assets and its program capacity, one could assure its long-term viability. Now he realized that this was not the case.

The old idea was that asset building in and of itself would assure the stability and sustainability of nonprofit organizations. This notion was built on the premise of permanence. Make an organization stable and it should stay that way. But the new thinking suggests that permanence cannot be guaranteed in the world of nonprofit organizations and perhaps in many cases shouldn't even be an aspiration, since it can lead to atrophy and irrelevance. Nowhere is that change more evident than in the attitude toward endowments. While there is no question that endowments, properly managed, should provide a permanent source of funds and can be very beneficial to organizations, in and of them-selves large endowments do not guarantee that an organization will be healthy for all time.

THE SYMPHONY ORCHESTRA
STABILIZATION PROGRAM

In 1966, program officers at a major national foundation designed a grants program with the goal of assuring the permanent stability of symphony orchestras in the United States. Their approach was simple. The foundation would provide money to build the endowments of leading orchestras. This money would in turn throw off a permanent revenue stream sufficient to expand programming and professionalize staff. In time, it was thought, these endowments would be so large that the long-term stability of orchestras would be taken care of and the foundation could move on to stabilize other kinds of organizations with the same type of approach. The resulting Symphony Orchestra Stabilization Program was budgeted at almost $70 million—a very significant figure in light of the total size of the industry at the time.

At first, the results of the program seemed to justify the foundation officers' optimism. Many part-time orchestras were able to offer year-round employment to their musicians by expanding the number of concerts and performing throughout the year. More trained professionals were added to the staffs in fund raising, marketing, and human resource management. Salaries increased both for musicians and for administrative staffs. The orchestras were growing in just the way the foundation officers had hoped. European tours, recording contracts, and critical acclaim were positive benefits of upgrading the American orchestra industry.

But as the years and decades passed, there were some signs that the program was not entirely on track. While the number of concerts offered increased, audience size did not. It was becoming more difficult to fill seats for individual concerts as overall annual admission figures did not keep pace with the increase in available seats. Musicians were getting restive and demanding higher wages—after all, the much-touted increases in endowments suggested that there was plenty of money. Perhaps most alarming, the growth in endowment income was not keeping pace with increasing costs. Deficits were climbing—exactly the opposite result from that predicted by the foundation officers.

At the end of the century, a major study of the financial condition of symphony orchestras[1] found that in two decades alone the industry income gap had increased tenfold. Costs had escalated to such a point that the cost of providing a concert to an audience member had increased from $5 in 1971 to $26 in 1991. Of that $26 cost, $15 had to come from fund raising, up from $3 in 1971. Orchestra endowments had grown as predicted but only by an inflation-adjusted 37 percent—not enough to cover the tenfold increase in the annual financial shortfall. By century's end, the industry and its funders were still scratching their heads, trying to figure out what they could do to solve the structural problems that this "stabilization" program had helped create. Ten years later, after a decade of economic instability, orchestras were declaring bankruptcy and the industry was in disarray. The full impact of an incorrect theory about sustainability had taken fifty years to wreak its havoc.

The case history recounted above has been carefully reconstructed from actual documents to illustrate the limits of endowments in assuring sustainability of nonprofit organizations. Endowments can help close the gap between income and expense by providing a regular stream of revenue to supplement other forms of earned and unearned income. But there are no permanent guarantees that endowments will assure long-term stability. Discipline is required. Organizational growth must be kept in check. Endowments themselves must be nurtured and must grow in order to keep up with inflation. "Borrowing" from endowments must be avoided except in extremely unusual and compelling circumstances. Finally, any restrictions in the use of endowment income must be consistent with the adaptability of the organization over time.

Four cases demonstrate the problems that can arise.

- Organization A has an endowment of $2 million and needs about $120,000 per year (or 6 percent of the total corpus) to meet its operating needs. A committee of the board invests the endowment aggressively so that it will yield income of approximately this amount. However, in time, inflation causes organizational expenses to grow, and the gap to be covered by the endowment grows to $150,000 per year. Since the endowment corpus remains at $2 million and is invested entirely to produce income, there is no way to produce the extra $20,000.

- Organization B is far more prudent regarding its use of income from its $2 million endowment. It has decided to utilize only 4.5 percent of the total annually. It reinvests the balance of its income so the endowment can grow. However, the unexpected loss of a major government contract together with a dip in the investment market leads to a substantial ($500,000) deficit for Organization B, and its board votes to "borrow" the required revenue from the endowment. Now that the value of the endowment has been temporarily reduced, there is not enough to meet operating needs, and the board votes to take more than 4.5 percent, thus eating into the corpus and leading to problems similar to those of Organization A.

- Organization C has managed quite nicely on its endowment for many years, utilizing only 4 percent and allowing its assets to grow. However, its unionized employees demand higher wages and benefits. No amount of explanation of the realities of income and expense satisfy the union representatives. They point to the $2 million endowment and say that it should be invaded so that the employees can receive a living wage. With the threat of a strike, the board votes to invade the principal, leading to an ever-increasing structural deficit each year until the endowment is used up.

- Organization D has raised its $2 million endowment through a capital campaign. It has promised donors in all written documents that proceeds from the endowment will be used to support an extremely popular student exchange program in a third world country. Political upheaval in that country requires that the student exchange program be discontinued. But because of the restrictions on the endowment, the funds cannot be used for any other purpose. A letter is sent to the original donors, asking that the restrictions be lifted. However, many of the donors have died and others do not give permission for the change. These restricted funds in the endowment sit invested, gaining income and growing, but not available to the organization.

Prudent organizations attempt to keep endowments as flexible as possible, not wishing to have to anticipate "in perpetuity" what activities the endowment funds should support. Others place time limits on restrictions, stating that after a period of years (perhaps twenty-five) the income from the endowment can be utilized for general purposes. Still others establish "wasting endowments," allowing principal and interest to be utilized so that either there is no endowment at the end of a specific time period or the restricted endowment has been replaced with unrestricted income placed in reserve. In every case, the goal is to maintain flexibility and an organization's ability to adapt.

With respect to financial management, most prudent organizations rarely take more than 4.5 to 5 percent of endowment principal each year for operating needs, and many take less. The balance is reinvested for capital appreciation, and the value of the endowment grows. Furthermore, the trend appears to be toward the total return policy. The endowment is invested for maximum growth without concern about the amount of income thrown off. At the end of each year, the endowment's total value (averaged over several quarters) is calculated. The organization then takes a specified percentage (perhaps 4.5 percent) of that value of the endowment for operating needs. This may be taken from endowment income if it is sufficient; but if the endowment income is not sufficient, the balance can come from the appreciation of capital in the endowment itself. Assets can be sold because they have grown so substantially.

Endowments are almost always valuable to an organization. Properly utilized, they should contribute to organizational sustainability, and they can be utilized as an emergency fund when things go awry, though always with a plan for how borrowed funds will be repaid, on a specific schedule and with interest. Their ongoing contribution to the bottom line helps many organizations deal with what is referred to as a *structural operating deficit*—a deficit that cannot be covered in any other revenue-producing or cost-cutting way. Yet overreliance on endowments to the exclusion of other mechanisms and strategies has gotten many organizations in trouble and has kept others from vigorously pursuing important income-producing or expense-reduction strategies. They must be regarded only as a part of the arsenal of sustainability strategies.

SIZE AND SUSTAINABILITY

Sustainability of nonprofit organizations (and their ability to adapt to change) can be affected by their size. Organizations can be too big. They can also be too small. Two very different organizations serve as illustrations.

Too Big

There have been many cases in which organizations have gotten too big to be sustainable as is clear in the following example.

THE SCIENCE EDUCATION COLLABORATIVE

The Science Education Collaborative (SEC) was founded to help schools utilize the myriad of resources available to them in their communities that could supplement their science programs. The basic premise behind the organization was simple. Many science resources were available to schools from universities, corporations, museums, and other institutions, but busy teachers, curriculum specialists, and others did not have time to find them. Many of these enrichment opportunities and supplementary materials were available free of charge. Others could be purchased at a substantial discount if several schools were interested. The SEC would act as a broker, an information disseminator, and a technical assistance provider.

The SEC began as a special pilot program within a larger education organization. But it was immediately so popular with teachers and schools, and it grew so rapidly, that tensions were created between the SEC program director and the parent organization's executive director. The board decided to spin off the SEC as a separate 501(c)(3) nonprofit corporation with some of the board members assuming leadership. The State Department of Education provided the initial funding for the organizational development work. It was hoped that school system members would provide for the ongoing operating costs through memberships.

Almost from the beginning there were unanticipated problems. The cost of operating an autonomous organization was higher than expected. The parent organization from which the SEC had separated itself continued to run its own science enrichment program, promoting it vigorously and causing identity confusion with constituents. Operating funds were short—while schools were willing to pay a modest sum for memberships, this was not enough to cover costs. An analysis of the situation led to a fateful decision—the SEC should attempt to grow out of its problems, taking on new programs and staff so that it might compete successfully with its local competition and garner national funding for its model programs.

The strategy worked well for the first five years. Special promotions and incentives were offered to schools, and the membership doubled. A talented proposal writer was able to secure seed funding for model programs in order to get them off the ground. The SEC was regarded as the leading local resource for science educators, and it received a number of awards for its work. Nationally, too, the SEC became known as an industry leader.

But after five years, sustaining the organization became impossible. Many of the initial grants were not renewed—the SEC's programs were now no longer new, and others were replicating them. Science teachers were becoming more sophisticated in their use of local resources and no longer needed a broker—indeed, several schools dropped their memberships, especially as the special incentives were discontinued and membership rates were increased to cover expenses.

Another fateful decision forestalled a realistic analysis of the SEC's situation. A major local funder decided that what the SEC needed was an endowment to cover the shortfall in its operating income. A major grant ($2.5 million) was provided on a challenge basis toward an eventual $10 million endowment. This was thought to be sufficient to solve the SEC's problems. All the

cash from the grant was provided before the SEC even conducted a feasibility study to determine whether there were other
funders to provide the match of $7.5 million.

A fund raiser was hired, utilizing a portion of the grant for that
purpose and diminishing the amount available for the endowment. Almost no money was raised the first year. Because the
SEC had counted on substantial income from the endowment, it
ran a large deficit and had to borrow from the endowment, beginning a downward spiral of revenue expectations. Even then, the
organization continued to operate at full tilt, adding staff to run
new, largely unfunded programs.

Today, the SEC no longer exists. Anger and finger-pointing
followed in its wake. Its original parent organization is once again
running science enrichment programs on a modest scale. There
is nothing left of the $2.5 million endowment gift. It was all
used up in the last dying days of the SEC. Many people wonder
what went wrong and how such a strong organization could have
floundered.

The story of the Science Education Collaborative demonstrates
how becoming too big can undermine sustainability. The assumption
that "growth is good" and that "bigger is better" has destroyed many
organizations and is being substantially rethought. Many funders
who fed the illusion by providing seed money for new programs or
endowment grants now believe sustainability can only be achieved if
organizations find an optimum size for healthy operation and are able
to adapt quickly as conditions change.

Too Small

It may seem counterintuitive, but organizations can also be too small
to be sustainable.

HAPPYSPRING, INC.

Happyspring, Inc. is a small conservation and gardening-oriented organization. It grew out of an effort to save thirty-five acres of undeveloped farmland and forest in a coastal town in Maine. When word leaked out that the owner of the property—a local dairy farmer—was planning to subdivide it into one-half-acre parcels, concerned citizens raised the money to buy the property intact. Happyspring, Inc. was created to receive tax-deductible contributions and provide stewardship of the property.

Initially, there was great interest in Happyspring. Nothing is more galvanizing to a group of conservation-minded individuals than saving beautiful property from developers. But once the purchase was accomplished, interest languished and the organization was taken over by ten local gardeners whose interest was in the unusual flora that grew on the acreage.

Over the next ten years, Happyspring operated mostly with unpaid labor. The budget was minimal, but the property had been so well maintained that volunteers could do most of what needed to be done. The $25,000 budget was adequate to pay for some property management and ancillary programming. Occasional nature walks and education programs were sponsored, and the group did a little fund raising.

Then, three events occurred in the same year and forced a reassessment. First, a hurricane washed out the access road, requiring over $40,000 for rebuilding. Second, a donor who had provided about a third of the operating budget ($7,500 annually) died and left no provision in her will for continued support. Third, younger people joined the board and urged the group to expand the education program and link it to the local public schools so that their children could experience the beauties of Happyspring. They urged the hiring of a part-time education director.

The ten board members who had provided the oversight for Happyspring, Inc. for almost a decade were tired. The changes that were now required convinced many of them that they had had enough. A younger trustee was willing to assume leadership and submitted some funding proposals to conservation-oriented foundations in the state. All were rejected. When called, foundation officials explained that there was a real question about the viability of the organization.

One foundation official did offer some assistance. He said that he would provide the services of a consultant to help the Happyspring board diagnose their organization's situation and determine whether it could be viable. Over the next three months, the consultant analyzed the situation and produced the following conclusions:

- First, Happyspring was land poor. It owned a piece of property that it could not comfortably manage and maintain.
- Second, the organization was people poor. There was no paid staff, no apparent board depth, and inadequate volunteer assistance to carry a program forward.
- Third, it was money poor. Its budget was inadequate to meet ongoing operational needs (not to mention capital requirements).
- Fourth, it was idea poor. There was no plan for how all these issues were going to be resolved.

In essence, Happyspring was too small to be viable. As an all-volunteer entity, it could not ensure that essential jobs would get done—or if done, get done well. While its beautiful property was an asset on the balance sheet, it was a practical liability because it required constant investment. Being small, the organization was not on the radar screen of local citizens who might support it. Most institutional donors would also not support it because of its small size and limited impact. Without that support and visibility, it was difficult to recruit the trustees who could change the situation.

Would money alone have helped Happyspring? Many people who find themselves associated with small organizations like to think that money is their only problem. They believe that a single major contribution or endowment gift could solve their problems forever. But large sums of money given to very small organizations often have exactly the opposite effect—they are destabilizing in the long term. For an organization without a strong organizational structure, a qualified staff, fiscal accountability, or a plan for how the money is going to be used, a large contribution often results in wasteful spending, unconsidered expansion, and a more severe series of structural problems over time.

Just Right

How does one determine the right size for a nonprofit organization to assure sustainability? How large is large enough and when is an organization too big? These questions are complicated by the fact that appropriate size will differ markedly for different types of institutions in different fields. A small college with a residential campus may be undersized at an operating budget level of $5 million, while an organization like Happyspring, Inc.—the conservation-oriented organization—may achieve operating stability at a $250,000 annual budget level.

Industry standards will certainly help determine the extent to which an organization needs to professionalize its manpower pool or whether it can rely on volunteers in prominent management roles. In a closely regulated industry like health care, paid professionals are the norm in top management positions. Similarly, one would not expect a university president to be a volunteer, nor any of his or her key associates (though there are undoubtedly occasional exceptions). On the other hand, a fairly sizable foundation giving a handful of large grants every year mostly to the same recipients may operate with a volunteer head and a group of independent contractors performing essential services, thereby reducing the size of the operating budget.

In determining the appropriate size and scope of an organization (and its programs, budget, staff, and physical plant), several key questions should be asked:

1. *Industry comparables.* What is the range of size for other organizations in the field that appear viable and healthy? (The answer to this question will vary by many factors, including geography and size of community, but there is still a range that can be determined.)
2. *Essential activity.* What is the minimum activity that must be

performed every year? Is there sufficient manpower that can be absolutely relied upon to get it done?

3. *Cost versus revenue structure.* How much does it cost to perform the minimum activities of the organization each year in a way that assures quality service and program delivery? Are there reliable revenue streams to meet this cost (with a little left over for contingencies)?

4. *Capitalization.* Are there sufficient reserves to meet unanticipated needs and cash flow requirements? Is there an endowment to cover any structural deficit? Are the reserves and other assets sufficiently liquid to be useful when needed?

5. *Visibility.* Is the organization large enough to be visible in the community (or service area)? Is its program impressive enough to attract leaders to the board and to command gifts from individual and institutional givers?

6. *Balance of supply and demand.* Is there sufficient demand for the amount of product and service being provided? If not, should the amount of product or service delivery be reduced or rechanneled?

MERGER OR CONSOLIDATION AND SUSTAINABILITY

Mergers and acquisitions have become a major staple of the business world. Small companies get bought up by larger ones. Enterprises in the same field see advantages to becoming a single entity with more clout. Efficiencies of operation and scale, issues of competition, and the ever-present consideration of the bottom line encourage myriad organizations to consolidate.

At the same time, the nonprofit world has largely resisted this trend, though the tide is beginning to turn. While nonprofits' challenges are similar, mergers have been much rarer than in the business world, and consolidations through acquisition are virtually nonexistent. Why has this been the case? Why did the mergers and acquisitions boom and the drive toward consolidation bypass nonprofit organizations? The answer is simple. Nonprofit organizations have not felt the same immediate pressure to consolidate because they have not been accountable to owners/shareholders looking for greater returns on investment.

In a nonprofit organization, voting members of the corporation do not have the same vital financial interest in seeing it perform efficiently.

They are generally volunteers who have little incentive to push for changes that could be wrenching in their short-term effects on programs and employees, although sound in the long term. Indeed, the employees of a nonprofit organization often have a personal interest in seeing it continue as it is, especially when their jobs are threatened.

Examples of nonprofit organizations resisting consolidation are common. One such example demonstrates the inherent resistance to change that works against a move toward greater efficiency and program effectiveness.

CONSOLIDATING SERVICES TO THE BLIND

After conducting a full-scale evaluation of its support to local nonprofit organizations, a community foundation in a major city determined that it could no longer support so many organizations set up to assist the blind. Most of these organizations had been around for decades, established at a time when childhood blindness led to a proliferation of employment training programs to ensure that blind adults would be able to find some kind of employment. Changes in medical treatment and changes in attitudes about the capability of blind people reduced the demand for these programs. The percentage of blind children decreased, while there was an increase in the number of blind people receiving a normal education and going on to very productive jobs and positions of leadership. As the evaluator put it in his report to the foundation: "The need for so many programs and organizations is no longer compelling."

The executive director of the foundation called a meeting at which representatives of the fourteen organizations serving the blind were present. He outlined the findings of the evaluation. "We continue to be committed to organizations serving the blind," he said. "But we believe the present situation can no longer be supported. There are too many of you doing the same thing. We are supporting too much infrastructure and too much inefficient duplication. We would like to see some kind of consolidation and modernization."

He suggested merger talks. "My board knows that this will

not be easy. There is much in the way of tradition, and each of you has a wonderful legacy and institutional history. We are prepared to provide $1 million to support the merger talks—to be divided in any way the fourteen of you can agree upon. Thereafter, a minimum of $5 million will be provided for implementation of a transition plan—more if we can be convinced that it is required. Ongoing support of programs for the blind will also continue from this foundation."

After six months, another meeting was held. The same representatives were in attendance. They told the foundation director that they had been unable to agree upon anything—even where to hold the talks. The boards of five of the organizations had refused to participate in any way, even if it meant an end of support from the community foundation.

This case history stands in sharp contrast to that of the Regional Health Network described in chapter 1. The board of the Health Network was able to diagnose the situation accurately, and its board came to the conclusion that continuation as a separate organization made no sense. Despite a proud history, the time had come to consolidate its operation with that of a larger organization in another state. Neither personal egos nor the obvious need of paid staff to retain a continuing source of income got in the way of a clear-headed assessment of larger questions. The questions asked were the right ones: Was there a better way to serve constituents? Could the job be done more efficiently, less expensively, with greater expertise? Was it possible or practical to try to keep the organization going? Was it time to look for a better way?

Without the constant interest of shareholders and without the practical threat of hostile takeovers that exist for profit-making entities, the actual pressures on nonprofit organizations to consider mergers, or consolidations generally, is remote. Even the threats of funders, constituents, and savvy trustees may seem benign. Funders may discontinue grants, constituents may seek service elsewhere, trustees may jump to another ship, and the organization may itself decline. But without a proactive effort at self-diagnosis, the substantive questions may be put off for years.

One practical suggestion is to get a group of organizations to agree to an objective analysis by an outside professional. Such an analysis should include:

- A description of field trends
- An assessment of the local (as defined by the organizations' service area) situation in light of these trends
- An evaluation of the various organizations' strengths and weaknesses
- A review of the competition (including competition from the profit sector)
- A comparative analysis of future options that might include the pros and cons of continuing with the same structures and programs, retaining the structures but modifying programs, seeking a merger or a strategic alliance, or formal organized abandonment of one or more of the entities.

If a group of organizations cannot be persuaded to share in such a study, any single organization can undertake the same kind of analysis to identify its options for the future.

COLLABORATION, CONSORTIA, AND STRATEGIC ALLIANCES

As the challenges facing nonprofit organizations have increased, many have found it useful to cooperate with other entities (both profit and commercial) and, in some cases, to form alliances. Such alliances stop short of mergers—they allow each participant organization to maintain its independence and autonomy. However, in many cases, they allow all the participants to accomplish more in terms of programming, to cut costs, to garner more income, or to achieve greater visibility and prominence.

The following examples demonstrate the range of opportunities available:

- *Consortium for student training in community health.* Five academic health centers in a major city work together to provide health-related service to underserved neighborhoods using teams of students. A central program office administers the overall fiscal and curricular operations for the program including fund raising. In addition, each center develops its own community-specific component program. The program has received both local and national visibility and funding by virtue of the strength of the partnership.

- *International archaeology consortium.* A graduate program in archaeology at a major university requires at least one semester of field-based research and has developed permanent relationships with organizations around the world. These organizations create supervised field experience in exchange for the low-cost, well-trained archaeologists from the university.

- *National fund-raising consortium.* Ten regional organizations in the same field have banded together to seek national funding for cooperative programs. Though each organization had limited geographic reach and therefore limited potential to raise national dollars, as a consortium they described themselves as a national network running a national program.

- *Regional fund-raising consortium.* In an analogous example, seven small land trust organizations, each with a budget of less than $100,000, formed a regional fund-raising group. Their motivation for doing so was that local foundations said that as individual organizations they were too small to meet the minimum guidelines for eligibility. However, as a group they exceeded the $500,000 minimum in applying for program support. The dollars, once received, were distributed to the organizations in proportion to their budget sizes.

- *Joint marketing/ticketing program.* Seven nonprofit theaters have set up a centralized ticketing function and cooperate on a joint marketing program. They share mailing lists and do joint mailings as well as cooperative promotion in one another's programs.

- *Block booking network.* Five organizations that bring musical events to a rural state in the West have set up a network. They agree in advance on the musical groups they wish to bring in and then offer a block of consecutive dates, thereby justifying the trip for the musicians and lowering the fees for the network participants.

- *Reciprocal membership.* Twelve national science museums run a reciprocal membership program. Members paying a higher fee receive as a benefit free admission to any of the museums on the list. Extra revenue from membership far outweighs the forgone admission fees.

- *Back-office savings.* An aquarium, a children's museum, and an art museum share marketing, financial management, and computer services. In each area, a single staff member housed at the largest of the organizations (the aquarium) reports to all three organizations and supervises departmental staff working for all three organizations. Costs are shared.

In recent years, many funders have seen the benefits of these kinds of efforts and have developed guidelines favoring organizations involved in some kind of collaboration. In some cases, this has resulted in some very powerful linkages where a number of organizations, working together, have identified and pursued community goals, achieved much greater visibility, and become much more sustainable as a result. In other cases, the results have been more practical—cost savings and efficiencies have been realized.

But the emphasis on consolidation and cooperation has also resulted in an inevitable push toward unconsidered initiatives and linkages. Some have been unsuccessful and short-lived. The participants have learned that collaborations cannot be achieved by fiat or created on a schedule to meet the exigencies of a grant deadline. Collaboration is a complex process. It must develop organically over time, and it must be beneficial to all involved if it is to be sustained.

THE BUSINESS MODEL AS A SUSTAINABILITY STRATEGY

As chapter 1 made clear, nonprofit organizations are different from commercial businesses in many ways, not the least of which is that the two have a fundamentally different raison d'etre. Commercial enterprises are in existence to make money. Nonprofit organizations exist to advance some beneficial purpose. Profit-making entities answer to owners/shareholders who evaluate performance on the basis of return on investment. Nonprofit organizations have no owners, no shareholders, and no investors in the conventional sense. If they make money, the funds remain in the charitable sector. While board members of commercial businesses serve the shareholders, trustees of nonprofit organizations serve the public and the public interest, answering to the regulating agencies that represent the public.

All of this is fundamental to the idea of nonprofit organizations. It is a long-held mantra that "nonprofit organizations are different." Yet, as the challenges facing nonprofits have increased, the differences between the profit and nonprofit sectors have shrunk in subtle ways. For example:

- It is far more common today to use a "bottom line" analysis in conducting an assessment of existing and future programs of nonprofit organizations. The initial question is no longer, "How well does the activity align with our mission?" It is, "Does the activity pay for itself?"

- Nonprofit organizations more frequently engage in activities whose sole purpose is to make money for the corporation. Sometimes these activities have no relation to the mission of the organization. In some cases, a separate profit-making subsidiary is created and/or taxes are paid on the "unrelated business income."

- Executive directors and other staff are rewarded for strong financial performance of the corporation. A bonus system is established and implemented when certain financial benchmarks are achieved. Similarly, poor financial performance becomes the basis for lower salary levels or terminations.

- Funders are less quick to respond to organizations in trouble and more frequently allow weak nonprofit organizations to fail. This seemingly Darwinian "survival of the fittest" approach derives from a realistic appraisal of the organizations' chances of success and an assessment of whether there is adequate demand for their services and programs.

- There is more frequent consideration of mergers and consolidations among nonprofit organizations. Some of the impetus for these mergers is generated internally by the organizations themselves, but a good deal of it is the result of pressure from funders.

- Partnerships between nonprofit organizations and profit-making concerns are more frequent. In the example of cause-related marketing campaigns, a manufacturer may launch a new product in alliance with a nonprofit organization. The manufacturer

helps its image (and, often, that of the product), while the non-profit receives a portion of the proceeds from sales.
- Nonprofit organizations have become more active in political advocacy to support positions beneficial to their self-interest.

Each of these practices is legal (though there are often constraints, especially in the area of political activity), and many are desirable under the right combination of circumstances. Implementing a more business-oriented, entrepreneurial, and commercial approach in nonprofit organizations is a trend that is on the increase, and it has brought about major turnarounds for organizations that were struggling. Sustainability—the watchword in the twenty-first century—has been achieved, at least for a time, using many of these sorts of techniques.

On the other hand, it is essential to keep in mind the ways in which nonprofit organizations are different from commercial businesses, if for no other reason than that others, who can affect the future of the nonprofit sector, will be doing so. Business people do not want nonprofits to use their special legally constituted beneficial position to compete unfairly or for less cost. As an obvious example, it seems unfair for nonprofit organizations to use their tax exemptions to achieve price advantages over profit-making businesses in the same market and with the same products. Many government officials, whose constituents and donors are heavily weighted toward those in business, share this view.

It is good to remember that the various advantages that nonprofits share and that were detailed in chapter 1 have been granted because the work they do and the way in which they do it justifies their special position. Tax deductibility of gifts and tax exemptions are two of the most important of these benefits, but there are many others. If the differences between nonprofit and commercial enterprises continue to shrink, then the rationale for preserving those benefits will diminish as well. In the end, these benefits are too valuable to lose.

LEADERSHIP AS AN ASPECT OF SUSTAINABILITY

Sustainability of nonprofit organizations depends upon many factors—no single magic bullet guarantees an organization's health and vitality. However, there is general consensus among experts that the long-term well-being of an organization is facilitated by something called *leadership*. Leadership in this instance is not an organizational attribute but an individual one, generally emanating from the person holding the top staff position—the executive director (who in some cases is called the president and/or the CEO [chief executive officer]). Leadership can also come from the head of the board (president or chairman), who in a nonprofit organization is almost always a different person from the staff head. In some organizations, these two individuals work together to provide team leadership.

The literature on leadership is vast and growing every year. It has become a subject of intense interest as more and more people see leadership as critical to the success of organizations of all types—profit, private nonprofit, and public. Leadership courses are taught at universities—not only in business schools but in other departments such as education and government. Leadership development programs are increasingly common in foundations, and seminars are provided by various organizations servicing the nonprofit sector and by independent consultants.

If there is consensus about the importance of leadership, there is little agreement about what, precisely, leadership is. Some experts offer a specific list of techniques; others describe key personal attributes of a leader. One writer will describe leadership as a science, another as an art. A book on the subject, titled *Leading with Soul: An Uncommon Journey of Spirit*,[2] emphasizes the spiritual side of leadership.

Some people believe that leaders are born, not made—that leadership qualities are part of an individual's intrinsic personality or that they are forged early in life. Others claim that leadership qualities can and should be taught. Some writers describe leadership as individual authority; others believe it is a process of group consensus where authority is consensual and earned. Advice abounds, but taken together the advice cannot be easily summarized.

It is dangerous to step into this confused morass. The temptation is to say that leadership cannot be defined, or that it is different things to different people, or that "if it works, it must be leadership." But none of these statements is particularly helpful. Instead, this chapter attempts to describe elements of leadership that can be found in a vast array of nonprofit organizations. These attributes are not the only ones that could be discussed, but they appear with great consistency and regularity and should be sought out in individuals and nurtured whenever possible.

Attributes of Leadership

What does one look for in a leader of a nonprofit organization?

Vision. An effective leader is one who has a clear vision of the future and the organization's place in that future. That vision must inspire people both within and outside the organization. When this quality of vision is lacking, the organization goes about its business each day with little more than precedent and habit as guides and little excitement to motivate its employees and volunteers.

- Vision means anticipating both opportunity and danger and convincing others of the importance of planning for them.
- Vision means understanding how the organization fits within a field and a community and being able to strategize about improving upon that position.
- A leader with vision has a strong and abiding commitment to the organization's mission that plays itself out in high-quality programs, and an overall commitment to excellence.

Community Engagement. A strong leader is externally directed (at least in part) and exhibits a well-developed knowledge of the community in which the organization is active. *Community* in this instance may be described by geography (though it can extend to a state, region, or the entire nation) and/or is defined by the field of endeavor, such as teaching hospitals, legal aid societies, or art museums.

- A strong leader has knowledge of constituent needs and an instinct for how to service them in a way that they will consider effective.
- Organizations with effective leaders demonstrate contextual appropriateness with their constituents. They know what constituents want, and how they want it. While this does not mean the leaders will simply do whatever their constituents ask, it does mean they will work together with them.
- The work that a leader does in the community creates substantive

relationships (both individual and organizational) characterized by mutuality of purpose.

• Effective leaders are willing to engage in change relative to community life. They recognize and respect change in their communities, and their work both reflects and causes change.

Organizational Management. Leadership is not the same as management, but there are aspects of management that are important to leadership. For example:

• Part of a leader's management role is to articulate the organization's mission and generate excitement among board and volunteers.

• An effective leader understands the importance of mission as a touchstone for organizational behavior—staff members are reminded continually and in various ways that their jobs relate to the mission.

• A good leader can make all staff members feel like they are part of a very special organization that matters and that they are critical to organizational effectiveness.

• Where effective leadership is present, there is a commitment to mutuality between the leader and staff, as well as between the board and the leader.

• Because a leader is skilled at overseeing all areas of management (though much of it may be delegated), the organization is able to respond to opportunities in dynamic and creative ways.

• The effective leader appears to have good instincts about the extent of risk that is desirable for the organization in its development.

Personal Attributes. Effective leaders often have a number of characteristics in common, many of which seem to come with maturity and life experience:

• Most have a well-articulated *personal* vision (as distinct from the vision pertaining to the organization, described earlier), and they demonstrate self-knowledge.

- Authenticity ranks high among the personal characteristics of leaders—that is, these are individuals who practice their personal values (or, as the colloquialism goes, "they walk what they talk").
- As a group, effective leaders are comfortable with change and ambiguity. In fact, many relish identifying opportunities and being creative agents of change.
- Effective leaders are individuals who are engaged with the world. In spite of working long hours in many cases, they are extremely knowledgeable about current societal issues.
- Most effective leaders have inquisitive, creative, and agile minds.

All of these personal characteristics allow effective leaders to find voice in the passion they demonstrate for their work.

IDENTIFYING, DEVELOPING, AND RECRUITING LEADERS

One of the major differences between business leaders and leaders in the nonprofit sphere is the manner in which they come to their positions. In business, it is quite common to find leaders who came up through the ranks. They are identified as future leaders early on, receive special training (both on the job and outside of the corporation), and are trotted out and tested for their roles. Corporations invest heavily in this process of leadership identification and development since so much is at stake. Effective CEOs are of extreme value to a corporation, as their often extraordinarily high compensation makes clear. Company performance and profitability depends, in many cases, on their qualities, talents, and abilities.

In nonprofit organizations, leaders (especially staff leaders) are more often than not recruited from the outside. It is the exception to find organizations that have identified a leader early on, developed that individual, and planned carefully for a smooth succession. When a strong leader leaves, the organization looks to other organizations, usually in the same field, hoping to recruit someone who seems to have the requisite experience and leadership qualities.

Part of the reason for this difference is that nonprofit organizations are generally thinly staffed, and there is not often the luxury of grooming a successor chief executive officer. Commonly, the people serving under the staff head are chiefs of departments or areas—like development, marketing, or finance. Their specialized skills are indispensable to the organization, and they cannot be spared for leadership development activities. For them to assume leadership roles, they must be recruited by other, generally smaller organizations where, it is hoped, they will learn their leadership skills on the job.

One of the effects of this difference in leadership development is that profit-making companies, working with potential insider candidates, can change course if it looks like the initial choice was a mistake. Many times, an heir apparent is identified and groomed but turns out not to be the right person for the job. Before any transition occurs, this individual is passed over and another candidate is identified and nurtured. While the disappointment to the individual and others around him or her may be substantial, the cost in corporate terms is minimal, much less than if the person had gone into the job and had to be removed later.

In nonprofit organizations, this ability to "try people out" is generally absent since leaders are recruited from the outside. This puts tremendous pressure on making the right choice without the benefit of having an individual work within the organization or the community at all. As one trustee put it, "we have to hit a home run every time. Even a single or a double isn't good enough." The challenge is even greater when the individual to be replaced has been a strong, effective, and longtime leader. With someone coming in from the outside, there is the inevitable comparison, a period of unreasonable expectations, and little time for acclimation. In some organizations where a leader has been in place for many years or even decades, an interim head may be hired to lessen the impact of unrealistic comparisons.

With board leaders, there is far more leeway to use the profit-sector model. Yet all too many organizations develop an automatic succession track with someone being identified as a potential chairman, put in the vice chair position, and automatically promoted to the chairmanship upon the resignation or term end of the existing chair. This can occur even when it is apparent that the identified individual does not display the leadership qualities required.

With respect to identifying and developing leaders, the following guidelines can be of assistance:

1. Whenever possible, evaluate the abilities of internal candidates. The identification process should begin early, well before the current leader intends to step down.
2. Consider the ultimate need for a new leader when hiring senior staff (below the executive director) or when recruiting trustees. Look for appropriate leadership potential that can be developed and tested.
3. Allow for on-the-job training experience and formal educational training.
4. When looking outside the organization for a leader, be clear about expectations. This goes beyond a job description. Identify the leadership qualities that are most being sought.
5. With outside candidates, be clear about the internal culture of the organization. If a consensus-type leader is being sought, do not pursue charismatic, authority-oriented types.
6. Give potential leadership candidates (and their families) an opportunity to spend time on site, interacting with board and staff.
7. When bringing candidates from out of town, give them ample opportunity to get to know the community.
8. Once hired, allow for a period of adjustment. Every leader needs time to acclimate to the organization and the community and build relationships.
9. Allow a new leader to put together his or her senior team. This may or may not include people who already are in the senior slots.
10. With respect to boards, identify any potential leader as early as possible. Give him or her an opportunity to display leadership qualities on the executive committee. Be prepared to change course if the individual identified does not live up to expectations.

NURTURING LEADERSHIP

The challenge of how to identify, develop, and recruit leaders raises the important question of how to nurture an effective leader once that person is in place. The track record of nonprofit organizations has been checkered at best in this regard. However, as the value of leadership has become increasingly apparent, many are finding ways to improve. Nothing is more sobering than losing an effective leader to another organization because he or she was taken for granted.

Based on the practice of organizations that have kept their leaders by treating them well, the following seems to be a useful checklist of dos and don'ts:

DO keep expectations reasonable even if the leader makes the job seem effortless.

DO NOT add tasks and responsibilities simply because everything is getting done and done well. Discuss any new expectations with a clear eye toward what may have to be delegated or given up.

DO provide adequate staff support. Remember that being a leader often requires a freeing up from routine and internal day-to-day tasks that can be done by others.

DO NOT assign tasks just because the leader is good at them—if they can be done by others, they probably should be.

DO provide adequate compensation. Remember that saving money by underpaying an effective leader simply makes a job in another organization that much more desirable. Be sure that benefits are figured into the competitive compensation analysis.

DO NOT underpay an effective incumbent leader simply because his or her salary has historically been below industry standards or has not kept up with inflation.

DO provide adequate time for professional networking and field-related work not directly related to the organization's day-to-day tasks (this can even include a specific number of days of outside consulting).

DO NOT assume that days away from the office on nonorganization business are days on which leadership tasks are not getting done. In many cases, the contacts made and the field reputation developed will have a very positive impact on the organization.

DO provide adequate personal time off. Burnout is the most serious complaint of nonprofit leaders today.

DO NOT assume that there is a direct relationship between hours worked and productivity.

DO provide time and compensation for leadership training opportunities.

DO NOT assume that an experienced leader knows it all or does not need to recharge his or her batteries with new information.

DO honor and value the leader. Appreciation and public recognition are energizing and contribute to good feelings about the organization.

DO NOT ever take the leader for granted.

CHECKLIST QUESTIONS FOR CHAPTER 10

1. To what extent has the organization directly addressed key questions relating to sustainability? How well does it meet expectations with respect to constituency service, effectiveness/efficiency, accountability, and leadership?

2. How do policies regarding the development and utilization of endowment funds either contribute to or detract from stability and sustainability?

3. What diagnostic process has been employed to determine whether the organization is too big or too small?

4. Would any type of merger or consolidation be beneficial?

5. What kinds of collaboration and strategic alliances have been explored?

6. To what extent does the organization employ a for-profit business model in its approach to problem solving?

7. What key characteristics are sought in a leader? How does the internal culture of the organization help determine these characteristics?

8. How are leaders identified, developed, and recruited?

9. How are leaders nurtured?

ELEVEN
Making Things Better

Jack Fox and Martha Whitney left their respective nonprofit organizations on the same day. Jack had been a volunteer at his church for two years. Martha had been employed as executive director of a shelter for battered women for four years. Both had begun their work with a feeling of optimism and a sense of service. But as the months and years passed, each was troubled by the fact that things were not always going smoothly in their respective organizations.

At the church, Jack couldn't quite put his finger on what was wrong. Certainly the shrinking membership base and the constant need for money were challenges, but he wasn't sure whether they were symptomatic of larger problems that no one in the church was willing to face. In Martha's case, she was able to diagnose what was wrong—there were not enough paid staff members, the building was inadequate, and the board was unwilling to raise funds—but she felt helpless to do anything about these problems.

Jack Fox and Martha Whitney are typical of many individuals in nonprofit organizations. They are good, committed people. They care deeply about the work their organizations are trying to do. But they feel stymied and frustrated, either because they cannot seem to use their talents effectively or because their organizations seem adrift and on the wrong track. Often the organizations are operating close to capacity with staff members overworked to the point of burnout and budgets strained to the breaking point. There never seem to be enough hours or sufficient money to identify and solve problems. People like Jack and Martha do not want to initiate personal conflicts, hurt people's feelings, or rock the organizational boat in any way. It is simply easier and less stressful to walk away from the organization and its problems.

The purpose of this chapter is to provide an alternative scenario for those who are committed to nonprofit organizations and want to make them better. These people should not be lost to the nonprofit world—they are too valuable. They should be encouraged to stay and contribute. This chapter will provide guidance on how to participate in a process of evaluation that can lead to improvements in an organization's operations and programs over time.

THE EVALUATION PROCESS

No nonprofit organization is governed or managed perfectly, and most have serious shortcomings in several areas. The ones that are most successful are able to get the board and staff to commit to a process for evaluating problems and making things better. This is done by taking a few important steps:

1. Accurately diagnosing the organization's current situation and identifying areas in which there are opportunities for positive change
2. Separating the problems into those that need immediate attention and those that might be dealt with later
3. Building board and staff consensus so that the identified problems can be dealt with honestly, forthrightly, and in a timely manner
4. Developing a realistic, affordable, multiyear schedule for implementing change
5. Continuing the diagnostic, evaluation, and self-improvement process year after year

Assessing Strengths, Weaknesses, Problems, and Opportunities

The diagnosis of an organization's current strengths, weaknesses, problems, and opportunities involves making assessments in several areas and evaluating the organization from several points of view. The process involves asking questions about how well the organization measures up to a predefined ideal. The following checklist provides an excellent starting point for a process of organizational assessment.

Mission, Image, and Case for Support

A. Mission. A strong organization is one whose purpose is relevant to current needs of the community it serves and to the requirements of a broad and well-defined constituency.

- Is the mission statement up-to-date or out-of-date (i.e., how closely does it actually conform to what the organization seems to be about)? How might the mission statement be reworded so that it is more reflective of the organization's purpose?
- Is the mission itself still relevant to the needs of those served? Can this be demonstrated in a concrete way that would convince a skeptic? Should the mission be broadened or changed in some way to become more relevant to contemporary needs?
- Who is being served (i.e., who are the clients)? Is this constituency sufficiently diverse, or is it too narrowly focused on a small group? If the constituency should be broadened, what concrete steps might be taken to accomplish this?
- Is there a compelling reason for the organization to exist? Are there other organizations doing the same work? Might strategic alliances or a merger mean greater efficiency and effectiveness in achieving the mission?

B. Brand/Image. The organization should be well known and well respected in its community and among its constituency.

- Does the organization's name mean anything to people in the community? What impressions and feelings are associated with the brand?
- How familiar are people with the organization's activities? Are there people who should know about the organization but don't? How can the organization's profile be raised?
- What is the organization's reputation? Is it well respected? Is there any old history or controversy that plagues its image? How can this be taken care of?

C. Case for support. The organization should present a compelling case for support both to its clients and to its contributors.

- How convincing is the organization's pitch to its users and its funders? Are the services, activities, and programs of the organization described in a way that will entice full participation?
- How well does the organization present an attractive alternative to its competitors?

- How clearly and simply are the financial needs of the organization outlined?
- Are contributors given a varied enough menu of giving opportunities? Are donors offered a way to meet their own objectives for name recognition or other needs?

Manpower Issues (Board, Staff, and Volunteers)

A. Board. Board members should be active, assuming general oversight of the affairs of the organization, taking responsibility for fund raising and allowing staff the space to carry out the day-to-day operational affairs of the organization without undue interference.

- Do board members know what is expected of them (does the organization have a trustee job description or board manual)? Do board members attend meetings regularly? Do they give and solicit money? Do they assume proper oversight of the budget? Do they engage in program and organizational planning?
- Are the bylaws structured in such a way that inactive or ineffective board members can be rotated off the board quickly and painlessly? Are there specific board members who should be encouraged to resign to make room for others who are more active?
- Do the officers assume proper leadership roles? Is there an effective committee structure?

B. Staff. The organization should have a qualified and well-trained staff that is large enough to carry out the tasks allotted to it. The organization chart should maximize the potential of the work force, and there should be clearly documented personnel policies that reflect a sense of fairness leading to good morale.

- What are the skills and qualifications of individual staff members? Does the organization have the best possible person for each job? If not, is the problem related to compensation, poor recruiting and hiring, or something else?
- Are there enough staff? Are their job descriptions complete and up-to-date? Is the organization chart appropriate?
- Are there personnel policies? Are they written down? Is there

a regular procedure for staff evaluation? Does it work? What is the level of staff morale? How can it be improved?

C. Volunteers. In organizations that rely heavily on volunteers, these individuals should be committed, given clear tasks, and rewarded for the work they do.

- Are there enough volunteers? Are there skills that are not being met by the current volunteer pool? How can more volunteers be found in the right areas of need?
- Are volunteer tasks and activities well organized and properly assigned? Are tasks described in writing? Is there a system of re-view and follow-up to make sure tasks are completed properly?
- Are volunteers serious about their work? Are they committed?
- Have they been oriented and told about the importance of the work they do? Is there a system that rewards them?

Finances

A. Financial management. The organization's finances should show prudent management, appropriate oversight and controls, and proper systems for predicting and tracking revenue and expense.

- Are the financial records kept accurately and statements produced frequently and promptly? Do key members of the board provide proper oversight and review the reports? Are there controls in place that meet generally accepted accounting standards? Is there timely outside review of the books?
- Do the balance sheet and the income statement show a history of prudent financial management? Is there an accumulated deficit, and if so, what strategies are there for eliminating it? Is there a cash reserve? An endowment?
- Are budgets prepared well in advance of the fiscal year? Is budget reconciliation done frequently enough to anticipate problems? Are cash flow projections available? Can revenue and expense projections and reports be analyzed for each activity and program? Are multiyear budget projections available?

B. Income and expense. Except under unusual circumstances, the organization should earn and raise enough money each year to pay its operating expenses.

- Is there an appropriate balance between earned and contributed income? (The ratio will vary depending on the kind of organization.) Is there a sufficient source of unrestricted income? Is the organization too dependent on a single donor or a few large contributors?
- Are costs reasonable given the service or product provided? Are there systems for analyzing and controlling costs?
- Does the organization operate at a surplus or deficit after all income (contributed and earned) is considered? If there is a pattern of operating deficits, what can be done to change this pattern?
- Is the fund-raising program well organized? Do board members and other volunteers carry out their responsibilities? Is information about donors collected, updated, organized, and used strategically? Are donors appropriately courted and properly thanked?

Activities and Programs

A. Resource audit. The organization's programs should meet the needs of the constituency and the community. They should be well administered.

- Are the programs and activities of this organization really needed or wanted and if so by whom? How much would people suffer if the organization went out of business?
- Which programs, services, and activities does the organization do best? How well do they meet the needs of clients and community? How can they be improved?
- Which programs, services, and activities does the organization do less well? Should they be dropped? If not, how can they be made more successful?

B. Positioning. The organization should appear to offer unique advantages to those who utilize its programs and services. It should be well regarded with respect to its competition.

- With which entities and activities does the organization compete?
- How well are its programs regarded in relation to its competition?
- How can the organization broaden its appeal to a wider group of constituents and strengthen the loyalty of current users?
- Might it be time to work more closely with the competition in providing service?

Planning and Evaluation

A. Planning. The board and staff of the organization should be involved in both short- and long-term planning at all times.

- How well defined are goals, objectives, and strategies for the next two years? The next five years? Is there a well-articulated plan that is providing a blueprint for action?
- How effective is the planning process? Who is involved and who is left out? How involved are the board, the staff, the constituency, and the broader community? Are new activities properly planned and piloted before moving into full implementation?
- Does the planning process take financial realities into account?
- Are conservative revenue and expense projections available? To what extent does planning involve multiyear budgeting?

B. Evaluation. Evaluation systems should measure performance against preestablished targets and standards. From time to time, evaluation should utilize the objectivity and expertise of outside professionals.

- How are the organization, in general, and its specific activities, in particular, evaluated? Are evaluations based on preestablished quantitative targets?
- How often are evaluations carried out and by whom? Are outside experts used in this process? To what extent is their advice heeded?
- Are planning and evaluation linked? How are the results of ongoing evaluation utilized in long-range planning?

SELF-ASSESSMENT VERSUS OUTSIDE EVALUATION

The diagnostic process just described can be done as a self-assessment, which relies on the talents and abilities of an organization's board and staff; alternatively, it can be done with the assistance of outside evaluators, utilizing the talents and knowledge of one or more professionals who are not associated with the organization in any way.

Self-assessment has many advantages. Those involved generally know the organization well. It doesn't take them a long time to get up to speed about the organization's history, community, constituency, and internal politics. It is inexpensive, because it does not require that large fees are paid to an outside consultant. It also can serve as a consensus builder inasmuch as those involved in the assessment process are the same individuals who will be responsible for making the necessary changes.

Yet some of these very advantages of self-assessment can work against the organization in the long run. Because those who are involved are close to the organization, they may suffer from institutional myopia. Because they have seen things operate in certain ways for so long, they may not be able to understand that there are novel alternatives that would actually lead to improvements. Additionally, they may, either consciously or unconsciously, be attached to certain individuals, procedures, programs, and activities that are not, in the long run, in the best interests of the organization.

For example, one would not expect a trustee who had underwritten a series of school-based public affairs programs for ten years to conclude that these programs were not as effective as similar ones offered by other organizations. An executive director who had spent several years training her assistant, with whom she feels a close relationship, might not feel inclined to look at an alternative staffing structure that excluded this individual.

Another danger with self-assessment is that there may be strong factions on the board or among senior staff, each with strongly held and differing opinions about particular issues. The factions will probably choose to disagree both about problems and solutions, and they may become quite personal in ascribing blame to individuals in the other camp. This is destructive and divisive and it usually means that someone from the outside with a fresh, objective vision should be called in to perform an organizational assessment or evaluation that at best might lead to a third way to resolve the issue as painlessly as possible.

Sometimes organizations resist calling in an outsider because board members or staff think they cannot afford the services of a consultant. However, it is important to keep in mind that there is a growing trend among institutional funders, such as foundations and public agencies, to pick up all or part of the cost of outside evaluation and assessment services. From the funders' point of view, money given for such projects—that in the end may lead to improved management, governance, programming, or planning—can be an exceptionally sound investment.

Regardless of whether or not an outside paid professional is used, it is always helpful to bring in an individual who is neither a board member nor a staff person to help out during the assessment period. Such a community member can aid in bringing objectivity to the evaluation process, spot areas of internal conflict, and lend a calming voice to the process of problem identification.

Building Consensus for Future Action

The process of building consensus among board and senior staff is critical as the organization moves toward a solution to its problems or decides to take advantage of new opportunities. The results of an organizational assessment can make people very nervous, particularly if they reveal problems. Unfortunately, some may regard these problems as a sign of personal failure even though, in many cases, the problems stem from very different sources—external changes in the community, new sources of competition, shifts in the priority of funders and underwriters, rapid organizational growth, staff turnover, or the failure of some new administrative procedure or system. In any case, an effort should be made to make everyone feel comfortable with the diagnosis of the problems. There must be broad consensus on what is wrong before the group can take effective action to do something about it.

An effective way to build this consensus is through one or more group meetings, such as retreats, involving board and senior staff. Typically, a retreat is led by a facilitator who has special abilities in leading group discussions and is fully familiar with the organization's challenges and the options that are under consideration for the future. The best of these meetings are those in which the participants are not simply there to receive information but are being asked to help formulate policy and direction. However, it is important, if decisions are to be made at the meeting, that the issues be clearly articulated, the options well structured, and the decisions formulated within pre-defined limits.

This chapter has offered some strategies for bringing about change and making improvements in a nonprofit organization. It has suggested that there are ways a nonprofit organization can set about diagnosing problems and making things better. Several areas need to be analyzed in the process of evaluation and change. The evaluation process itself can reveal organizational strengths and weaknesses and can provide the basis for developing goals and objectives for the future. Different names are sometimes attached to the evaluation process to indicate different kinds of emphases (e.g., management review, program evaluation, marketing audit, or financial assessment), but the overall intent is the same—to establish a baseline of consensus around organizational problems and to identify areas where there are opportunities for positive change.

Evaluation, either through self-assessment or outside evaluation, is generally a positive experience, but there are certain inherent dangers. One is the tendency for board and staff to become discouraged because they have been overly self-critical. They forget that they are measuring themselves or being measured against an ideal that no organization ever achieves. As the assessment process unfolds and they compile long lists of organizational deficiencies, they begin to question their own competence and the judgments of others. This can be dangerous and destructive. The purpose of the assessment is not simply to be negative. It is to develop an agenda for change.

It is also extremely important to realize that organizations cannot be changed overnight and that the process of problem solving and change is generally best managed on a gradual and ongoing basis. Certainly every nonprofit organization can do what it does more effectively. Put another way, every nonprofit organization has room to make improvements. The challenge for trustees and staff is to manage the changes in such a way that the effects are positive and long lasting.

NOTES

ONE: UNDERSTANDING NONPROFIT ORGANIZATIONS

1. Unless specified otherwise, data in this paragraph comes from the National Center for Charitable Statistics, Number of Nonprofit Organizations in the United States, 1999–2009, http://nccsdataweb.urban.org/PubApps/profile1.php?state=US, accessed January 14, 2011. Note that new reporting requirements imposed by the IRS in 2010 resulted in loss of tax-exempt status for 275,000 organizations (Stephanie Strom, "I.R.S. Ends Exemptions for 275,000 Nonprofits," *New York Times*, June 8, 2011, http://www.nytimes.com/2011/06/09/business/09charity.html), although some of these revocations are being disputed at the time of the writing of this book.

2. Kennard T. Wing, Katie L. Roeger, and Thomas H. Pollak, "The Nonprofit Sector in Brief: Public Charities, Giving, and Volunteering 2010" (Washington, DC: The Urban Institute, 2010), 3. www.urban.org/publications/412209.html.

3. Stanley J. Czerwinski, "Nonprofit Sector: Increasing Numbers and Key Role in Delivering Federal Services," GAO-07-1084T, a testimony before the Subcommittee on Oversight, Committee on Ways and Means, House of Representatives, July 24, 2007, 1. http://www.gao.gov/new.items/d071084t.pdf, accessed January 13, 2011.

4. Agency for Healthcare Research and Quality 2008 Medical Expenditure Panel Survey http://www.meps.ahrq.gov/mepsweb/data_stats/summ_tables/insr/national/series_1/2008/tib1.pdf, accessed January 13, 2011, Table I.B.1.

5. *Giving USA 2010*: The Annual Report on Philanthropy for the Year 2009, Center on Philanthropy at Indiana University, 2010, vi.

6. Wing, Roeger, and Pollak, 6.

TWO: THE BOARD

1. The word *trustee* is used here to describe a person serving on the board of trustees. Sometimes this group is referred to as the board of directors, in which case those who serve are called directors. However, the directors who serve on the board are not to be confused with a staff person with the same title, such as an executive director, a program director, or an artistic director. In general, directors who are board members do not serve on the staff and are not paid.

2. While statutes governing nonprofit or charitable corporations do not specify that trustees may not be compensated, it is generally expected that the majority of trustees will not be. In some cases, the IRS, in reviewing applications for tax-exempt status from certain types of organizations, will require that a provision be included in the corporate charter specifying that trustees may not be compensated. In some nonprofit organizations, the chief executive officer and the artistic director (both of whom collect a salary) do sit on the board ex officio, often without a vote. In almost all nonprofit organizations, however, the vast majority of board members are not compensated, so that the spirit of independence from financial self-interest on the part of the board is maintained.

3. In many cases, creditors threaten to sue individual trustees if their claims on the organization are not met. However, given the laws in most states, they have no legal standing in this regard even if they can prove gross negligence.

THREE: ASSEMBLING THE WORKFORCE

1. Generally, the board of trustees hires the executive director. The executive director hires other staff. In large organizations where staffs are sizable, division heads often hire the people who work under them. In the most decentralized organizations, where each employee is hired by his or her immediate supervisor, it is advisable to involve staff colleagues working in the same department in the recruitment and interviewing process. No matter what hiring procedure is used, it is always advantageous to have more than one person forming an impression of prospective employees even if one person ultimately will make the final selection.

FOUR: PERSONNEL POLICY

1. The term *benefits* as used here may include, but is not limited to, vacations, sick days, personal days, maternity and paternity leaves, other leaves of absence, medical insurance, private retirement plans, life insurance, disability insurance, and other forms of nonsalaried compensation. Social security, workers' compensation, and unemployment insurance may also be considered benefits to the employee, although they are not discretionary—that is, they are the employee's right by law.

2. Employees of nonprofit 501(c)(3) organizations are covered by unemployment insurance by virtue of their employment. The organization itself, however, must be careful to understand its options and liabilities. At the federal level, the organization is exempt from paying unemployment taxes (FUTA). At the state level, laws vary, and it is important for a nonprofit organization to check the procedures. In many states, the organization has an option to participate in the unemployment insurance program. If state unemployment insurance (usually assessed as a percentage of total employees' salaries) is paid regularly and an employee is subsequently laid off, the state pays the unemployment compensation and the organization pays nothing. If the organization does not pay into the state unemployment insurance fund (and nonprofit organizations usually have the option of not participating in the system) and the employee is laid off or fired, the state pays the unemployment benefit and then charges the organization the full cost of the claim. Nonprofit organizations that are certain they will have no employees collecting unemployment may decide not to pay into the system. Others may wish to do so. Still others may wish to establish their own self-insurance fund, putting aside a certain portion of the employees' salaries into a separate bank account for a time until they feel confident that they are protected against unemployment liability. (Note: Unemployment benefits cover only salaried employees, not independent contractors.)

3. When an employee works according to a *flextime* schedule, he or she substitutes one set of working hours for another but works the same number of total hours. If the employee works *overtime,* he or she works additional hours beyond the number originally required.

4. The individual's title may be president, executive director, administrative director, artistic director, general director, or something else, but he or she is at the top of the organizational chart.

SIX: FINANCIAL MANAGEMENT

1. Technically, it is not permissible to use restricted funds for purposes other than those specified by the individual or organization imposing the restriction. However, organizations occasionally are tempted to borrow from their restricted funds to cover short-term cash needs. The rationale generally given is that the organization will pay back the restricted funds prior to needing them and in the meanwhile such a temporary transfer of funds helps the organization avoid more expensive borrowing. This practice is common among nonprofit organizations, but is it legal? According to one accountant consulted on this matter, the practice is legal so long as the organization has secured a letter of credit from a lending institution (or individual) that commits sufficient funds to replace the restricted funds should the organization be unable to repay the restricted obligation. It is, of course, *not* legal when the donor clearly prohibits such borrowing. Some boards establish formal policies

about this type of borrowing, including who may authorize the borrowing and how much (percentage of grant) may be borrowed. In any case, a repayment plan should be required prior to any such borrowing.

SEVEN: FINANCIAL STATEMENTS AND FISCAL PROCEDURES

1. Many organizations do both fund accounting and departmental or program accounting. A fund may include a number of projects or departments. A project or a department may span funds as well, for example, when a particular program is supported by both unrestricted and restricted funding.

2. In most organizations, the net assets or equity figure portion is adjusted only at year end; it does not change during the year, and the changes in the total net assets are reflective of the net income (or loss) from the income statement. Again, for a profit-making corporation, this equity could be the owners' original investment, which is augmented or reduced by any subsequent profit or loss.

3. Note that one of the requirements of FASB was that organizations must recognize pledged contributions as revenue at the time of the pledge, no matter when the pledge is to be paid. Some organizations do not do this until the time of the audited statement, since people feel that recording pledged contributions as revenue any earlier overstates revenue and creates a false sense of well-being on the part of those reviewing the financial statements. To the extent that this recording is done, the line item on the balance sheet reporting uncollected pledges is generally called Contributions Receivable.

4. One of the results of the FASB changes is that funds previously classified as deferred revenue (for example, a restricted grant received in advance of the project it is funding) may now be classified as temporarily restricted net assets. However, some revenues will still be classified as deferred.

5. The balance sheet allows someone to calculate the equity of property owned by the organization. The value of the property is shown under Assets and the outstanding debt on the property is shown under Liabilities. The amount of equity in the property is the difference between these two figures. Thus in figure 7.3, the equity is calculated as $305,362 minus $154,840, or $150,522. Interest payments do not appear on the balance sheet but are shown on the income statement.

6. On year-end audited statements, there is generally a section at the bottom of the Statement of Activities (income statement) that indicates the increase (decrease) in net assets, which is actually simply a different name for net income (loss). This line is followed by the following reconciliation:

Increase (decrease) in net assets	$5,221 (same as net income)
Net assets at beginning of year	$130,707 (from prior year's balance sheet)
Net assets at end of year	$135,928 (sum of the above)

This net assets figure must also be broken out among unrestricted, temporarily restricted, and permanently restricted net assets, which is done with a Statement of Changes in Net Assets report. Alternatively, the income statement may be presented with three columns, one for each of the net asset categories.

7. Organizations may adopt different versions of this system, but keeping a "paper trail" to indicate approval of invoices and time/method of payment is essential.

8. The IRS requires different forms for different budget sizes: Organizations with gross revenues of less than $50,000 must file form 990-N (a simple e-postcard filing); organizations with budget of less than $200,000 and assets of less than $500,000 must file Form 990-EZ; all others must file Form 990.

9. Samples of policy documents that can be adapted to fit a specific organization are readily available online (including for some policies, from the IRS itself). Two possible sources are the National Council of Nonprofits (www.councilofnonprofits.org) and the Free Management Library (www.managementhelp.org).

EIGHT: FUND RAISING

1. A recommended book that includes much material on social media and fund raising is Beth Kanter and Allison Fine's *The Networked Nonprofit* (San Francisco: Jossey-Bass, 2010).

2. The Internal Revenue Service has various tests to determine types of nonprofit status. One of these tests looks at the sources of revenue. For example, if more than a designated percent comes from a single donor, this can "tip" the organization into another category with different requirements. Organizations that receive a high percentage of total income from a single donor should seek legal assistance and consult relevant government web sites such as http://www.irs.gov/pub/irs-pdf/p557.pdf.

3. In this section, the term *corporations* refers to large business concerns that have organized giving programs. While smaller local businesses, described earlier in this chapter, are also corporations, the nature of their philanthropy is quite different from what is described here. It is on a much smaller scale, is primarily restricted to the local giving area, and is generally not as carefully organized as the giving programs of larger corporations.

4. From "Venture Philanthropy: Evolving from Theory into Practice," Working Paper #8 from Wolf, Keens & Co. (now Wolf Brown).

5. Cf. especially Thomas Wolf, *How to Connect with Donors and Double the Money You Raise* (Medfield, MA: Emerson & Church, 2011).

TEN: SUSTAINABILITY AND LEADERSHIP

1. Thomas Wolf et al., *The Financial Condition of Symphony Orchestras* [Washington, DC: American Symphony Orchestra League, 1992 (now League of American Orchestras)].

2. Lee G. Bolman and Terrence E. Deal, *Leading with Soul: An Uncommon Journey of Spirit* (San Francisco, CA: Jossey-Bass, 1995).

INDEX